THE REBEL TRUMPET AND THE MOSQUITO FLEET

Two Full-Length Novels on the American Civil War

GORDON D. SHIRREFFS

WOLFPACK
PUBLISHING
—— EST 2013 ——

The Rebel Trumpet and The Mosquito Fleet
Paperback Edition
Copyright © 2023 (As Revised) Gordon D. Shirreffs

Wolfpack Publishing
9850 S. Maryland Parkway, Suite A-5 #323
Las Vegas, Nevada 89183

wolfpackpublishing.com

Paperback ISBN 978-1-63977-323-7
eBook ISBN 978-1-63977-322-0

THE REBEL TRUMPET AND THE MOSQUITO FLEET

THE REBEL TRUMPET

To Mary Kay Johnson, my adopted niece, who I am sure will someday be a writer

CHAPTER ONE

The eleventh New York Volunteers, the Fire Zouaves, waited in the hot woods, listening to the steady, distant thudding of the artillery guns and to the irregular firing of musketry, which sounded like the popping of grease in a gigantic skillet. Beyond the dusty woods, across a high banked and sluggish stream, the gun smoke hung close to the broken ground, mingled with the yellow dust churned up by wheels, hoofs, and marching feet.

The fighting had been going on for hours, but the Eleventh was not yet baptized by battle. The hot July sun and the dust of the Virginia roads had played havoc with the once bright uniforms of the Fire Zouaves. The red pants and caps, short blue jackets, and white gaiters had lost their freshness, and all were now a neutral, dusty color, stained by sweat, but the heavy silken presentation flags at the center of the mass of waiting men were still bright, although they hung listlessly in the quiet air.

Lieutenant Colonel Farnham rode slowly along the line of his regiment of five hundred men. He looked almost nonchalant and cool as he rode, but anyone with half an eye could tell he was mentally gauging the Eleventh, wondering what would happen when they would be thrown into the battle that had swayed back and forth for hours, with the advantage first on one side and then on the other.

"Colonel, sir! When do *we* go in?" big Gershom Bates asked.

Farnham waved a hand. "Soon enough, my man," he said with a smile.

Bates whipped out a huge bowie knife and flourished it. "We'll go through them rebels like a greased pig at a lodge picnic!"

"That's the spirit, Bates!" Farnham called as he rode on.

Drummer Steven Ames of *A* Company shoved back his red, tasseled cap and wiped the sweat from his face. He looked down the line of his company. He wondered if they were all as scared as he was. The long march from Centreville had been hard enough on them, and Steve's drumming had aroused them at two o'clock that morning after a poor night's rest. Now it was late in the afternoon, and the battle that Bates had confidently predicted would be over in less than an hour had begun to stretch on and on, with no sign of the rebels running from the hard-fought field and with the firing increasing in volume.

"Worried, kid?" asked little gap-toothed Walt Mawson.

Steve shook his head. He looked down at his long legs in their baggy Zouave trousers and tight white leggings and wondered if they'd carry him to the fighting when the Eleventh's time came.

"That's where a cavalryman has it all over us infantry-men," said Walt philosophically. "We get scared, and our legs give out, while a cavalryman's horse will always carry him along no matter how scared his rider is."

Gershom Bates swaggered up and down the line of *A*

Company, eying the quiet and apprehensive men. "Why don't they send in us Fire Zouaves?" he bellowed.

Sergeant Mike Hogan shifted a little from where he rested with his back against a log. "Your time will come, me bucko," he said quietly.

Bates twisted his long mustachios. "It'd better, Sergeant! I'm not going back home to New York City without a bagful of rebels!"

"The war will last long enough for ye to get your fill."

Bates placed his hands on his hips and looked up and down the company line. "Not to my way of thinking," he said." It will be a short war, Sergeant."

Most of the men nodded as though they wanted to believe the big braggart.

"All wars are supposed to be short," said Hogan. He yawned. "They always are —at the beginning."

Bates eyed the noncom as though he was the very incarnation of pessimism. "I say this one won't last longer than this afternoon, that is after the Eleventh gets at those rebels."

"Hear, hear," said Walt Mawson.

Hogan yawned again. "How many wars have ye been in, Bates?" he asked dryly.

Gershom Bates opened his wide mouth, and then he shut it. Mike Hogan had trapped him there, for Bates had never heard a shot fired in anger, while Mike had fought in the British Army in India and had served with Garibaldi in Italy as one of 'the thousand,' the red-shirted patriots who had fought for Italian freedom in 1860. Bates swaggered off down the line, and Hogan grinned. "Now, if Bates was a real veteran," he said to the men near him, "he'd be lying down resting instead of doing his fightin' with his big mouth."

Steve touched his dry lips with his tongue. He was dry, but water was scarce. He had placed a smooth pebble in his mouth to start the flow of saliva, a trick he had learned in the deserts of New Mexico and Mexico as a young boy. His canteen was about half full, whereas most of the green men about him had drained theirs dry long ago.

"Wish you was back in Mexico, kid?" asked Walt Mawson as he pulled off his left shoe and inspected a blister on his heel.

"*New* Mexico," said Steve.

Some of the men laughed nervously. It was a standing joke in *A* Company, which had started since that day in New York City when Steve had enlisted in the Eleventh as a drummer boy and had given outlandish New Mexico Territory as his home. New Mexico, to most of the city-dwelling members of the regiment, was away out back of beyond.

All through the hot and dusty woodsmen lay on their arms, listening to the muttering and smashing of battle across the sluggish stream that wound through the broken scrub timberland. The Eleventh New York Volunteers were part of Willcox's Brigade of Heintzelman's Third Division. The rest of the brigade was as green as the Eleventh, the Thirty-eighth New York, the First Michigan, and the Fourth Michigan. The only trained troops in the whole brigade were the regulars of Battery *D*, Second United States Artillery.

Walt Mawson stood up and peered through the smoky, dusty woods. "Some army we got," he said proudly. "Lookit, all them men waiting like us to wipe out the rebels."

"'Tisn't an army yit," said Sergeant Hogan. "'Tis an armed mob, green as the hills of me native Killarney."

Some of the men looked angrily at the placid Irishman.

Steve stood up beside Walt Mawson. The woods were full of men, and here and there, men drifted along, stopping to squat and talk with men of other regiments. They walked and talked and carried news from one unit to another, trying to fit the pieces of the puzzle together to get a clearer picture of the battle. In time, men like them would become the famed 'newswalkers' of the Army of the Potomac and the Army of the Tennessee.

An armed mob, green as the hills of Killarney, thought Steve.

Raw as it was, the Union army was certainly colorful. Washington, D. C, had been filled with regiments from many states and in many different uniforms. There were volunteers and militia with a seasoning of smart regulars: the silk-stocking Seventh New York Volunteers, wearing their smart gray uniforms; the First Rhode Island Volunteers, wearing serviceable gray pants, dark-blue flannel shirts, slouch hats turned up at one side, and with long-haired Kady Brownell, wife of a sergeant, and his company's color-bearer; the fighting Irishmen of the Sixty-ninth New York Volunteers, with their bright emerald-green flag. Then there were the Seventy-ninth New York Volunteers, composed of Scots, many of whom wore tartan trousers and diced Glengarry caps, and the First New Hampshire Volunteers, who had appeared in Washington with sixteen baggage wagons, a brass band led by a drum major in a bearskin hat, a hospital wagon, and a contingent of nurses in gray traveling dresses and straw hats. There were other picturesque regiments, such as the Garibaldi Guards, the Thirty-ninth New York Volunteers, wearing jaunty red jackets and plumed *Bersaglieri* hats, a melting-pot regiment composed of Hungarians, Swiss, Germans, Italians, Frenchmen, and Spaniards, with a few Cossacks thrown in for good measure. There were at least four or five regiments of Germans in the army, too, good soldiers whose commands were given in their native tongue.

"Lookit him!" cried out Walt Mawson.

Steve turned to see a mounted courier splashing across the stream with a folded dispatch in his mouth.

"What's the news?" yelled Gershom Bates.

The courier snatched the paper from his mouth.

"Dispatch from General McDowell to Washington!" he called out. "We're winning! We've taken the Henry House plateau and have the rebels on the run!" Then he was gone through the woods, leaving a fleck of damp yellowish foam from the lathered horse on the back of Steven Ames's left hand.

"I told you so, Sergeant," crowed Bates to Hogan.

"The battle is not over yit."

"We'll be in Richmond in a week!" said Bates.

Most of the men were on their feet, with broad grins on their dusty, sweat-streaked faces.

"Too bad we didn't get a chance to show them how the Fire Zouaves fight!" thundered Gershom Bates.

Walt Mawson glanced sideways at Steve with a shamed look on his face. "I ain't sorry, Steve," he said. He swallowed hard. "I guess I ain't cut out to be a hero like Gershom Bates is."

"He sure talks like one," said Steve quietly.

"You ain't as afraid as me, kid. You been shot at before, ain't you?" He looked closely at Steve. "By Apache, Navaho, and suchlike?"

Steve nodded.

"In Mexico, wasn't it? Makes a difference, don't it? I mean, you're used to it."

Steve looked away as he tightened up the snares on his big field drum. "I don't think anyone ever really gets used to it, Walt."

Sergeant Hogan nodded. "Aye," he said quietly.

Captain Michaels came down the line. "Play the long roll," he said to Steve. "We're moving up, drummer."

Steve took his sticks from the brass drumstick carriage, which was hooked to the wide white-web drum sling. He took the drummer's stance and began to beat the instrument. All through the woods, where Willcox's Brigade had been waiting, other drummers took up the steady rolling.

There was a rattling and clashing of equipment as the

Eleventh New York fell in dressed ranks and then waited for the command to move out.

In a few minutes, the regiment moved out of the hot woods into the still hotter Virginia sunshine, in a column of fours in double time.

The regimental commander and his aide splashed through the little stream, followed by the colors and by *A* Company, the color company. Here and there, men dropped from the ranks to scoop up some of the sluggish water. "Watch it!" roared Sergeant Hogan. "Ye drink that swill, and ye'll be no good to your country or to yourselves for the rest of the day!"

The water felt good on Steve's blistered feet as he slogged on at the head of the company with his drum hung across his shoulders by the trail ropes, bumping and banging against him. "What stream is this, sir?" he asked Captain Michaels.

The officer turned. "Bull Run," he said with a funny grin. "No one ever heard of it before, and no one will ever hear of it again after this day."

They passed over a chopped-up area of land, stippled with dusty scrub trees, double-timing all the way. Now and then, a man staggered from the ranks and fell over, sick from the heat and exertion.

"Close up! Close up!" yelled officers and noncoms.

They reached a road and followed it. Ahead of them, across the smoky fields, they saw a low plateau wreathed in battle smoke, on which perched a two-story house. Beside the house, there were two Union batteries in roaring action, while on the far side of the hill, rebel guns answered back in defiance.

The Fire Zouaves came up from the Sudley Springs Road, with their rifles at right-shoulder shift, slogging toward the sound of the heaviest firing, with the bright colors slanted forward to lead them on, while behind the regiment was left a broad trail of exhausted men.

There was a continuous rattling of musketry from the

right, while from the left came the steady thudding of the guns. Colonel Farnham drew in his horse and whipped out his sword to show his regiment the line to form upon. The tired men staggered into position and looked toward the enemy.

The two Union batteries were magnificent as they blasted flame and smoke, recoiled, were swabbed, loaded, aimed, and fired again and again. The sweating, smoke-blackened gunners looked like demons from the nether regions as they served their roaring charges.

"Regulars those," said Captain Michaels as he mopped his red face. "Captain Griffin's Battery D, Fifth U. S. Artillery and Captain Ricketts' Battery I, of the First U. S. Artillery, the West Point Battery. They've been engaged most of the day hotly."

Steve felt his stomach roll a little in fear. He was tired and thirsty, and now fear had come to roost on his shoulders and keep him dreary company. A dead man lay in a hollow about fifty feet from the company, with clawed hands resting on the edge of the hollow as though he wanted to climb out and join the Zouaves. There were many other men scattered across the smoky fields like tumbled bundles of old clothing, and some of them were not good to look upon.

Steve glanced down the company line, and he knew most of the men were as scared as he was. But they were good material, formed by Colonel Elmer Ellsworth, of Chicago Zouave fame, from the rough and tough volunteer firemen of New York. Ellsworth himself had been slain by a hotel owner in Alexandria because he had taken a Confederate flag from the roof of the hotel, and his men of the Eleventh New York had sworn vengeance.

The roar of the battle seemed to increase, and there was a steady slapdash of musketry fire, while above it all, the hoarse shouting of men and the frenzied screaming of wounded and frightened horses could be heard. On the far side of the plateau, a line of men had formed in the shifting smoke, and the sun glinted on the bright bayonets as if on shards of broken mirror. They wavered in the heavy firing of the Union batteries.

"Why," said Walt Mawson in an odd, surprised voice, "them are rebels!" He swallowed hard. "They ain't running away neither, Stevie."

Gershom Bates stood a few feet ahead of his squad, with his rifle at present bayonet and a fierce look on his mustachioed face. "Let 'em come on!" he cried.

Little Walt Mawson looked back down the slope. He edged away from his squad. "They's a wounded man down there," he said vaguely to no one in particular. "Maybe I'd better help him to the rear. Looks like a friend of mine from Hoboken."

Mike Hogan leaned casually on his rifle and glanced sideways at the little man. "Stay right where you are, Mawson," he said quietly.

"He'd better!" yelled Gershom Bates fiercely. "We want no cowards in the Fightin' Eleventh!"

Steve half-closed his burning eyes. A memory had come back to him of the time his father's freighting wagons had been attacked by Mescalero Apache on the dreaded *Jornada del Muerto* in New Mexico. Steve had been nine years old then, but he had known how to load rifles beside his mother and pass them on to the fighting teamsters.

There was a dull thud, and one of the Zouaves stepped from the ranks as though to get a better look at the enemy.

"Get back into ranks, Hillman!" yelled the captain.

Hillman turned a little, then fell heavily onto his back to look up at the sky with glazed eyes that did not see.

Steve's mother had died just as quickly, with a Mescalero arrow in her heart, right beside Steve in the wagon, that terrible day on the Jornada.

Steve opened his eyes wide, trying to drive the thought of death from his mind. The bursting shells looked like great swabs of cotton tinged with red and yellow, and there was death in every one of them.

It all seemed so vague and unreal, and there was a deep sickness in Steven Ames. Virginia was a long way from New Mexico, and yet he felt just then that they were one and the same in violence and death.

"You all right, Steve?" asked Walt in a shaky voice.

"Yes."

"You're a drummer," said Mike Hogan. "Go ye to the rear to help with the wounded."

"No," said Steve. In time of battle, the orders of the company commander were signaled by a drum. Steve would be needed before long.

The whole Henry House plateau was a mass of struggling men. Riderless horses galloped through the melee, frantic in their terror.

"Stand fast, Zouaves!" called Captain Michaels.

The wavering line steadied.

Volley fire roared from a rebel brigade, and here and there, Federal units began to drop back, slowly at first, and then a little faster. Some men pitched away their rifles, while others smashed them against rocks and trees. There was an odd feeling in the smoky air, the subtle turn of battle. No one could really say what it was, but it was there just the same. More and more of the Federals fell back, and then some of them began to run. But there was no cessation of firing from the two Federal batteries led by Ricketts and Griffin; it seemed as though they planned to win the battle alone.

The smoke was thicker now, laced with sparkling red and yellow flashes. Captain Michaels went down on one knee and waved a hand back and forth in front of him as though to clear away the smoke for a better view of the battle.

"Saints preserve us!" yelled Sergeant Hogan. "Captain, sir, look ye to the right!"

Cavalry was forming near the fence line on Bald Hill,

led by a big man with a flowing beard and a black ostrich plume in his slouch hat. The trotting cavalrymen obliqued from column to deploy into line, and then a trumpet seemed to shriek in joy, and even above the crash of battle, the sound of the trumpet was like a silver bell, sending a thrill down the backbone of rebel and Federal alike.

Commands rippled down the ranks of the Eleventh New York, and the command wheeled to the right to face the charge with five hundred rifles." Fire!" came the sharp command. The rifles flashed in a long, irregular volley of hazy bluish smoke laced by red flashes. Few of the Zouaves could see the effect of their volley because of the thick, drifting smoke, but the sound of that silvery trumpet carried through to them.

"Load!" commanded the company commanders.

"No! No!" yelled Mike Hogan. He thrust out his rifle at charge bayonet. "Meet them with the steel!"

It was too late to rectify the tactical error. The rebel troopers came through the smoke. Gershom Bates stared at the naked steel saber coming at him, threw down his rifle, and scampered down the hill, hurdling a fence while he yelled in fear. "We're whipped! Run for your lives!" His red cap blew off and revealed his shorn scalp.

"Stand fast, Zouaves!" called out little Walt Mawson. "Don't run! Meet them with the steel, lads!"

Steve stared at the little man. A knot of Zouaves, encouraged by Mawson's steady voice, stood fast with him to meet the roaring charge.

Then the cavalry struck the first of the waiting line, and it was chaos. Some of the men met the charge with the bayonet, while others stood staring stupidly at the troopers, with their ramrods still in their rifles and their jaws agape as they saw the great horses crash through the regiment. Some of the horses leaped at the yelling Zouaves as though they were clearing a fence, for few of them were trained cavalry horses, but rather, hunters turned into war horses.

"Beat the rally!" yelled Hogan to Steve.

Steve raised his sticks and began to beat as hard as he could while the silver trumpet screamed above the sound.

"Run!" yelled a red-faced corporal.

"Stand fast!" cried Walt Mawson.

Steve played as he had never played before, but it was no use, for the Eleventh were breaking like reeds in front of the cavalrymen. A horse struck Steve's drum and smashed it like a dropped pumpkin. Steve tried to get his silly little dress sword from its sheath. A fleeing Zouave knocked him down.

He saw Walt Mawson fighting like a tiger to get to him, swinging his rifle by the barrel and yelling like mad. He reached Steve and gripped him by the collar to drag him to the safety of the stone fence a few feet away. "We'll hold them!" cried the little man.

The rebel trumpeter galloped past, and his instrument flashed in the bright sunlight as he played the charge again and again, but the left side of his gray shell jacket was black with blood.

The Zouaves were hopelessly broken. The few of them who stood fast were knocked down or killed, and one of those who went down forever was little Walt Mawson, fighting to the last.

Steve got his back against the fence. "Stand fast!" he cried hoarsely.

"Look out, kid!"

The cry came from behind Steve. He turned to see a great bay horse falling down toward him while its hoofs lashed out and its rider fought to keep his seat. Then the hoofs descended and struck Steve on the left shoulder, driving him down beside the fence. The whole world seemed to dissolve into a chaotic, whirling pool of utter blackness, while through it all came the silvery voice of the rebel trumpet until that too faded away.

CHAPTER TWO

BULL RUN—JULY 1861

I t was dusk when Steven Ames opened his eyes
again. There was a vague recollection of hearing
shooting and yelling and thudding of hoofs on the
hard ground, mingled with periods of unconsciousness,
and like everything else, that hot mad day, it seemed
unreal a nightmare.

He was pinned against the stone fence and above him
was the dead bulk of the bay horse. Only the fact that
Steve lay in a slight hollow at the lower edge of the fence
had saved him from being crushed to death, but he could
not get out from under the animal. He passed a shaking
hand across his face, and it seemed swollen and crusted
until he realized that what he felt was dried blood. His
head throbbed as his field drum did when he played the
long roll.

A strange, haunting sound came to Steve, and he
knew it was the pitiful moaning of wounded and dying
men, coming eerily through the dimness. He raised his
head, wincing with the savage thrust of pain through it.
His left side throbbed, but it didn't seem as though he
had any broken bones.

He looked past the head of the horse. Here and there, over the cluttered field of battle, he saw moving pools of dim yellow light as men walked about with lanterns, looking for the wounded. Now and then, they would kneel beside a body, then arise to thrust the bayoneted rifle into the ground close beside the body as a marker. Other men staggered up the slope, carrying wounded men on improvised litters formed of rifles and blankets. Steve narrowed his eyes. The uniforms looked alien to him, and he knew they were rebels. He craned his neck to look down toward the Sudley Springs Road. A column of men, followed by rolling guns, tramped along it, and as they passed a fire, he saw the rebel flag at the head of the column.

He lay in a semi-deserted part of the field, although men passed back and forth not a hundred yards from him. Somewhere, out of his sight, a man was crying for his mother in a pitiful, racked voice.

Steve moved and felt the stones of the fence give a little, and he grimly wondered whether it had been his body, driven by the weight of the horse, that had loosened the stones. He shifted slightly, got one arm up, and began slowly to shove back the heavy stones until he could work his way out from under the horse.

The first body he saw was that of little Walt Mawson. His face was calm and peaceful looking. Walt Mawson had died like a hero, fighting to the end in his first battle, while Gershom Bates had run off.

There wasn't any doubt now in Steve's mind that General McDowell had been soundly defeated. There was one thing he *did* know for sure, and that was that he had to get away from the battlefield or spend the rest of the war in a rebel prison. He was too used to the freedom of his home in New Mexico to live long in a filthy prison.

He unclasped his sword belt and dropped the ineffectual dress sword beside the shattered drum. Crawling along the fence line, he found a half-full canteen lying beside a dead rebel trooper. As he raised it to his lips, he heard a faint, moaning cry from a clump of brush on the other side of the fence.

Steve stared into the dimness. Something was moving about beside a fallen horse. A head raised, and Steve knew he had been seen. "Watah!" the voice cried out, and there was a Southern intonation in it.

Steve stopped the canteen and drew out the knife he had brought from New Mexico with him, a parting gift from Hernán Calvillo, his boyhood friend in Santa Fe.

"Watah!" called the rebel again huskily.

Steve tested the edge of the keen knife with his thumb. If the fallen man raised the alarm when he saw the Zouave uniform on Steve, there would be little chance for Steve to escape, crippled as he was. Steve began to crawl along the fence line, and the cold sweat broke out on his face from the pain of his side.

"Watah, comrade!"

Steve raised his head again. There were some litter bearers not a hundred yards away, and one of them had turned to listen to the sound of the wounded man's voice.

"What's wrong, Dan?" asked the other litter bearer.

"Heard a man calling for watah, Clay."

The other man laughed dryly. "They all are, Dannie." They walked on with their limp burden.

There were plenty of rebels close enough to hear the man if he made an outcry when he saw Steve, and yet Steve knew he could not let the man lie and suffer because of his terrible thirst. Steve held the canteen in one hand and the knife in the other, ready to use either one. He meant to escape from that battlefield, and no one was going to stop him!

He crouched beside the fallen horse and looked down at the rebel in the dimness. He was a slight man, smaller than Steve, and his groping hands were like those of a child. One of the hands gripped Steve's right wrist and gripped it tightly enough to make him wince. "Watah?" asked the man.

Steve nodded. He unstoppered the canteen with his teeth and held it toward the rebel. "Where are you hit?" he asked before he placed it to the man's mouth.

There was a moment's hesitation. "Left side... high up... close to heart..."

"You can have water then."

The eyes seemed to bore through the dimness. "*You a Yankee?*"

Steve tightened his grip on the knife. It was a weapon he hated to use, although he had seen plenty of knife play at home.

"You heah me?" asked the man.

"What difference does it make?" asked Steve quietly. He held the canteen to the lips of the wounded man, crouching close beside him to stifle any outcry. It was then he realized that the rebel was hardly much older than he was.

The rebel finished drinking and rested his head against the horse beside him. "Poor Dandy," he said.

"Who?"

"My horse. Got a bayonet through the belly. But he kept a going, Yank."

There was a faint light in the eastern sky. The moon was rising.

"Don't worry, Yank. I won't cry out."

There was something lying beside the wounded rebel. It shone dully in the darkness. It was a trumpet. Then Steve remembered the trumpeter who had gone past him at a gallop, putting his whole soul into his music with his left side shot to pieces.

"Who won?" asked the rebel.

"I'm not sure. But your people hold the battlefield."

"Then we did win!" There was no triumph in the voice.

"Yes," said Steve. He glanced back over his shoulder.

They were still alone in their private section of the battlefield.

"Colonel Stuart said we would win. He knew."

"Colonel Stuart?"

The boy nodded, then winced in pain. "Colonel James Ewell Brown Stuart. Commander of the First Virginia Cavalry. We call him Jeb Stuart. It was us who smashed your line, Yank."

"I know," said Steve dryly.

The boy coughed. "We wavered a little when you *all* volleyed us, but the colonel called out to me. 'Dacey Curtis,' he yells, 'you play that there silver trumpet like you never did before.' And I did, Yank..."

"I saw and heard you, reb."

Steve placed the canteen beside Dacey. "Good luck," he said. "I have to go now."

The hand gripped Steve's wrist with surprising strength. "No... you wait a bit..."

Steve placed his mouth close to Dacey's left ear. "Listen, rebel," he hissed. "Looks like I'm the only real live Yankee left on this battlefield, and I don't aim to sit around here waiting until they find me! I don't want to sit out the rest of the war in a reb prison eating corn pone, grits, and sowbelly!"

The boy smiled. "They ain't so bad, but I won't cry out, Yank."

Men moved about beyond the fence, looking for wounded. Steve lay low.

"Anyone ovah theah?" a man cried out.

Steve wet his lips and gripped his knife.

"Seems like we heard voices ovah theah!"

Dacey Curtis did not move or cry out, and the men moved slowly off.

"You're a fool," said Steve. "They might have saved you, Dacey. You're bad hit."

"I said I wouldn't cry out, Yank. I got something to tell you."

"It can wait."

Steve raised the knife, and the boy's eyes turned full upon him, but there was no fear in them.

Steve began to cut away the blood-stiffened material of the gray shell jacket. The moon was starting to shed light on the field through low, ragged clouds. Steve looked closely at the wound, and then he turned away, sickened by what he saw.

"No use, eh, Yank?"

Steve pulled the jacket over the wound.

"No use?" persisted the boy.

"You'll be all right."

"No... I know."

Steve wiped the sweat from the boy's face and then peeled off his own shell jacket. He rolled it and placed it under Dacey's head.

"Thanks, Yank."

"My name is Steve. Steven Ames."

"Steve, then. Where you from, Steve? They said you Frenchy-looking soldiers was from New York."

"That's right, but my home is in New Mexico."

Dacey coughed. "That's a long ways from heah."

"Yes. I've got to go now, rebel."

The boy raised his head. "Hand me that trumpet, Yank."

Steve picked up the beautiful instrument and placed it in Dacey's dirty hands. The boy passed a caressing hand along it. "Pretty," he said softly. "Jeb Stuart said it would turn a coward into a hero when he heard it played right. 'Got magic in it,' my father said. He brought it from Mexico with him. Captured it in the wah we had down theah. Captured it from a Mexican lancer, but the trumpet had French words written on it."

"So?"

"My father always said it could do anything if you played it with heart."

Steve nodded. He could still remember the First

Virginia Cavalry smashing into the ranks of the Fire Zouaves and of how the silver trumpet, played by a mortally wounded boy, had spurred on the cavalry.

The moon was now shining on the low hills. If Steve was to make good his escape, he'd have to leave right away.

"I know you have to go, Steve," said Dacey.

"Yes."

The dirty hands passed up and down the trumpet. "This shouldn't be lost, Steve."

"It will be found with you, Dacey."

"No. It has to be passed from one soldier to another, Steve."

Steve stared curiously at the boy.

"My father got it from the trumpeter of the Mexican lancers that way. On his death bed, my father gave it to my brothah James. Brother James died of camp fever at Harper's Ferry and left the trumpet to me. He was trumpeter for Jeb Stuart, and I stayed on to fill his place."

"I've got to go, Dacey," said Steve desperately.

"In a minute, Steve." Dacey raised his head and placed the trumpet in Steve's hands. "Take care of it," he said thickly.

"But I'm a Yank, Dacey!"

The eyes opened wide. "Don't matter none. This war is madness anyway. That's what my mothah said when I left for Harper's Ferry to get the trumpet. Fathah against son and brothah against brothah. Today you and me fought against each othah, and tonight you tried to help me. Take the silver trumpet, Steve. Don't use it against us rebels. Try to use it to help each othah. I don't know how, but I know you'll find a way." The head raised, and the blue eyes were fierce in the moonlight. "But if you use it wrong, you'll pay for it if I have to come back from the grave."

"Take it easy, Dacey."

"That trumpet has been to too many wahs. 'Bout time

a beautiful thing like thet was used for good instead of evil."

The beautiful instrument felt cool and alive in Steve's hands.

Dacey Curtis rested his head on the shell jacket. "Good-by, Steven Ames," he said quietly.

Steve stood up. "I'll go and get one of your doctors."

"They'll take you prisoner."

"It doesn't matter."

The boy smiled. "You see? The trumpet is already working its magic on you, Steve."

Steve opened his mouth and then shut it. The moon shone on the boy's face. His eyes were wide open, but they did not see, and there was a calm smile on the still, pale face.

"Good-by, Dacey Curtis," said Steve. He slung the silver trumpet over his shoulder by the yellow silken cord and then walked to the north toward the thick woods, and he did not look back as he walked, but the moonlight reflected from the polished surface of the trumpet.

On the Henry House plateau, a tall, bearded man looked down on the battlefield. "What's that shining in the moonlight, Hastings?" he demanded of an officer beside him.

The officer stared. "Nothing, sir."

"Might be an escaping Yankee."

The officer smiled. "There isn't a Yankee left on this field, sir, who isn't dead, wounded, or a prisoner of war."

"All the same, there's something moving down there."

"Moonbeams, sir, nothing but moonbeams. The moonbeams of victory for the Confederacy."

"Yes, I think you're right." Colonel Jeb Stuart kneed his horse away from the fence and rode toward the camp-fires of the victorious Southern army.

CHAPTER THREE

The broiling August sun was beating down upon the tent, forming curiously mottled patterns on the dirt floor. There was scarcely a breath of wind, and when the wind did blow a little, it brought with it the stench of the nearby Tiber Canal where the decaying offal of the government slaughterhouses floated in the filthy waters.

Hoarse commands came to Steven Ames as he lay in his tent. *A* Company was out on the hard-packed drill field not far from the company street, going through the motions and times of loading and firing under the whiplash voice of Sergeant Michael Hogan.

The fever Steve had contracted on his long march through the night rain from the field of Bull Run had finally laid him low, and he was not the only one. Twenty percent of the company was ill with fever in the filthy tents. Five times in the past two days, the burial wagon had passed down the company street. If it kept up, the Fire Zouaves would lose more men in the camp than they had at Bull Run.

Steve felt under his sagging cot for his canteen. He

sipped a little of the warm water and then wet his hand
to cool his burning forehead. As he placed the canteen
back on the floor, his hand touched the canvas-wrapped
silver trumpet that he had brought from the battlefield.
It had been stolen once by a man from *B* Company and
recovered by Sergeant Hogan while Steve had been
delirious with fever. Sergeant Hogan had said it would
bring a fine price in a Washington hock shop.

Steve closed his eyes. He could still see the drawn
face of Dacey Curtis. Two weeks had gone by since the
battle, and the Federal troops had fallen back to defend
Washington. The rebel papers were screaming that it had
been total defeat, that the North was whipped, that one
Southerner could whip a dozen Northerners, and so on
and so on. Washington itself was full of Southern sympa-
thizers, many of whom had stood on street corners in the
drizzling rain, smirking as they saw the dispirited Federal
troops straggle back into the city.

A drum thudded lifelessly in the hot, still air. A detail
of cavalrymen trotted past the Zouave camp, sending
yellow dust swirling into the tents.

Steve coughed and sat up, holding his head in his
hands. The tent seemed to tilt and whirl, and there was a
deadly fear within him that he, too, would end up in the
growing graveyard just beyond the camp. Suddenly, with
all his heart and soul, he wished he was back in the cool,
clear air of his native New Mexico, and he knew he was
homesick. These people were not really his people. Some
of them he liked, such as Sergeant Hogan and Captain
Michaels, and he missed his friend Walt Mawson, who
had died at Bull Run.

A shadow fell across the floor of the tent, and Steve
looked up to see a young officer, wearing the bare
shoulder straps of a second lieutenant, smiling at him.
Steve got to his feet and managed a passable salute.

"Sit down, Steve," the officer said.

Steve sat down gratefully. "How did you know my name, sir?"

The officer looked about the littered tent. "Volunteers, all right. Regulars would never leave a tent looking like this."

Steve felt a little angry, but the officer's smile disarmed him. "It takes a little time to train men, sir."

The officer nodded. He sat down on a cot and placed his sword between his knees. He rested his hands on the sword and studied Steve. "How do you feel?"

"All right, I guess."

"You don't look like it, Steve."

Steve shook his head. "I guess all of us will have to go through a bout of fever sooner or later."

"I hope not. I'm Lieutenant Lloyd Bruce, Third United States Cavalry."

"Pleased to meet you, sir." Steve eyed the officer. The Third was well known to him, for they garrisoned posts throughout New Mexico, and as far as he knew, they were still stationed in the territory. "The Mounted Rifles," he said.

Bruce smiled. "I see you know the *old* name."

"Yes, sir. The Brave Rifles."

"I came here to look you up, Steve. I'm glad I did. This is no place for you."

"It's *my* regiment, Lieutenant."

The dark eyes studied Steve. "Is it? New York Volunteer Firemen. Toughs and roughs from the tenements. Why did you enlist in the Eleventh?"

Steve shrugged. "I was in school, and it was spring. The bands played, and the flags waved, and then the President called for volunteers. I knew how to play a drum. The rest was easy."

"I would probably have done the same thing. Well, gather your gear together. You're coming with me."

"I don't understand, sir."

Lieutenant Bruce reached inside his blouse and

brought out some papers. He held one of them up between two fingers. "This is your honorable discharge from the Eleventh New York Volunteers."

"But, sir...!"

Bruce took up another paper. "Wait! This is your enlistment in the First New Mexico Volunteer Infantry, now stationed near Santa Fe, Territory of New Mexico."

Steve stared at Bruce. "You're moving too fast for me, sir. Maybe it's the fever. Maybe you don't exist at all."

"You can pinch me—that is, except that it isn't exactly military courtesy to do so."

"But why am I to leave the Eleventh?" Steve stood up. "I did my duty! I was knocked unconscious on the field and came back to my regiment when I was able to do so! That's more than many of them did. Gershom Bates ran away when the cavalry charged us, and we haven't seen him since!"

"You don't understand. How old are you, Steve?"

"Eighteen, sir!"

Bruce thrust a tongue against the inside of his cheek.

"You might be. You're big enough. But..."

"Seventeen, then!"

Bruce rubbed a hand against his jaw.

Steve wet his lips." Sixteen?" he asked in a small voice.

"Fifteen, Steve. I know for a fact."

"What happens now?"

"There are plenty of fifteen-year-old lads in the army. Yes, and younger lads than that too, but it is required for them to have their parent's consent for enlistment."

Steve's eyes narrowed.

Bruce went on. "I've heard you are a good field drummer, Steve. Learned to play from old Sergeant Honus Schuster, retired, of the Seventh United States Infantry. Am I right?"

"Yes, sir." The officer knew far too much, thought Steve.

"Sergeant Hogan says you are the best field drummer in the Eleventh."

Things were beginning to fit together now.

"The fact is, Steve, you did not have your father's consent to join the volunteers. Therefore, you have committed fraudulent enlistment. Your father wrote to your schoolmaster, who in turn located you in the Eleventh New York. He passed on that information to your father, who at that time was in Independence, Missouri, ready to leave on the Santa Fe Trail with a government wagon train under his charge. I can assure you that there was some mighty fast action after that.

"Your father wrote to Senator Chavez in Washington. The senator contacted the War Department. There's no need of my telling you how much weight your father and uncle can pull in government matters when they wish to."

Steve nodded. "Yes," he said dryly.

Bruce held up the papers. "Therefore, it was easy to get your discharge from the Eleventh and have the papers made out for your enlistment in the First New Mexico. This time, with your father's permission."

"I won't leave the Eleventh, sir."

Bruce stood up, and his eyes hardened. "You're wanted home in New Mexico, Steve."

"I won't run away like a whipped pup!"

"Attention, Drummer Ames!"

Steve stiffened.

"Now listen to me, soldier! We've gone through a lot of trouble to get these papers cleared and to find you! I haven't much time left in Washington, and I don't intend to waste it arguing with you!"

"But, sir, Sergeant Hogan says this will be a long war, that every man is needed. We haven't been licked yet, sir. One battle doesn't win a war."

"I agree with you, Ames."

"That's why I want to stay here rather than go to New Mexico and sit in a garrison for the rest of the war."

Bruce came closer to Steve. "I can see you know little of what has been going on in the rest of the country while you've been serving here. There will be plenty for all of us to do in New Mexico."

Steve couldn't help smiling. "What does New Mexico have to do with the war, sir? Away out back of beyond. The lost colony of the United States."

"The last information I have is that Texas Mounted Rifles are on the move from San Antonio toward El Paso del Norte. It's also rumored that a column of Texas rebels plan to invade New Mexico."

Steve grinned. "Some rumor. What would they gain by that, sir?"

"Would you believe me if I told you that Luke Comfort learned that information?"

The grin faded away. "The best scout in the Southwest! I've never heard of him bringing in any wrong information."

Bruce nodded. "I have orders to join the Third Cavalry in the District of New Mexico as soon as possible, carrying important secret dispatches from the War Department to Colonel E. R. S. Canby, district commander. Your father requested that you accompany me. By a little manipulation, it was arranged that you get discharged from the Eleventh, enlisted in the First, then go with me as my orderly to Santa Fe."

Things were moving too fast for Steve. He passed a hand across his burning forehead.

"As of right now, Drummer Stevens Ames, you are on detached duty from the First New Mexico Volunteers, District of New Mexico, to act as mounted orderly to Second Lieutenant Lloyd Bruce, Third United States Cavalry, District of New Mexico, a courier from the War Department, Washington, D. C, to Santa Fe, Territory of New Mexico, via Independence, Missouri, and the Santa Fe Trail."

Steve couldn't help laughing at the mock-solemn air

with which the young officer had made his speech, and he knew he would grow to like Lieutenant Bruce very much on the long and arduous trip to Santa Fe.

Bruce placed Steve's enlistment paper in the First New Mexico on top of the boy's cased drum, and then he looked steadily at Steve. Steve took a pen and a bottle of ink from Corporal Duffy's footlocker. He squatted down beside the drum and signed the paper, then watched while Lieutenant Bruce signed it. Bruce then administered the oath to Steve.

Steve looked about the hot tent. He'd miss the members of his mess.

"Are you well enough to travel now?" asked the officer. "I have two horses waiting for us at the head of the company street."

"I can ride, sir. I can *always* ride."

"That's what I've heard. Like a centaur, Senator Chavez said. You should be in the cavalry, Steve."

Steve flushed.

"Get your gear together," said Bruce.

Steve picked up his haversack and put his personal things into it. He picked up the silver trumpet and then looked at his new field drum, which had replaced the one lost at Bull Run.

"Is that all you have?" asked Bruce.

"Yes, sir."

"We'll have to get you out of that Zouave uniform and into regulation blues."

Steve looked quickly at him.

"No offense, Steve, to you and the gallant Fire Zouaves, but you'd look a little silly chasing Kiowas near Plum Buttes in that getup."

Steve nodded. "It is a little gay for that purpose, sir."

A hoarse command sounded at the head of the company street. Feet thudded against the hard ground in the unmistakable rhythm of marching men. Steve walked to the door of the tent. *A* Company came down the street, rifles at right-shoulder shift. More commands rattled out, and the company swung from column to company front and grounded arms. The dust floated over the line of tents.

"Smartly done," said Bruce.

"Dismissed!" roared Sergeant Hogan. He wiped the sweat from his face and then came toward Steve and the officer. He saluted. " 'Tis hot work, but it has to be done before we can best the rebels at their own game, sir." He eyed Steve. "So ye're leavin' the regiment?"

"Yes, Sergeant. As though you didn't know."

Hogan avoided Steve's hard stare. "Well, 'tis for the best, me boy. This is no place for ye. Go home to New Mexico Territory. From what the lootenant has told me, thayer might be a bit of a fightback, thayer too."

"Oh, sure, sure," said Steve dryly.

"Don't *ye* be too sure thayer won't be! Ye wait! 'Twill be a long war and a hard one! Ye know that country, and ye know them people. 'Tis me honest belief they can use ye thayer and that ye'll get a bellyful of fightin' before ye are much older."

The men of the company stood about leaning on their rifles instead of going to their tents. Steve turned to the officer. "I'd like to say good-by to my messmates, sir."

"I expect you to."

Steve walked to the company and shook hands all around.

"We'll sure miss your lively drumming," said big Sam Donald's.

"Except at reveille," said grinning Orton Rybal.

"The best of luck to ye, Stevie," said Corporal Duffy.

It was hard to look at the smiling faces. Steve waved a hand and went back to the officer and Hogan.

"Now, mind ye, Steve," said the sergeant, "ye have the makings of a good soldier in ye. Remember what I taught ye!"

"How can I forget?"

"Repeat the soldier's catechism once more for me!"

Steve snapped to attention. "Keep my eyes open and my mouth shut; be first in the mess line and in the pay line; never volunteer for anything under any circumstances!"

Hogan nodded in deep satisfaction. "Aye, ye'll do, son." He looked at the trumpet. "Ye'll take that along, no doubt?"

"Yes."

"A strange story about that. Somehow, I have a feeling that thayer is magic in that horn. 'Tis the Irish in me, no doubt."

"No doubt," said Bruce with a smile.

Steve squeezed the trumpet. It has to be given from one soldier to another, Dacey Curtis had said.

"A beautiful instrument," said Hogan.

Take the silver trumpet, Steve, the dying boy had said. Don't use it against us rebels. Try to use it to help each other. I don't know how, but I know you'll find a way.

"We'll have to leave," said Lieutenant Bruce. "We can get a train out of here in three hours. Time enough to get you outfitted, Steve."

Steve held out his hand to Sergeant Hogan. Hogan took it in his ham of a hand. "Good luck, me boy. May the wind be always at your back and a light in your path."

"A fine Irish thought," said Bruce.

Hogan's eyes were suspiciously bright. "No. 'Twas Robbie Burns said that."

The two of them walked along the dusty company street. As far as the eye could see, there were tents in the fields and on the hills, while the sun flashed on brightly scoured shovels as earthworks were being dug to defend Washington. There was a steady, low murmuring of many voices. The sun also shone on brass gun barrels and on the bayonets of the pacing sentries. Drumbeats and bugle calls came on the warm wind.

"You'll never forget this place," said Bruce.

"No, sir."

"Some memories have a way of staying with us."

"Yes, sir."

The officer clapped Steve on the back. "But you'll be glad to have a horse beneath you and to feel the dry prairie wind against your face."

Steve smiled. He could almost feel that clean, dry wind now, sweeping across miles and miles of plains to the land of New Mexico, where wolf-fanged mountains stood etched against an incredibly blue sky dotted with cotton-puff clouds sailing steadily along. It would be good to go home.

CHAPTER FOUR

GLORIETA PASS, NEW MEXICO TERRITORY—SEPTEMBER 1861

A shaft of lightning flashed across the sullen sky and seemed to lance into the huge, somber bulk of El Pilon. For an instant, the eerie light revealed the rugged walls of the deep canyon, stippled with shaggy piñon and juniper trees, and then the canyon was in darkness again. There was a distant thudding of the drums of the Thunder People in the gorges.

Lieutenant Lloyd Bruce turned in his saddle, resting a hand on his cantle pack.

Steven Ames turned too. "What's wrong, sir?"

"How far are we from Santa Fe now?" asked Bruce.

"About eighteen miles."

"I wish we had stayed at Koslowski's Ranch, as they asked us to."

The night was dark again. The two horses followed the dim road at the bottom of the deep pass. Steve swung his single-shot Sharps carbine from where it was slung at his side so that it rested across his thighs. A heavy navy cap-and-ball Colt pistol was holstered at his right side.

Steve's dun tossed its head. "What is it, Zouave?" asked Steve quietly. The mount had been waiting for him at Independence, a gift left for him there by his father, and there was no mistaking his father's fine hand in picking out horseflesh.

"They said Jicarilla Apache had been troublesome in here the past few months," said Bruce.

"They won't attack two well-armed soldiers, sir."

"Don't be so cool about this!"

Steve grinned a little in the darkness. "We've come eight hundred miles across hostile Indian country with nothing happening. Nothing will happen this close to the end of our trip, sir."

Bruce waved a hand. "Don't be too sure about that!"

There was a spit of rain in the night air. Steve looked up at the dark sky as a faint web of lightning traced a course across it. Bruce had been in a hurry ever since they had left the wagon train behind them at Las Vegas, in New Mexico, to push on ahead to Santa Fe. They had been safe enough on the long trail from Independence. Few Indian tribes would attack a well-armed caravan unless they had overwhelming numbers. They had received too many bloody noses from fooling around with the tough caravanners.

The wind keened up the canyon. Steve shivered a little despite the warmth of his thick issue blouse. He had been completely outfitted in Washington before he had left there—dark-blue blouse, light-blue trousers, a forage cap with the infantry trumpet insignia on it, which he had personally made sure was just a mite too small so that he could perch it jauntily on one side of his head as he had seen the Regulars do.

"Wait!" said Bruce.

They drew rein and sat their horses in the darkness, listening to the moaning wind. It was a familiar place to Steve, for he had often traveled through there with his father's freighting trains. But tonight, it seemed different, a strange alien difference that began to bother him.

"Jicarilla's won't attack at night, sir," said Steve.

"I've heard that one before."

"Their souls will wander forever in darkness if they are killed at night."

Bruce passed a hand along the barrel of his carbine and then touched the locked dispatch case that was slung at his side, and that never left him awake or asleep. "They said I was to proceed as fast as possible to Santa Fe," he said, almost as though he was talking to himself. "Hurry! Hurry! Hurry!"

Steve eyed the young officer. Lieutenant Bruce had undergone quite a change since he had left Las Vegas, and the importance of the dispatches had unnerved him more than Steve had realized.

"They said there were *ladrones* in here, too," said Bruce.

Steve nodded. "There always are thieves in here, sir." He patted his carbine." Few of them have the nerve to attack soldiers, though, sir. They like the odds with them."

"Perhaps."

The officer looked back down the canyon. "I think we had better hole up until dawn."

"That's a favorite attacking time for the Jicarilla's, sir."

Bruce cut a hand sideways to quiet Steve. The officer was brave and intelligent, but it hadn't taken Steve long to find out that he knew next to nothing about hostile Indians. Another thing Steve had learned was that Bruce didn't like to be reminded about his ignorance of Indians. He knew Steve had been raised in the frontier country among skilled Indian fighters and scouts, such as his own father, and the knowledge of that had seemed to irritate the officer.

Steve couldn't help himself. "It's better to travel at night in Indian country and hole up by day, sir," he said.

"I'm in command here! We can't see to shoot in this murk!"

"They won't..."

"Be quiet, soldier! I've heard enough of your expert opinions! Is there any place along here where we can get shelter from the coming rain?"

"Half a mile up the road, Lieutenant, there's a place where a rock overhang would provide shelter. There's a spring there too and grazing for the horses. It's a favorite camping place of my father's."

"Good!"

The rain was pattering down on the dry leaves when Steve led the way from the rutted road toward the dim bulk of the great rock overhang to the south. Steve swung down and took the reins of both horses as Lieutenant Bruce peered about. "This looks just fine, Steve," he said.

Steve nodded. It would be a long, hard wait for him until dawn. He didn't like the idea at all, but there was nothing he could do about it but sweat it out until they got on the road again.

Bruce was still nervous. He prowled back and forth as Steve took his gum-rubber talma from his saddlebag and put it on. "This is a long way from the war," growled the officer.

Steve led the horses to the shelter and leaned against Zouave, listening to the steady pattering of the rain. The very air seemed full of the electrical odor of the lightning discharges and the fresh smell of the rain, but there was something else in the air, too, the odor of fear.

Bruce put on his talma and walked to the far end of the rock overhang with his carbine in his hands. Steve eyed him idly in the faint light from the Hashes high overhead. Suddenly Steve stiffened. Something had seemed to move in the darkness beyond the officer.

Steve walked toward Bruce. "Maybe we had better go on, sir," he suggested.

Bruce shook his head, then walked farther out from the rock. It was then that Steve saw the sudden movement in the brush, and he opened his mouth to yell, but it was too late.

The warrior seemed to appear from nowhere, with a raised knife in his hand, and even as Steve darted forward, he saw the knife dart down against the back of Lieutenant Bruce. The officer grunted and went down on one knee, and his carbine fell from his limp hands.

Something grated on the rocks behind Steve. He whirled and instinctively cocked and raised his carbine. There was no time to aim at the racing Jicarilla. Steve fired and knew he had hit the warrior, for he staggered back and fell heavily.

Steve turned again, just as a brilliant lance of lightning shot down the pass, to see the first warrior crouching beside the officer, slashing away at the strap that held the dispatch case at Bruce's side.

There was no time to reload the carbine or draw pistol. Steve remembered his Zouave training. He darted forward, reversed the carbine, and drove the steel-shod butt hard against the head of the warrior. The warrior looked up with wide eyes and then fell beside the officer. There was no time to lose. Steve had been told time and time again by Lieutenant Bruce that nothing mattered except getting those dispatches to Santa Fe, despite anything that might happen to him.

Steve snatched up the dispatch case and ran toward his dun. He swung up onto the horse and slapped him with the carbine barrel. Using his spurs, he galloped toward the road. He glanced back as he rode, and in the cold illumination of the lightning, he saw the set face of Lloyd Bruce and knew that he was dead.

Three warriors seemed to rise from the very ground as Steve reached the edge of the road. They raised their weapons, but Steve sank the steel into the flanks of the dun, and the big horse smashed into the three warriors, scattering them like chaff. "*¡Madre de Dios!*" one of them screamed as he went down.

A gun flashed behind Steve as he bent low and lashed Zouave on down the road, and it seemed to him as though the slug picked at his left sleeve. He raced to the west as the rain came down in a slashing downpour.

Steve rounded a huge rock shoulder and then reloaded as he let the dun ease off a little. It was still a long way to Santa Fe.

He looked back, although there was nothing to see. He had grown to admire and respect Lieutenant Lloyd Bruce during the long journey from Washington. The officer had fulfilled his duty but had died almost in sight of his goal, and it was up to Steve to finish the mission.

The road was empty. There was a cold feeling within Steve, for there had been something wrong about those Jicarilla's back there. In the swift and deadly flurry of action, there had been little time to think, but now the reaction set in, and he felt sick. They *never* attacked at night.

The dispatch case bumped against his side, and he cast away his sickness. This was war. A man-made comrades and lost them quickly in time of war. One way or another, by separation or by death, comrades left and were never seen again, but a man's duty stayed with him always. Those dispatches must get to Santa Fe, and Steven Ames, of the First New Mexico Volunteer Infantry, was the one who had to get them there.

CHAPTER FIVE

SANTA FE, NEW MEXICO TERRITORY—SEPTEMBER 1861

The rain was still falling when Steve Ames reached the first adobe houses of Santa Fe. There was a faint tinge of the false dawn in the eastern sky. The houses seemed to squat despondently in the wet, with their brightly painted doors and small, secretive windows, while from the flat roofs, muddy water poured out of the spouts, forcing Steve to ride in the center of the narrow, winding street.

There was little joy in him at his homecoming. When he had first left Washington with Lieutenant Bruce, he had still been a little bitter about leaving his friends in the Eleventh New York. Then he had grown to accept the idea of returning home, and gradually he had learned that he had really wanted to return home all the time. But now it seemed as though he had left part of himself back there in lonely Glorieta Pass with Lieutenant Bruce, as he had also left a part of himself at Bull Run with Walt Mawson and Dacey Curtis.

He skirted a rushing irrigation ditch, then rode toward San Francisco Street and followed it to the wide deserted plaza with the long bulk of the Governor's

Palace dominating the northern side. Beyond the plaza, he rode toward the narrow street where his father's house was. The cold, wet wind moaned ceaselessly through the cottonwoods and willows.

He turned into the street and looked eagerly down it. It hadn't changed a bit in the two years he had been away. He remembered the day he had left there in a stiff, store-bought suit, bound for the Santa Fe Trail, to end up eventually at Albright's Academy for Boys and Young Gentlemen in New York City.

He dismounted in front of the great door that had been cut into the thick adobe walls to permit carriages to pass through into the patio. It was studded with square-hewn bolts and heavy metal fittings. He tried the handle of the smaller door that was let into the big one, although he knew well enough it would be locked. *Ladrones* prowled the streets of Santa Fe at night, looking for every opportunity.

Steve took off his cumbersome talma and then walked down the side lane to where a great tree hung a thick branch over the wall. He had climbed that tree many a time, both to get in and to get out of the house, without his father's permission, of course. He gripped the branch and swung up his legs to get a toe hold in the niche that had eroded itself into the adobe wall. It was a matter of seconds to pull himself along the wall, then drop lightly atop the roof of a storehouse. He walked to the edge and let himself down into the wide, flagged patio.

The great house was built in the form of a rough square, with rooms on the west and east sides, the great hall on the north side, and stables and storage rooms on the south side. The patio had been his mother's kingdom in the old days, where she had tended her flowers and shrubs, had fed the birds and squirrels and had done her sewing.

There wasn't a light on in the house. He crossed the puddled patio and opened the door that was the inner entry into the patio, then passed through the dark passageway to the outer door. He lifted the heavy bar from its metal supporting arms and eased back the huge door. Then he led Zouave into the patio and to the stables.

It was dawn when he came out of the stable. He carried his gear into the little hallway that led into the long, low living room. He lighted a Rochester lamp on the old Spanish Colonial table and then paused to look about himself. The room had not been changed.

The lamplight glistened from the top of his mother's rosewood piano, which had been brought at great expense over the Santa Fe Trail. His father's polished Hawken rifle was missing from the wooden pegs over the beehive fireplace, and he knew then that his father was not at home.

Steve took off his wet forage cap and damp blouse and hung them on a chair while he looked about the familiar room. Piñon wood was stacked vertically in the fireplace, and he took flint and steel and struck a light. The dry wood crackled sharply, and he warmed his hands at it.

"Does the house look any different, Steve?" the quiet voice said.

Steve jumped a little, then turned to see his uncle standing in the doorway that led to the bedrooms. Carter Ames was a tall, bearded man, a good many years older than Mark Ames, Steve's father. His eyes were gray, and there were times when there was a fierce light in them, for Carter Ames was a fighter. Steve stood up as his uncle came to him, then drew him close in a bear hug. "You look more like your father every day," he said, "but there is a strong touch of your mother in you too."

"Where is Father?"

"Down south. On territorial business. Your father acts like a man obsessed since this war started. He's trying to hold New Mexico for the Union all by himself, it seems."

Steve nodded. He might have known that.

"You've grown a lot and filled out, Steve. You'll soon be as big as your father."

Carter Ames sat down and studied Steve. "How was the battle, Steve?"

"Pretty bad, Uncle."

"They all are. It was a foolish thing for you to do."

"There were a lot of boys younger than myself there."

Carter Ames nodded. "Yes. I would think so. Where is Lieutenant Bruce?"

Steve looked away.

"What's wrong, boy?"

Steve turned. "Lieutenant Bruce was killed by Jicarilla's late last night in Glorieta Pass."

Carter Ames leaped to his feet. "Good heavens! The dispatches!"

Steve walked to the hallway and got the wet leather case. He handed it to his uncle. "I managed to get away from the Jicarilla's with them, sir."

"What happened?"

Steve quietly told the story.

"You've got courage, boy," said his uncle. "Thank God you came through safely yourself."

Steve fingered the bullet hole he had found in his left sleeve. "I was lucky it was so dark and that they weren't mounted."

"I cannot imagine why they'd attack at night." Carter Ames touched the dispatch case. "Bruce knew how important these dispatches were. He was a fool to come through that pass with just a boy as an escort. No offense to you, Steve, for you played the part of a man. Thank heaven you were there!"

"I knew they were important, sir."

"You have no idea how important, son."

Steve warmed his hands at the fire. The thought of

the tight little fight in the pass had chilled him. "I'm not so sure they were Jicarilla's, though, sir."

The gray eyes half closed. "No? Why not?"

"First, you know they don't like to fight at night."

"Yes."

"Then, when I knocked down the warrior who had killed Lieutenant Bruce, the lightning flashed, and I got a good look at him."

"So?"

"His eyes were light, sir. And he had blond hair. The whole incident was odd. Jicarilla's attacking at night. A warrior with fair hair. Then, when the warrior had downed Lieutenant Bruce, he didn't snatch at his weapons as most Apache would do, for you know how they value fine weapons, but instead, he grabbed for the dispatch case."

"Yes," his uncle said softly.

"When I broke for the road, Zouave crashed into three more of them, and one of them cried out in Spanish as he went down."

"Zouave?"

"My horse, sir."

"I see." Carter Ames looked into the crackling fire.

"Perhaps they were *ladrones* disguised as warriors, sir."

"No... I do not think so, Steve. You know little of what has been going on here. Someone knew that those dispatches were coming through Glorieta Pass in the hands of Lieutenant Bruce. There are forces working here in New Mexico determined to turn the territory over to the Confederacy. There are other forces, just as determined, who work to save New Mexico for the Union. True, many people in the East think this territory is hardly worth bothering about, but they are blind fools!"

"What do you mean by that, sir?"

"I'll tell you when we have eaten. Get out of those wet clothes. I think there must be some of your old clothing in your room. I'll have time to whip up some grub for us while you're changing. It wouldn't do for Colonel Canby to see you in a messy uniform and with an empty belly."

Steve walked to his room at the far end of the hallway. It was just the same as it had been the day he had closed the door on it two years ago—the whitewashed walls, neatly hung with calico sheeting on the lower four feet to keep the whitewash from rubbing off on one's clothing; the crudely carved bedstead with the thick woolen trade blankets on it; even the little carved *Santo* stared woodenly at him from its niche in the wall. The Ames were not Catholics, but they lived in a predominantly Catholic community, and Steve had become accustomed to their ways. Old Rosa Abeyta had worked in the house after his mother had died, and she had placed the *Santo* in the niche to stand guard over Steve while he slept.

He took some of his old trail clothing from the great wooden wardrobe. Though they had fitted him rather loosely two years ago, now he had a hard squeeze getting into them, but they were warm and dry. He carried his damp clothing into the living room and hung it near the fire.

In a little while, his uncle came into the room from the kitchen, bearing a heavily laden tray. Carter Ames smiled. "Warmed-over frijoles and hard bread. All I have left from last night. I don't eat here very often now that we have no housekeeper. Rosa married again and lives south of here with her new husband, Eusebio Campos, the muleteer. I haven't been able to get a decent housekeeper since then."

"Smells good to me."

Carter Ames placed a pot of chocolate near the fire to warm. Steve noted that the dispatch case hung from the old man's wide belt and that the butt of a pistol showed from his pocket. He was a well-known lawyer in the territory and had sat as a judge in territorial courts. He was a powerful factor in the land and a courageous man, but above all else, he was a Union man, and as long as men like Carter Ames would fight for New Mexico Territory, the Confederacy might get a rough comeuppance. Of that, Steve was quite sure.

———

CARTER AMES SHOVED BACK his plate and then walked to the fire. He placed more piñon wood on it and warmed his big hands at the cheery blaze. He spoke over his shoulder to Steve. "Times are troublous here, Steve. The war will soon be felt here as it has been in the East."

"Just Indian raids, sir, and we've lived through quite a few of them."

The old man turned. "No, there's more to it than Indian raids. We've had them before, and we'll have them again. Right now, it's Texans bothering us. Texas Mounted Rifles! They already hold southern New Mexico and part of Arizona as well."

"Probably just a bluff, sir."

The fierce eyes seemed to lash out at Steve. "Bluff? You're talking just like the rest of the fools who cannot, and will not, believe those Texans mean business! Supposing those rebels do attack and conquer New Mexico? Do you know what they stand to gain?"

Steve shook his head. He still thought his uncle was building up a big case out of nothing.

"If the Texans conquer New Mexico and capture the vast military stores at Fort Union, they could arouse Southern sympathies all over the Southwest. They could gain many recruits, arm them, then strike west through Arizona to attack California. Once California was in their hands, the Union might suffer a blow that would lose the war for them."

"How so, sir?"

"California and the rest of the Pacific Coast have fine

deep-water ports. The Pacific slopes are covered with fine timber for shipbuilding. There's the Mare Island Navy Yard and the Benicia Arsenal. Ships from all over the world could bring their goods to the Pacific Coast, sell them to the rebels, who in turn would freight them across California, Arizona, New Mexico, and Texas, thence into the Confederacy! Do you follow me?"

"Yes, but the Union navy can blockade the Pacific Coast as it is now blockading the Atlantic Coast and the Gulf of Mexico, sir."

Judge Ames snorted. "Maybe! But did it ever occur to you that the Federal government gets most of its gold from the California mines? What happens if the rebels get possession of the California gold mines and the silver mines of Nevada?"

Steve paled a little. "I never thought of that."

"You'd better! The whole country had better! You don't run wars without gold and silver, son. The Romans could have told you that. Another thing: all we've got to hold New Mexico, the key to the whole situation, is a handful of Regulars backed by local militia and volunteers, and a great part of those militia and volunteer units are composed of native New Mexicans. Now, these men are brave enough, but they have an inherent fear of the *Tejanos,* as they call the Texans, and there doesn't seem to be much we can do about it."

The old man walked to a roller map that hung on the wall over a side table. He pulled it down, then placed the lamp on the side table so that the yellow light illuminated the parchment, and Steve saw that it was a great map of the Southwest. The old man began to talk again, and as he did, so he traced the course of his talk with a spatulate finger, and some of his past words began to make greater sense to Steve.

"The whole territory south of Albuquerque is practically a ghost country now, Steve. Apache are ripping through it from one end to the other. Ranches, *Placitas,* and mines have been abandoned. The few troops we have down there can hardly hold the Texans back, much less patrol hundreds of square miles of deserts and mountains to hold the Apache in check."

Carter Ames began to touch crosses marked on the map in red ink. "You see these crosses? They mark the sites of half a dozen forts, once manned by Regular troops that have been shamefully abandoned! Forts Bliss, McLane, Breckinridge, Buchanan, Fillmore, and Stanton. All we have left in the pathway of the advancing rebels is Fort Craig, on the Rio Grande near the Valverde Fords. If Fort Craig falls and our troops are driven from the field, the rebel flag will be flying over Santa Fe within a week after that."

Steve walked to the map. He could clothe that paper with buttes and mesas, springs, water holes, trails, and roads. He knew them well enough.

"After our recent disaster at San Augustine Springs," said his uncle, "our Regular troops at Fort Stanton abandoned it and set fire to it, then retreated to Fort Craig. For all we know, the Texans may have occupied Fort Stanton too."

"What happened at San Augustine Springs, sir?"

"Cowardice and treason! Major Isaac Lynde surrendered the entire garrison of Fort Fillmore after a shameful retreat from the fort itself. Seven companies of the Seventh United States Infantry and three companies of the Mounted Rifles. He surrendered five hundred well-trained and well-armed soldiers of the Regular army to three hundred poorly armed Texans without firing a shot! It seems incredible, but it did happen. Luke Comfort is down there now investigating the incident."

Steve smiled at the recollection of the scout. "I hope the Apache don't get him."

Judge Ames snorted. "Apache get Luke Comfort? He can travel through the middle of their country and never be seen while he can see them. That's why the Mexicans call him *El Espectro*."

"The Ghost. It suits him all right."

The judge sat down and looked into the dying fire. "We are forming many new units here to fight against the Texans or any other rebels who figure on attacking us, but I doubt the value of most of these units. The people here have depended on U. S. troops ever since the American Occupation in 1846.

"There are not enough Americans to fill up the units and give them Yankee strength, so to speak. Then too, in addition to the Texan threat, there are thirty to forty thousand hostile Indians running loose in the Southwest."

"We have some good men working for the Union, though. Ceran St. Vrain commands your regiment, the First New Mexico Volunteers, and Kit Carson is his second in command. Those two men are worth at least a battalion apiece."

The judge filled the chocolate cups. "There are Southern agents working throughout the territory to incite the Indians and the native New Mexicans against the Union. They tell wild stories of the terrible *Tejano's* and of how they each carry two huge razor-edged bowie knives, double-barreled shotguns, a brace of revolvers, and lassos with which to hang any prisoners they catch. It is said too that they ride half-wild mustangs who have been trained to bite and kick their enemies."

Steve whistled softly.

"Trouble is, Stevie, that most of those wild tales are heartily believed by the native New Mexicans, at least those who have no education, and there are a lot of them. Our eastern politicians have forgotten us. They are so concerned with the war in Virginia and Tennessee they have forgotten their back door is wide open and banging back and forth in the wind of invasion. The Southwest, and possibly the entire Union, is in terrible danger here. The odds are high against us."

"And I thought I was leaving the war behind in Virginia!"

The fierce eyes studied him. "We need all the help we can get, Steve. Your place is rightfully here in New Mexico with your father and myself, as well as with all your friends, and before this Avar is over, you'll be playing a man's part in it like a good many other boys about your age, Steve."

Steve stood up and walked to the door." If you'll excuse me, sir, I'll attend to my horse."

"Go ahead, Steve."

Steve hesitated at the door and then turned. "If those were not *ladrones* who killed Lieutenant Bruce, they must have been Southern agents. And, if they were, why would they use a disguise such as they did?"

The old man stood up and came closer to Steve. "Because it is entirely possible that those men may have been well known here in New Mexico Territory, men who do not want their identity known, at least at this time."

"But why?"

The gray eyes half closed. "Because they are waiting to see which way the ball bounces, Steve, obviously, they want the South to win and will do everything they can to further the Southern cause, but if the South does not win, then they can still play the part of loyal Union men."

"That's about as sneaky a way as they can do it, sir."

A big hand closed on Steve's shoulder. "They play both sides, son. I'd rather have an enemy face to face with me and know he was a man of honor and who believed in his own cause. But such men as we have just spoken about have no honor and care not a whit about it. They seek personal gain only."

"Why can't they be rooted out?"

The old man spoke in a low, tense voice. "Because some of them are in high places, positions of trust, we don't know for sure who they are or what their game is. There is only one thing we can do. Be ever alert!" He placed his hand on the butt of his pistol.

Steve opened the door and walked out on the patio. He had come home to a boiling pot of intrigue and suspicion, and he knew now that the war had come to New Mexico as well as to the rest of the United States. There was no place in his great country and no person who would not be affected by it, directly or indirectly, one way or another.

The air was bright and fresh, with no sign of rain in the clear morning sky. There was a winy freshness in the mountain wind, now warmed by the sun and carrying with it the odors of thyme, sage, and mint. Bright pools of water dotted the Magged patio. The rolling of a drum came from Fort Marcy, which overlooked the city. The echo had hardly died away in the nearby hills when it seemed to be mocked by the soft tolling of a chapel bell.

Zouave whinnied softly from his stall, and Steve went to feed the great dun. Steve's mind was racing with all that his uncle had told him, and he realized now that there was great danger in New Mexico as well as in Virginia and Tennessee, and that his wish to see action in the war could just as easily be fulfilled in his home country as it could be in the East. Suddenly he felt older, as though he too would have to play the part of a man, and he determined to do the best he could. He was a soldier, and a soldier served where he was ordered to serve, and Steve's place was in New Mexico Territory.

CHAPTER SIX

SANTA FE, NEW MEXICO TERRITORY–SEPTEMBER 1861

The sun was well up when Steve and his uncle left the house and walked toward the plaza. Country people urged their shaggy little burros along with cudgel blows as they hurried toward the market. Ragged peons in dirty, grayish trousers and shirts shuffled through the mud of the street. The old familiar odor of the city seemed to settle about Steve —piñon smoke, the strong odors of many horses and burros, the perfume of flowers threading through it all.

Two-wheeled *carretas* groaned past on shrieking, ungreased wheels, and the ringing of metal on metal came from a nearby blacksmith shop. Steve shook his head. "Santa Fe hasn't changed much," he said.

"Not outwardly, Steve, but underneath the peacefulness, there is a lot of tension."

They entered the plaza and walked toward the low Governor's Palace. Rows of country people sat beneath the shade of the long roof that ran the length of the palace and shielded the sidewalk. Heaps of melons, shiny while onions, potatoes, apples, and squash lay on squares of dirty cloth. Long strings of scarlet chili pods hung from the great posts of silvery wood that supported the roof overhead. The canvas stalls stretched along the west side of the building. Pigs grunted, turkeys gobbled, and vendors shouted their wares along the line of stalls. Here and there were stolid Indians from the pueblos, muffled in cheap trade blankets, saying nothing but watching everything.

Steve and his uncle walked into the dimly lighted palace. A sergeant major of Regulars sat at a desk. "Good morning, Judge Ames," he said with a smile.

"I must see the colonel at once, Sims."

The sergeant major stood up. "Just a moment, sir." He walked into a hallway, and they could hear his voice mingled with that of another man. In a moment, he was back. "The colonel is in conference. Captain DeWitt will see you, though."

Carter Ames nodded shortly. "Come on, Steve," he said.

They walked down the hallway and entered a small room. An officer sat at a desk. He stood up as Carter Ames entered. "Good morning, Judge," he said cordially.

"Morning, Captain. This young man is my nephew, Steven Ames, just arrived from the East. Steve, this is Captain Milas DeWitt, one of Colonel Canby's aides."

DeWitt held out a hand to Steve and smiled as Steve saluted. "A real soldier?" he said with a faint tinge of satire in his cultured voice.

Carter Ames nodded. "Steve fought at Bull Run with the New York Volunteers."

The curiously light-blue eyes of the officer studied Steve. "I don't suppose you're too proud of that, Steve?"

Steve flushed. The man was trying to annoy him, and Steve had a feeling that his uncle didn't care too much for the officer either. "The Union troops fought well, sir," he said. "It was a battle that could have gone either way. In my opinion, the rebels were luckier than we were."

"Perhaps. Perhaps." The officer looked at Carter Ames. "I'll take the dispatches, Judge."

"They are for Colonel Canby, sir."

"The colonel is very busy. When he is through with his conference, he must leave for Galisteo. Let me have the dispatches, and they'll be in his hands so that he can study them on his trip."

Judge Ames glanced at Steve. Steve raised his head. "The orders were that the dispatches were to be placed in Colonel Canby's hands, Captain."

A muscle in the officer's left cheek began to twitch a little. "Perhaps you didn't understand me, young man."

"He did, DeWitt," said the judge. "But he has his orders."

"From whom?"

"From Lieutenant Lloyd Bruce, sir," said Steve. "He told me to deliver these dispatches personally to Colonel Canby and to no other person."

"So?" The officer leaned forward. "And where is this officer, may I ask?"

"Dead in Glorieta Pass, DeWitt, "said Carter Ames. "Ambushed and murdered by Jicarilla's. The boy got the dispatches and broke through the Jicarilla's to get here with the case."

DeWitt held out a hand. "I'm sorry to hear about Bruce. Good work, young Steven Ames. Now I must have those papers."

"No, sir," said Steve.

For a moment, the room was very quiet. Then Captain DeWitt leaned forward. "Perhaps you don't understand," he said slowly and clearly. "I represent the colonel. The colonel is too busy to bother with such matters as these. Now give me that case!"

Carter Ames seemed to grow a little in height, and his eyes took on the fierce, frosty look Steve knew so well. "You seem to feel that these dispatches are rather trivial, sir," he said coldly. "Such is not the case. An officer died to get them here. My nephew fought his way through Jicarilla's to get them here. They go into Colonel Canby's hands and into no one else's! Now maybe you understand!"

Captain DeWitt straightened up. "What right have you to interfere in military affairs, sir?"

Carter Ames waved a hand. "This is not a parade ground at West Point, Captain. This is New Mexico. We New Mexicans are all interested in military affairs, and as a member of the military committee of the territory, appointed by Governor Connelly himself, I see no reason why I should not take an interest in the defense of this territory."

"Well spoken, sir," a quiet voice said behind Steve. He turned quickly to look at a tall officer wearing silver eagles on his shoulder bars.

Carter Ames turned. "Here is Colonel Canby now, Steve. Give him the dispatches."

Steve saluted and handed the case to the officer. Canby smiled. "I expected an officer to deliver these, young man."

"Lieutenant Bruce was killed last night in Glorieta Pass by Jicarilla's, sir. At least..." Steve's voice trailed off as he saw the look in his uncle's eyes.

"At least what?" questioned the colonel.

Steve swallowed. "Nothing, sir."

"My nephew was riding with the lieutenant as orderly, Colonel," said the judge quickly. "Bruce was killed, and Steven here got the dispatches and rode to Santa Fe with them."

The colonel studied Steve. "My personal thanks to you, Steven Ames. Come, Judge, let's look these over."

"Steve, wait outside for me," said Carter Ames.

"No," said Canby. "Let him come too. He risked his life for these dispatches. It's only right to assume he wouldn't reveal their contents."

Captain DeWitt started to come around his desk, but

Canby stopped him with a wave of his left hand. "DeWitt, I want you to go to Galisteo for me."

There was an odd look in DeWitt's eyes when the three of them left the office.

Canby seated himself at his desk and fiddled with the dispatch case lock. "You have the key?" he asked Steve.

"No, sir. Lieutenant Bruce carried it in his boot. There was no time to get it."

"And why not?"

Steve allowed the ghost of a smile to drift across his face. "I was a little busy at the time, Colonel."

Canby nodded. He took a knife from a desk drawer and began to slit the thick leather of the case. "You are sure you were ambushed by Jicarilla's?"

Steve looked at the judge. The judge nodded. "No, sir," said Steve.

Canby's head snapped up. "What do you mean, sir?"

Steve explained what had happened.

Canby leaned back in his chair and looked at Carter Ames. "What do you think, Judge?"

"How many people knew about those dispatches?"

"Here?"

"Yes."

Canby steepled his fingers. "Myself, you, Judge, your brother Mark, Governor Connelly, Captain Florian, and Captain DeWitt."

"No others?"

"Not to my knowledge."

Carter Ames rested an arm over the back of his chair. "There must have been a leak somewhere then."

"Yes."

"My brother Mark is down south and has been down there ever since he came back from Independence. You know I kept my mouth shut, and certainly, the governor did. I know you didn't speak about the papers to anyone but those people you have named."

"That leaves Captains DeWitt and Florian," blurted out Steve.

Colonel Canby's eyes were a little cold when he looked at Steve. "Both trusted officers and gentlemen. Captain DeWitt has been traveling through the northern parts of the territory for the past few months on defense business."

"And Florian?" asked Carter Ames.

Canby flushed a little. "He has been here. The man is careless and perhaps a bit of a fool, but he is no traitor, sir."

"Let us hope not, Colonel."

Canby took out the dispatches and began to scan them swiftly, and his expression changed from one of hope to one of disappointment. Finally, he looked up. "I had hoped for better news. I had requested many stands of arms, Springfield, or Enfield.58 caliber rifles. Instead, they say they will send me a shipment of large-calibered Austrian muskets and other junk picked up from foreign governments eager to sell their antique equipment to the gullible Americans so that they can rearm themselves with the latest weapons at our expense.

"The government expects little action here in New Mexico, and they intend to transfer my Regulars back east where they are more sorely needed!"

"I had expected some information on when my troops will be paid, but there is nothing here mentioning pay at all. The Regulars have not been paid in nine months, and the Volunteers have never been paid at all.

"They say I might get help in time, but for the time being, I must hold this territory with the troops I have, less the Regulars."

Carter Ames smashed a fist down on the arm of his chair. "Great news! Supposing the Texans find that out? It is probably their fear of the Regulars that has made them move so slowly thus far. The Texans had poor arms until Major Lynde delivered the best we had to them by his surrender at San Augustine Springs. Supposing they find out we're getting foreign stuff with which to arm our men. Those Texans will not have to shoot us out of the territory. They'll laugh us out!"

Canby rubbed his jaws. "There is more news. There is information about a rebel column coming up through the Panhandle of Texas to attack us, and perhaps another one up the Pecos."

"Great! Great!" snapped the judge.

Canby stood up and looked out of the window into the patio. "If all this information had gotten into the wrong hands, it would have speeded up the rebel invasion. I know you two gentlemen will keep it to yourselves. Perhaps I should have kept it to myself rather than to put fear into others."

"We're not whipped yet, Colonel."

"No...but things are getting worse. We're a long way from help here, Judge." The colonel turned. "How was the trip on the Santa Fe Trail, young Ames?"

"The Kiowas tried to cut off some of our men. Pawnees trailed us, trying to get at our horses and mules. Three hunters were killed near Salt Bottoms. There was hardly a time, sir after we reached the Arkansas when we weren't being watched by hostile Indians."

Canby nodded. "I expect travel on the trail to be closed before too long. We cannot afford to spare enough troops as escorts. In time we'll be cut off completely from the East. It is then we'll have to fight with our backs against the wall." The colonel held out his hand to Steve. "Thank you in the name of the territorial government for your courage and loyalty in bringing these dispatches safely to me."

Steve shook the officer's hand and then stepped back and saluted.

"Wait for me outside, Steve," said his uncle.

Steve walked out of the office and through the hallway past DeWitt's office, but the officer wasn't at his desk. Steve stopped outside underneath the great roof and watched the busy market business.

"You mustn't think me hard to get along with, Steve," a voice said behind him.

Steve turned. It was Captain DeWitt, booted and spurred, with his saddlebags hanging over his arm. "You were doing your duty, sir," said Steve quietly. *At least I think you were doing your duty*, he thought.

"You must understand that an aide must act as a buffer, so to speak, between a superior officer and those who might annoy him with trivial matters."

Such as dispatches from Washington, thought Steve.

"I don't want you or your uncle to think I have anything personal against either one of you."

"We don't, sir."

"How did the Federal troops behave at Bull Run?"

"We fought well. We were green, and they were green. They had better leadership, I think."

"Still, I wonder if we can be sure of the final victory?"

Steve stared at him. "Have you any doubt, Captain?"

DeWitt laughed. "Certainly not! But we must take Bull Run as the measure of things until other battles are fought."

"My regiment fought well enough. We made mistakes. When Stuart's cavalry charged, we tried to reload after firing a volley when we should have met them with the bayonet. Experienced troops wouldn't have done that. We were smashed. We made mistakes at Bull Run, and so did they, but we made the biggest mistakes. The biggest one of all was in thinking we had the battle won before it had really been settled. It won't happen again."

"On to Richmond," said DeWitt dryly.

"One battle doesn't decide a war, sir."

"No, it doesn't, but here in New Mexico, we have

rancher majors and storekeeper colonels. The policy here seems to be to promote a man for *whom* he knows rather than for *what* he knows."

"There are not enough trained men to meet the emergency, Captain. That's what my colonel said."

DeWitt nodded. He looked across the plaza and seemed to talk almost to himself. "There will be great opportunities here for the right man. Opportunities to be snatched and developed when the time comes, and to the devil with the hindmost."

Steve looked at him surreptitiously. There was a faraway look on the handsome face of the aide.

An orderly brought up a fine gray horse and saluted DeWitt. DeWitt turned and smiled at Steve as the orderly placed the saddlebags on the horse. "Perhaps we shall serve together yet, young Ames. I may need a good orderly when the time for fighting comes. If you do your duty as you did last night, I can't think of a better choice for an orderly."

"Thank you, sir."

DeWitt mounted, returned Steve's snappy salute, and then kneed his gray through the crowds in the plaza, followed by his orderly.

"That'll be the day," said Steve aloud.

Carter Ames stopped beside Steve. "A strange man," he said as they walked back toward their house.

"How so, sir?"

The judge looked around at the straight back of the aide. "West Point graduate. Left the service a year or so before the war and went to Texas and Mexico. Some say he was in business down there. Others say he was a spy for the abolitionist movement. No one really knows. But he came back into Federal Service when Fort Sumter was fired upon and was offered the position of aide by Colonel Canby because Canby knew DeWitt was acquainted with this country and the people. He's been of invaluable help to the colonel. They say he's slated for a high command when the fighting starts. I have no doubt but what he'll do well at that too. He's an expert shot with rifle and pistol, and they say he fences like a musketeer and rides like a Cossack."

"High praise, sir. It isn't like you to give one man so much praise."

Carter Ames tugged at his beard. "No, Stevie," he admitted. "There's one thing I know for sure about Captain Milas DeWitt."

"And that is?"

"I don't like him!"

They walked on to the house, and once they were inside, the judge looked at Steve and took him by the arm. "The colonel is well pleased with you. I suggested you be kept here in Santa Fe as a messenger, orderly, and so forth, for the time being at least."

Steve flushed. "I'd rather be with my regiment."

"You can do better work for the Union here."

"How so?"

Carter Ames looked behind him as though someone might be eavesdropping. "You speak Spanish like a native, Steve. You know and like these people, and they know and like you. A smart lad like yourself can keep out of sight and keep his eyes and ears open and his mouth shut. Do you follow me?"

"Yes, sir!"

The judge winked. "I knew you would!"

"What do I do first, sir?"

"Get out of that uniform. Few of these people know you've been in uniform. None of them know you're in the First New Mexico. Get into civilian clothing and get out and see your friends in Santa Fe. Learn all you can."

"Is that all, sir?"

"It's a beginning, Steve. The colonel was quite impressed by you." The judge walked into the house.

Steve shook his head. He had wanted to let his

friends see him in uniform. He heard Zouave whinny, and he went in to see the big dun. The words of the colonel swirled through his mind. "In time, we'll be cut off completely from the East. It is then we'll have to fight with our backs against the wall."

CHAPTER SEVEN

The rumor of the missing government wagons had developed into a story of fact, and little else was being spoken about in Santa Fe. Twelve heavily laden wagons had left Fort Union, near Wagon Mound, bound for Fort Marcy at Santa Fe via Las Vegas and Glorieta Pass. They had passed through Las Vegas, and somewhere in the vicinity of Starvation Peak, they had vanished.

Steven Ames stood in the plaza near La Fonda, the great inn of Santa Fe, and listened to a trooper who was telling some of the people what had happened.

"It was a strange thing," the trooper said. "The wagons were in good shape, most of them almost new, and the teams were good ones. I was part of the escort under Sergeant Mason, ten troopers in all. Near Starvation Peak, we saw some Jicarilla's lurking about in the brush up ahead of us, so Sergeant Hampton takes six of us after them, leaving three troopers behind with the wagons. The teamsters were armed, so there wasn't too much to worry about. The Jicarilla's took off like jackrabbits, and we were about to return to the wagons when we saw an army officer standing on a low ridge near the road. He yelled at us and waved his arms, and then the Jicarilla's dragged him from sight."

"Sergeant Hampton led us in a charge up that ridge, and when we got to the top, we saw the officer being dragged down a canyon. Hampton leads us on, and suddenly we got a volley from ambush, full in the face, and Hampton goes down dead along with another man."

"By the time we got into cover, the Jicarilla's was gone. We waited half an hour, and then Corporal Grady scouts ahead. No trace of the Jicarilla's at all, but we did find part of the officer's uniform. By then, it was getting dusk, so we took the bodies back toward the wagons. We went slow because of the bodies, and we weren't too anxious to run into another ambush."

"Well, we reached the place where the wagons had been, wasn't hide nor hair of them there, friends. Nothing but a little manure on the road. No tracks. No horses. No wagons. No men. Nothing."

A man whistled softly.

The trooper wiped the sweat from his sunburned face. "I tell you, it gave us an eerie feeling to be standing there in that empty road with two dead men lying across their saddles and not a trace of twelve government wagons and their teams."

"What was in the wagons?" asked a clerk from Houghton's general store.

"New government rifles, powder, ball cartridges, caps, bullet molds, lead, medicinal stores, saddles, harness sets, sabers, and some cases of artillery shells. There was a pair of brass mountain howitzers, too, dismounted, but it doesn't take long to put them together. Besides all that, there was sacked flour, beans, and a lot of other food supplies."

"Some haul," said the clerk.

"Jicarilla's, you think?" asked a bearded militiaman.

The trooper shrugged and thrust out his hands, palms upward. "*¿Quién sabe?* Who knows? All I know is that the wagons vanished." The trooper turned and walked toward the street that led to Fort Marcy.

Steve shoved back his wide-brimmed hat. The troops were in short enough supply as it was. The loss of those wagons was a hard blow to the territory.

"*¡Amigo mío!*" a voice cried, and Steve was hit with full force between the shoulder blades. He staggered and turned around to look into the smiling face of Hernán Calvillo, a boy with whom he had gone to school in Santa Fe and with whom he had been expelled more than once.

"*¡Querido amigo!*" yelled Steve. He hurled himself at Hernán and gripped him about his slim waist, lifting him up and dumping him hard on the dusty ground.

"Son of a goat!" cried Hernán as he pounded Steve on the back with both fists.

"*¡Hombrecito!*" coughed Steve as he scrambled on top of his friend.

"Here! Here!" a man cried out. "No fighting here, boys!"

They looked up through the wreathing dust in surprise. "Fighting?" asked Steve. "I was just greeting Hernán here. I haven't seen my *amigo* in two years."

Hernán was laughing so hard there were tears in his eyes.

The man shoved back his wide-awake hat and scratched his bald head. "Well, I'll be switched," he said. "Friends? I'd hate to see you two together if you were enemies."

Steve got up and pulled Hernán to his feet. Hernán gave him the *abrazo,* wrapping his arms about Steve's shoulders and thumping his back. "How you have grown!" he said. "Perhaps it was the salt air in Nueva York?"

"No," said Steve with a grin. "I was right puny there,

but when I crossed into New Mexico on the way back, I grew four inches and put on twenty pounds!"

The New Mexican's eyes were wide. "Is this true? Come, we leave at once. I, too, would grow four inches and put on twenty pounds."

They walked toward the Governors' Palace, and the dark eyes of the smaller boy hardly left Steve's face. "You did not forget Hernán then?"

"I have to admit I never got expelled once from Mr. Albright's Academy for Boys and Young Gentlemen."

"Is that why you joined the army?"

They laughed again. Steve held the arm of his best friend. "Where have you been?" he asked. "No one seemed to know."

The gay face saddened a little. "My father and mother died with the smallpox. For a time, I lived in Taos with Tio Gaspar, but he was a hard man to get on with. Then I lived in Galisteo with Tia Theresa, but she has seven children, and there was little to eat. So then I went to live with Tia Rosa, who used to keep house for you, and there I am learning the trade of a muleteer from Tio Eusebio Campos. He is a good man. Far too easy on me, Tia Rosa says."

"I am sorry to hear about your father and mother."

"*Gracias, amigo.* But they are with God now. Happier perhaps than they were here, for life was always hard for them."

"Can you stay with me for a time?"

Hernán shrugged. "Why not? My aunt and uncle have gone to a wedding in Las Vegas, and they left me here on the way. They say I get into too much trouble."

"So?"

Hernán grinned. "I do not like weddings anyway." He threw back his shoulders. "So I will stay with my *compañero!*"

"What do you think about those missing wagons, Hernán?"

"A strange thing! How is it possible to make twelve big wagons vanish into thin air? Perhaps it was the work of evil spirits." Hernán swiftly crossed himself.

The sergeant major came across the plaza, carrying a uniform over his left arm. He beckoned to Steve. Steve and Hernán hurried to him. The sergeant major held up a blouse and a forage cap that had crossed brass saber insignia on it with the numeral three above them. "This look familiar, Ames?" he asked.

Steve examined the items. There was a crooked seam on the elbow of the left sleeve that he remembered sewing himself. "Yes, sergeant major," he said quietly. "This was Lieutenant Bruce's blouse. I sewed up that seam one night by firelight near the Cimarron Crossing."

The sergeant major nodded. "We never did find his body, you know. This cap and blouse were found by Corporal Grady and his men when they were ambushed."

"They were supposed to have seen an officer," said Steve.

The noncom nodded. "Yes, wearing these items. It couldn't have been Lieutenant Bruce. Who could it have been?"

The three of them looked at one another, then the sergeant major turned away. "I'll tell Captain DeWitt what you told me," he said.

"Do," said Steve politely.

The noncom looked sharply at him, then walked away.

Hernán looked to the east. "It would be interesting to go there and see if we could find those wagons," he said. "I have a horse. He is small and sad, but he travels surprisingly well."

Steve grinned. "You know something, *amigo?*"

"What is it?"

"I, too, have a horse!"

"Then let's go! This place palls on me, *amigo!*"

They hurried toward the Ames house. It would be

more than a thirty-mile ride, and they would have to camp out overnight, but both of them were well accustomed to sleeping under the stars.

———

BOTH HORSES STOOD in the patio, saddled and with cantle and pommel packs. Hernán had been right about his horse, whom he called by the noble name of El Diablo. Steve had buckled on his pistol belt and had placed his Sharps carbine in its saddle scabbard while he had rounded up a short-barreled Wells-Fargo Colt for Hernán and a muzzle loading Enfield carbine, which had once belonged to his Aunt Rosa's first husband, Adolfo, the gardener.

"What will your uncle say?" asked Hernán as he tightened the girth on El Diablo.

"Nothing."

Hernán looked surprised. "Now that is news! Why, *amigo?*"

Steve grinned. "He's not here, that's why. He left for Taos yesterday on territorial business."

"And your father?"

"I haven't seen him since I left for New York two years ago. He's down south somewhere."

"On territorial business."

Steve looked at him quickly. "How do you know?"

Hernán shrugged. "Who doesn't know? He is a well-known man. Owner of a freighting business. Once an officer in the Army of Occupation that came here many years ago. A good friend of the governor and of the military commander. What else would he be doing?"

"You know a lot, *chico*."

Hernán smiled crookedly. "I know too much. There is very little that goes on in this territory that is not known to Hernán Calvillo, the all-seeing one."

El Diablo turned his head and dropped his ears,

raising a right hindfoot. Hernán jumped away. "Oh, no, you don't, *Caballo mío!*" he cried out.

Steve eyed the disreputable horse. "He sure knows you," he said dryly.

Hernán nodded. "He has heart this one. A real bravo. A drinker of the wind."

"You'd never know by looking at him, *amigo.*"

"Do not let appearances deceive you." Hernán sidled close to his sad-looking steed and patted him on the neck. "See? The fire in him?"

El Diablo stood hipshot with his eyes half closed, as though asleep on his feet, but Steve could see one evil eye studying him, and he wisely kept away from the rear end of El Diablo.

"That is a fine *Caballo* you have, Steve," said Hernán.

Steve nodded as he slapped Zouave on the rump. "My father bought him in Independence for me and left him there until I picked him up."

"Your father is the wise one with the *Caballos,*" said Hernán. "See, he is a coyote dun. One of the race that dies before tiring. He will always be in the lead, *amigo.*"

"*Brio escondido*," said Steve. It was a phrase well known to both of the boys. *Brio escondido*, "the hidden vigor." The dun had never tired on the long trip from Independence, and on that terrible night when Lieutenant Bruce had died, and Steve had saved the dispatches, Zouave had been like a part of Steve as he had ridden down the Jicarilla's and fled at a steady mile-eating pace through the pass to the slopes above Santa Fe.

Hernán led his mount toward the door, and then he turned. "But you must report that you are leaving," he said to Steve.

"Report to whom?"

"To the army, *amigo.*"

"I left the army in Washington, *Hombrecito.*"

"So? Are you not a drummer assigned to the First New Mexico Volunteers?"

Steve eyed his friend. "How did you know that?"

"*¡Ea pues!*" Hernán snapped his fingers.

"Go on," demanded Steve.

The ingratiating smile flowed over Hernán's face like the shadow of a swift cloud on the slopes of the Sangre de Cristo's. "I said I was all-seeing, Steve."

Steve nodded sourly. He might have known. Word got around Hernán's people with the speed of light.

"So you will report, *amigo?*"

Steve wet his lips. There had been little for him to do in Santa Fe in the days he had been there. His uncle had said Canby had been pleased with him and that he was to be kept in Santa Fe rather than to serve with his regiment as a messenger, orderly, and so forth. Steve had done little but walk around town and see his old friends and learn the latest news, all of which was already well known to Colonel Canby and to the meanest hostler at La Fonda inn.

"Steve?"

Steve shook his head. "Lead your horse down the side lanes," he said. "I'll meet you on the pass road out of sight of town."

"*¡Bueno!*" Hernán opened the outer gate and led El Diablo through it. In a little while, Steve heard the clopping of hoofs on the side lane west of the great house.

Steve looked about the quiet patio. Both his father and his uncle were gone on territorial business, so they couldn't stop him. Colonel Canby was too busy to bother about the activities of a humble drummer boy in the First New Mexico. Steve had been given to believe that his immediate superior was Captain Milas DeWitt, but in the time Steve had been in Santa Fe, the captain had not bothered with him nor he with the captain. It was simple enough. He would go with Hernán. They'd certainly never miss the two of them in Santa Fe, and perhaps he and Hernán could find out something about those mysteriously vanished wagons.

He led Zouave to the gate and opened it, leading the
dun out into the sunlit street. He ground-reined the
horse, then walked back into the house, closing the great
door and barring it so that he could leave by the smaller
door and lock it behind him. As he reached for the door
latch of the smaller door, he suddenly remembered something. The silver trumpet! He had carried it from Washington with him and had placed it within the wardrobe in
his room.

He stood there for a while, wondering if he should
take the trumpet with him or not, then decided against
it. The going might be rough, and he wanted no harm to
come to it. He went to his room and got the instrument.
For a moment, he uncovered it and eyed it, remembering
where and how he had come by it. It seemed so long ago,
and yet the voice of Dacey Curtis seemed to pass through
Steve's mind, handing the trumpet on to him. Big chance
there was for Steven Ames to use the trumpet to help
either Yankee or rebel or both. New Mexico was too far
away from a smoky battlefield in Virginia and the
bequest of a romantically minded boy who was dying
even as he spoke.

Steve covered the trumpet and carried it into the
living room. There were many *ladrones* in Santa Fe, but
they knew better than to steal anything that might be too
easily identified. Gold and silver were what they wanted.
Still, the trumpet had silver in it; its very tone let anyone
know that. Steve opened his mother's piano and placed
the trumpet inside it. He softly closed the rosewood lid,
looked around the big room once, then left it.

He led Zouave down a side lane and through narrow,
winding streets until he was south of the town, near the
road to Albuquerque; then, he cut across country to pick
up the road leading southeast to Glorieta Pass.

The wind was fresh and dry as he rode, and in the
distance cloud shadows chased themselves along the
purple mountain slopes. He eyed the rough country to

the east. Somewhere within those jumbled mountains was the secret of the lost wagons. Slowly he forgot about Bull Run, Dacey Curtis, the silver trumpet, Santa Fe, Captain DeWitt, and everything else except the fact that he had a fine horse beneath him, an open road, a good companion, and an adventurous quest.

CHAPTER EIGHT

SANGRE DE CRISTO MOUNTAINS—OCTOBER 1861

Steve Ames opened his eyes and looked up at the dim roof of the cave. It was cold in the predawn darkness, but he was snug enough under his thick trade blanket. He raised his head and saw the shadowy outline of Hernán's steeple hat against the outer light. A cold wind was keening up the pass below the cave.

They had ridden swiftly from the time they had met on the road until just after dusk when they had stopped to make their camp. The horses were picketed in a shallow box canyon a quarter of a mile from the cave. It was a procedure both of them had learned in Indian country, for a snorting or whinnying horse would give away a camp.

What troubled Steve was the fact that the road from Las Vegas, which trended almost due south then turned northwesterly through the Sangre de Cristo's by way of Glorieta Pass and Apache Canyon, had been safe enough from the predatory Jicarilla's for some time before the war. There was always plenty of traffic on that road. Santa Fe Trail caravans, stagecoaches, parties of well-armed traders, and troops of cavalry had made it a bad place for

raiding Indians. It was true that the war had given
Indians a rather free rein in New Mexico, but even so, it
had sent more and more troops traveling both ways
through the passes.

Yet Lieutenant Bruce had been killed eighteen miles
from Santa Fe, presumably by Jicarilla's, and the twelve
wagons from Fort Union had vanished like melting snow
on the lower slopes of the Sangre de Cristo's on a warm
day, and no one had any idea what had happened to them.

Hernán moved a little. He was swathed in a thick
serape, and his carbine barrel thrust itself up from
beneath the serape like a stalk of ocotillo. He looked like
some strange thorny growth of the desert as he sat there,
watching the canyon below the cave.

"Hernán," said Steve.

"*¿Si?*"

"See anything?"

"Nothing but ghosts, *amigo*. This is a haunted place,
Stevie."

Steve sat up. "Let's eat and get out of here."

Hernán arose and stretched himself. "I do not like
this place. As I said, it is haunted."

Steve snorted. "By what?"

Hernán shrugged. "Many things. You know the Pecos
Ruins. They say there were once over two thousand
Pueblo Indians living there. The Conquistadores treated
them harshly. Apache and Comanche raided them.
Smallpox and mountain fever did the rest. In 1540,
according to the padres, they had two thousand people.
Now, in 1861, there is no one left there."

The dark eyes studied Steve. "You do not believe
some of their spirits are still in this place?"

"*¿Quién sabe?*"

"Many travelers have been killed by Jicarilla's and
ladrones in here. You can see the crosses over their graves
almost every mile. Do *they* not haunt this place?"

Steve placed dried meat and cold beans on their tin

plates and uncorked his big felt-covered canteen. "I'm interested only in a particular type of ghost, *amigo mío*."

"Yes?"

Steve looked up. "The ghosts of twelve wagons loaded with military supplies."

There was a long silence, and then Hernán spoke again. "And the ghost of Lieutenant Bruce?"

Steve nodded.

"You do not believe those were Jicarilla's who killed him?"

"No."

"White men?"

"Yes."

Hernán gnawed at the dried beef. "I know of the Jicarilla's. They used to live far north of here, but the Comanches drove them south. For a time, they adopted the Christian faith and accepted Spanish rule, then they joined their cousins the Mescalero's and raided both Pueblo and Spaniards alike. But they have not been active in this pass for a long time, Steve."

"No."

Hernán digested his thought as he had the beef. "Then what are we looking for, *amigo*?"

Steve stood up. "Not ghosts, *amigo*, that is for certain."

They gathered their gear together and left the cave to go to the horses. The false dawn was graying the eastern sky, and they could see the seven-thousand-foot bulk of Starvation Peak dimly against the coming light. It was said that over a hundred colonists had taken refuge up there when pursued by Indians long ago and had starved to death. More ghosts thought Steve.

————

"THIS MUST BE THE PLACE," said Hernán as he stopped leading El Diablo and looked up at Steve.

Steve nodded. There was a ridge to their left a short distance from the wagon road, the only true ridge for miles.

They led the horses transversely up the ridge.

"Look here," said Hernán. He placed a finger on what looked like splashes of quicksilver on the rocks. He has eyes like an eagle, thought Steve. They were bullet splashes and quite fresh too. There was something else on a flat rock ledge, a dark stain, and both of them knew what that was. Men had died right there.

Steve squatted on the ridge top and looked down at the road while Hernán scurried through the brush like a hunting beagle.

The canyon was well lighted, and the road wound along like a tattered ribbon. There was no sign of life except for a hawk hung like a scrap of charred paper high in the updraft over the canyon.

Steve scanned both sides of the road with his uncle's field glasses. The old man would have been angry at him for taking the glasses, although he hadn't used them himself for years. They were good German glasses, made by Vollmer of Jena, and Carter Ames thought a lot of them. So did Steve.

Hernán pattered back down the slope." Look," he said. He held out his hand. He held the string-tied tops of paper cartridges, the type of cartridge that is contained with powder and ball in stiff paper. The top of the cartridge is bitten off by the shooter; then the powder is dumped into the rifle barrel, followed by the ball, and finally the paper as a wad to hold them in place.

Such cartridges were common enough, but it probably marked the place where the Jicarilla's had been firing on the troopers.

"See anything?" asked Hernán as he dropped the papers.

"I'm not sure." Steve handed the glasses to Hernán.

"Look across the road at that little grove of trees. There's a dry wash behind it."

Hernán took the glasses and studied the place. He whistled softly. "Let's take a closer look, Stevie."

They led the horses down the ridge and across the road, tethering them among the trees. Every now and then, both boys scanned the heights, and at such times they tightened their hands on their gunstocks. It was quiet in the canyon, almost too quiet.

Steve went down on one knee and studied the tracks in the bottom of the dry wash. There had been no rain in that country since the night he had ridden into Santa Fe. Here, on the hard gravelly bottom of the wash, could be seen faint hoof and wheel tracks, a good hundred yards from the wagon road. Steve looked down the road both ways and saw no place where big army wagons could have been hidden, nor did it look as though wagons could have been hauled over the ridge to the north of the road.

Steve stood up and looked up the wash. It seemed to vanish into the heights south of the road.

"Who would take wagons in there, Steve?" asked Hernán thoughtfully.

Without another word, they went back to get their horses, then led them slowly up the wash, between brush-lined banks, until they could no longer see the road behind them but only the brush and to the south of them the rugged heights of the canyon wall.

The wash banks became higher and higher until at last, the boys were walking in a narrow gorge, and it didn't seem as though anyone would take a wagon through there, but now and then they saw where metal-tired wheels had scoured into the harsh, gravelly earth, and there were horse and mule droppings all along the way.

But still, the gorge wall got higher and higher until they were walking in a semi dimness, cut off from the early morning sun, and a cold wind blew against their faces as they kept on.

Hernán wet his lips. "Perhaps these are not the wagons?" he suggested vaguely.

"Who else would haul wagons in here?"

Hernán shrugged. "Who else?" he echoed.

They had covered several miles, it seemed, and they expected the narrow slot in which they walked to close in at a dead end, but suddenly it widened. They had been climbing steadily, and Hernán looked up fearfully at pieces of whitened driftwood that had caught in crevices and on ledges high above them. The place would be a death trap in a flash storm." How did the sky look to you, *amigo?*" he asked quietly.

Steve glanced at him. "Bright. Why?"

"You saw no clouds?"

"None."

"You are sure?"

Steve scratched his chin. "Come to think of it; I saw some heavy clouds forming over Starvation Peak just before we came in here."

"¡*Dios en Cielo!*"

Steve grinned as he walked on.

The gorge widened, and although they covered long stretches in which they saw no signs of wheels or tracks, there was always something that led them on —a broken branch of brush, an uprooted rock. Both boys knew that a rock settles with its heavy side down and that in time the part beneath the surface becomes darker; therefore, a rock with its heavy and dark side up had been displaced.

They came out into a wider canyon, and beyond it, they could see a notch against the sky. The canyon was as lonely as the grave, and the simile made Steve feel a little nervous.

Hernán shoved back his heavy steeple hat and wiped his face. "If we keep on this way, Steve, I'll be back in Galisteo before dusk."

Steve nodded. He was a little puzzled. He was sure they were following the tracks of the missing wagons, but why were they headed this way? If the Jicarilla's had stolen them, they would have looted their haul, taking what pleased their odd fancies and ruining or burning the rest. The wagons would have been abandoned or burned, and the horses and mules were taken for transportation or food. No Indian likes to use a wagon, and in certainty, there was little enough area in their hidden haunts where a wagon could be used.

"Shall we go on?" asked Hernán.

"Why not?"

"Why not, indeed? We can come out on the Galisteo road and ride north to Santa Fe. A nice, roundabout ride, in which we learn nothing, my little goat."

"Don't be too sure, *Hombrecito*."

The sun was high now, and the heat of it flooded the canyon as they crossed toward the far side; in a place where water had flowed across soft flats, they found deep, rutted tracks where the wagons had been pulled across.

"It must be *ladrones*," said Hernán thoughtfully. "No Indian would take such pains to get these wagons through here."

"*Si*," said Steve quietly. "But no *ladrone* would be caught with a government wagon and government mules and horses. The troopers shoot first and ask questions later. You know that as well as I do."

They rested in the early afternoon, picketing the horses in a hollow. Steve lay back with his hat tilted across his face. According to Hernán, they would come out into the Galisteo Valley area, which was about twenty miles due south of Santa Fe. Roads led south and southwest from the area, through the mountains, and there were many little communities throughout. Scarcely the place for anyone attempting to smuggle stolen government goods through without being seen, for the people were noted for their curiosity about travelers.

There were quite a few pueblo ruins in the Galisteo Valley, nine of them in fact, two on the north side and seven on the south side in the Galisteo Basin. No Indians had lived in them for over half a century, and the simple farming people of Galisteo left them strictly alone because of their superstitions concerning the brooding relics.

Hernán came prowling through the brush and scrub trees. "It is as I thought," he said quietly. "The wagons have passed through the notch, but where have they gone from there?"

"All we can do is follow the tracks."

Hernán squatted beside Steve. "Supposing we catch up with the thieves?"

Steve shoved back his hat and sat up. "Why..." His voice trailed off.

"*Si,*" said Hernán wisely. "We left Santa Fe to find the wagons, although we did not expect to find them. But we found the tracks. The wagons could not have flown from here. Therefore they went through the notch. How much farther can they have gone?"

Steve stood up and reached for his carbine.

"Eh, *amigo?*" asked Hernán.

Steve looked at him. "Do you want to go back?"

Hernán looked at the jumble of mountains through which they had come, and the memories of that narrow gorge with its shadows and brooding thoughts was a little too much for him. "No," he said quietly.

"Then we go on! *¡Vamanos!*"

They led the horses toward the notch.

Hernán wet his lips, then shifted his carbine from one hand to the other, constantly drying the free hand from sweat. Not until they had cleared the notch did he seem to get confidence back into himself. "Eh," he laughed. "I was afraid of an ambush back there, *amigo!* How foolish can one...." His voice stopped short as the sound of a breaking stick came to them. A bush high on the slopes to the left of them seemed to blossom in white and red, and Hernán's steeple hat was removed from his head as though by an invisible hand. The echo of the shot slammed back and forth in the notch and then died away.

The two boys slapped their horses on the rumps and dived for cover in a brushy wash. They eyed the quiet slopes.

"Jicarilla's?" said Hernán at last in a curiously dry voice.

"No Indian can shoot like that, *amigo*! That was almost two hundred yards from here."

"*Si.*"

They scanned the slopes. Steve uncased his uncle's glasses and studied the area. There was no sign of life.

"Let's go," said Steve.

"Where?"

"To the Galisteo Valley, of course!"

Hernán smiled faintly. "Perhaps we should go back the other way?"

"We'd have to pass through the last part of it after dark."

"*Si.*"

They crawled along to where the horses had stopped beside a rugged upthrust of rock and led them down the slope. Steve looked to the left as they passed the place where the hidden marksman had been. There was an opening into the heights. It was then he saw the movement of the brush, and he threw a shoulder against Hernán, driving him to the ground as the marksman fired again, and this time El Diablo was struck on the flank. He reared and snorted and took off at a dead run down the valley, with a worm of blood trickling down his dusty flank.

The boys lay flat on the stony ground. Steve cocked his Sharps and checked the range up to the place where the thin smoke drifted amidst the brush. Two hundred yards at least, a long shot, and nothing to sight upon.

Hernán crossed himself.

Steve wet his lips. They were in good cover. Zouave was in a hollow. "Stay here," he said quietly to his companion.

He inched his way along the slope until he was a good fifty yards from Hernán, then cautiously raised his head. There was something alien on the slope, a darker patch of shadow, and the brush moved a little, although there was no wind.

Steve flipped up his backsight and set it at two hundred yards. He rested the heavy barrel on a rock and sighted it on the place where he saw the brush moving.

Something protruded through the bush like a snake, and the sun glinted on a rifle barrel. The barrel was pointed down toward where Hernán lay hidden.

Steve cuddled down against the stock of his carbine. He picked up the knife-blade front sight of the carbine with his eyes and settled it squarely into the notch of the rear sight. He moved the carbine a little until he was sighting approximately where a man would be lying if he was holding that rifle through the brush.

Hernán moved quickly. The rifle spouted flame and smoke, and at that instant, Steve pressed the trigger. The Sharps kicked back hard against his shoulder, and for a moment, his sight was obscured by the smoke of the discharge. Then he saw a movement in the brush. A man had stood up, dropping his rifle. Gripping his right wrist, he buck jumped through the brush to vanish into a jumble of rocks and scrub trees.

"Good shooting, *amigo*!" called out Hernán cheerfully.

Steve reloaded. "Yeah," he said dryly. "Thanks for setting him up, but as good as he is, he might have put a slug through your thick head!"

Steve crawled to Hernán, and they lay there a long time looking up the slope, but there was no sign of life.

The rifle lay in the sun below the brush where the marksman had been hidden when he had fired.

Steve placed his carbine beside Hernán. "Keep me covered," he said.

"Where are you going?"

"To get that rifle."

"But we have good guns, *amigo!*"

Steve nodded. "But not that one." He slid into a gully and trotted along it until he reached a thick brushy patch. As he angled up the slope, with his cocked pistol in his hand, there was no sound or sign of life. The valley below him was as peaceful looking as one could imagine.

He crawled toward the rifle and got it, looking about on the ground as he did so. Bright flecks of blood were on the rocks. He peered up the slope toward that mysterious opening but thought better of trying to see where it went.

Steve went back to join Hernán, and they examined the rifle. It was new; a .58 caliber Springfield with the government stamp upon it.

"What does it prove?" asked Hernán.

Steve tapped the stamped serial number on the rifle. "Someone has a record of the rifles carried in those wagons. Maybe this is one of them."

"So?"

Steve pointed toward the dim opening in the heights to the south. "Where would that go?"

"Into the Galisteo Basin, not far from the southern ruins."

"What's in there besides ruins?"

"Nothing much. A deserted mission. A few abandoned houses." Hernán wet his lips. "You're not thinking of going up there, are you?"

"We'd be fools to try. Someone wanted to keep us from going up there. He did a good job. We'd better get out of here. I have a feeling it wouldn't be too healthy in here after dark."

Hernán breathed a sigh of relief. "You know, *amigo*," he said quietly, "I have exactly the same idea."

They walked toward the far mouth of the valley with Steve leading Zouave. A horse whinnied in the distance, and El Diablo appeared, galloping loosely. He stopped near Hernán and whinnied softly. Hernán examined the wound. "It is only of the flesh," he said with a smile. "I will see to it in Galisteo." He patted the ungainly horse. "You see how he loves me?"

Steve nodded.

Hernán turned to pick up his carbine, and as he did so, El Diablo's ears went back, and before Steve could yell a warning, the horse had neatly planted both hind hoofs against the seat of Hernán's baggy pants, driving him swiftly into a thicket of catclaw.

Steve pulled Hernán from the thicket. The boy shook his fist at the horse. Tears of rage and pain were in his eyes. Steve couldn't help laughing. "See how he loves you, *amigo*?" he said.

Hernán picked up his carbine, rubbed the seat of his pants, and set off down the valley, the very picture of outraged dignity.

Steve thrust the rifle he had found through the straps of his cantle pack. Taking the bridle reins of both horses, he followed Hernán. Now and then, he looked back toward the place where he had wounded the mysterious rifleman. Something was up there—something that was well guarded. Even now, sharp eyes might be watching them.

It would be best to stay in Galisteo that night. Then, in the morning, they could go into the Basin and scout about, acting the part of hunters, for Steve fully believed that those missing wagons were somewhere within a few miles of him.

CHAPTER NINE

GALISTEO, NEW MEXICO TERRITORY—OCTOBER 1861

Galisteo was sleeping in the late afternoon sun. Green clouds of cottonwoods seemed to rest against the dun hills. The dying sun turned the thick-walled adobe houses into golden cubes, accented by the blue-painted doors and the scarlet strings of chilies that hung from the projecting roof beams. A wraith of smoke hung low over the little village, mingling with the late afternoon haze.

"Is it not pretty?" asked Hernán of Steve.

New Mexico was a dream in September and October. The war seemed so far away, and yet the bullet hole in Hernán's hat seemed more real than the beautiful Galisteo Basin.

The air was crisp and winy, and now and then, the quiet was broken by the high, clear bugle notes of prairie larks. The beautiful birds fluttered about the water tanks and the bright flowing irrigation ditches. The larks, with their white-bordered tails and their golden breasts with jet-black necklaces, caught the eyes of the boys as they rode along.

"Even the mockingbird cannot imitate the prairie lark," said Hernán. "Listen!"

The bugle call seemed to ring in the quiet air.

"The lark has no death in its soul, my mother used to say," said Hernán softly.

As they reached the outskirts of the town, they could see the little *Pajarito's* 'swallows' thick around the houses.

Steve wrinkled his nose. The sandy streets were littered with offal amidst which pigs, dogs, and chickens rooted for scraps while half-naked children added to the swarm. The odor of piñon smoke mingled with the stench of the rotting waste in the streets.

They rode toward the little plaza. Hernán turned in his saddle. "They have organized a militia company here. Many men have joined it. But the weapons are all junk. They could have used some of those fine rifles which were in the missing wagons." The boy waved a hand. "These are simple people, and they do not like war, but they are willing to fight for New Mexico."

How well will they fight? Thought Steve. He didn't want to hurt his friend's feelings, but he knew how little value was placed on these peon soldiers by the territorial officials. They knew little about weapons and shooting as compared to the tough Texas rebels who had been raised in the saddle and teethed on pistols and rifles.

"Look," said Hernán, "there are two officers! One of them is Capitan Padilla of the militia. I do not know the other one."

"I do," said Steve quietly. It was Captain Milas DeWitt. He kneed his horse toward a lane between two adobes, but it was too late, for the officer had seen Steve. DeWitt spoke quickly to Captain Padilla. Padilla saluted and walked off while DeWitt came toward the two boys. Steve slid from his saddle and stood at attention, awaiting DeWitt.

The light-blue eyes were curiously cold as DeWitt returned Steve's salute. "What are you doing here,

Ames?" he asked. He glanced quickly at Hernán, then back at Steve." Have you brought a message to me from Colonel Canby?"

"No, sir."

"Then what are you doing here?"

Steve swallowed. "We came through the mountains east of here from the pass road."

DeWitt looked past Steve toward the hazy purple mountains. "Through there? There is no road."

Hernán flashed his best toothy smile. "*Sí, Capitán* but we found a way."

"So? On whose orders did you come through there, Ames?"

There was no use in trying to wriggle out of it. "No one gave me orders, sir," said Steve quietly. "I went on my own."

The muscle began to twitch in DeWitt's left cheek. "Come with me," he said sharply. He led the way to a large house at one side of the plaza and entered it. He stood by the fireplace in the low-ceiled living room, with his hands clasped behind his back. A field desk had been set up in the room, and it was covered with forms and papers. Several boxes of military impedimenta stood next to the wall, and there was a rack of rusty and pitted muskets near the fireplace. Probably the useless pumpkin-slingers that had been allocated for the defense of New Mexico Territory! They looked as though they would be more dangerous to the shooter than to the target.

"You realize, of course," said DeWitt, "that you are absent without leave?"

"I do not think so," said Hernán brightly. "He lives at home, has no uniform and nothing to do, so—" He stopped short as he saw the look on Steve's face.

DeWitt raised a hand. "It was only through your uncle's say-so that we allowed you to idle your time away in Santa Fe, Ames." He smiled coldly. "It seems as though military discipline comes second after political influence in the territory. It so happened yesterday that I wanted you to ride with me down here to Galisteo and act as a translator while we swore in new recruits for the militia company."

"I'm sorry, sir."

"That doesn't matter! There are other things more important than that! Why did you ride out to Glorieta Pass? Why did you come through those mountains?"

"We had an idea we might find those missing wagons, sir."

"So? Patrols from Fort Marcy and Fort Union combed that country looking for them."

Hernán grinned. "It must have been the combs without the teeth, *Capitán*! For we found out where those wagons went!"

DeWitt stared hard at the two boys. "You did? Tell me about it. Not you, Ames, your friend there."

Hernán quickly told the story.

DeWitt motioned to Steve. "Get that rifle you found."

Steve went outside and took the rifle from the cantle pack. He brought it inside. "I thought we might be able to check the serial number of this rifle against the serial list of the rifles that were in the missing wagons, sir," he said.

DeWitt took the weapon and glanced at it. "Yes, perhaps." He looked up. "But you saw no wagons?"

"No, sir."

"You actually think the tracks you saw leaving the pass road were made by the missing wagons?"

Steve shrugged. It was a habit he had acquired from Hernán. "*Quién sabe*, sir? Who knows?"

DeWitt smiled faintly. "Wagon and hoof tracks have no serial numbers, unfortunately for us."

Hernán guffawed, slapping his thighs. "That is a good one, *Senor Capitán*! The *senor Capitán* is a wit. I..." Hernán swallowed hard as he saw the frosty look in the officer's eyes.

"Supposing you hadn't met me here, Ames, would you have returned to Santa Fe tomorrow?"

"No, sir," said Steve boldly.

"What would you have done?"

"Gone into the south Galisteo Basin to find those wagons."

"You think they are there?"

"I'm sure of it, sir."

"You were warned to stay away by that hidden marksman. Weren't you afraid that you might never come back from the Basin?"

"No, sir."

Hernán grinned. "Had you seen Steve shoot that man through the arm, you would not think we are afraid to go into the Basin, *Senor Capitán*!"

DeWitt leaned the rifle against the wall. "Perhaps not. But that is man's work. Have you boys a place to stay here?"

Hernán waved a hand. "There is my Tia Theresa, but she has only two rooms and little to eat."

DeWitt nodded. "There is plenty of room here. Can you forage for your own food?"

"I was a Zouave, sir," said Steve proudly.

"Yes...well, do what you can. But one thing! You are leaving for Santa Fe first thing in the morning. Under orders! I'll take care of the south Galisteo Basin with some of the militiamen we have here."

"Yes, sir!" said Steve.

"Dismissed then!"

The two boys walked outside. Hernán spat into the gutter. *"No, Bueno!* No good! That one makes me ill."

Steve shrugged. "He's right. I had no business leaving Santa Fe. We're lucky he wasn't a little tougher on us."

"He can't hurt Hernán Federico Telesfor Donaciano Gaspar Melchior Calvillo!"

Steve looked surprised. "Who are *they?*" He ducked the wild swing Hernán made at him.

———

IT WAS dark when they left Tia Theresa's little house at the edge of town near the canal. Steve's money provided the materials for *cabrito el homo,* in the preparation of which Hernán insisted his Tia Theresa had no equal throughout all Nuevo Mexico, and Steve was inclined to think that Hernán was more a dutiful nephew, rather than a real gourmet.

They stopped near the crumbling tower, built many years ago as protection against the Indians, then allowed it to decay in times of peace.

There was a faint tinge of moonlight in the eastern sky, which just served at the time to make the night's darkness seem more intense. Tia Theresa had filled them in on all the activities of Galisteoans from newly born Serafina Velarde to old Panfilo Ochoa, who was said to be one hundred and two years old and still cut a fine dancing figure at the local fandangos. She had spoken with pride about Capitan Luis Padilla and his fine company of militiamen, Galisteoans all, who would drive the hated *Tejano's* first into the Rio Grande and then into the Gulf of Mexico, without raising a sweat.

"Tia Theresa knows many things, *amigo,*" said Steve.

"That is true."

"She spoke of so much my poor ears are tired."

"That is so."

"She is a veritable mine of information."

"Of a certainty!"

Steve leaned against the side of the tower. "But she said nothing about strangers in the Galisteo Basin. Nothing about strange wagons."

Hernán plucked a stalk of dried grass and thrust it into his mouth. It gave him the look of a wise little burro as he spoke around it. "Tia Theresa not only knows many things, *chico,* which she is willing to tell one and all, but she is also a wise woman who knows when to keep her mouth shut."

Steve nodded. "I had the same feeling, *amigo.*" He looked at the eastern sky and the growing moonlight. "But why?"

Hernán chewed at his grass. "It is better to keep one's mouth shut at times. She is a widow with seven children to support. Does it matter to her who has stolen twelve government wagons?"

"Those stores in the wagons might have helped protect her from the Texans."

"Pah! And does it matter to her whether this territory is ruled by *yanquis* or *Tejano's?* Not a whit!"

"But she was afraid of something."

"That is true." Hernán came closer to Steve. "There are men here in Galisteo who do not work too hard at the farming or the woodcutting, yet they always seem to have money. You understand?"

"Yes."

"These wagons. They vanish from the Glorieta Pass road and are spirited through the mountains toward the Galisteo Basin, where they again disappear. Think you not that someone must have seen them?"

"Yes."

Hernán shrugged and held out his hands, palms upward. "If you lived here, a peaceable person, and knew about such things, would you poke your nose into them?"

"I don't know."

"Tia Theresa knows. So do lots of other *paisanos* here in Galisteo. Keep the mouth shut, and the throat does not get slit."

Steve shivered a little in the cold, searching wind that suddenly swept down the street, scattering trash, and dry leaves ahead of it. "Let's go to the house," he said. "We can have a fire there."

They walked down the dark street. Galisteo went to bed early behind locked doors and sealed windows. Memories of Jicarilla and Mescalero raids were not too dim in that country.

Captain DeWitt was not in the dark house. The boys went to the room at the rear of the house that he had allotted to them. It was spacious and clean, with a huge and ancient wooden bedstead. Hernán lighted sweet-smelling candles and then lighted the firewood in the beehive fireplace. He squatted on his heels, looking into the dancing flames.

"Of what are you thinking, *Hombrecito*?" asked Steve as he took off his jacket and gun belt.

"This Capitan DeWitt. He likes you?"

"I don't think so."

"There is something strange about him."

"How so?" Steve pulled off his boots and dropped onto the bed, resting his chin on his crossed hands so that he could watch the dancing flames.

Hernán shrugged as he took off the serape he had flung across his shoulders. "His mouth says one thing; his eyes say another."

"I agree."

"He is a bitter man, *amigo*."

"That is so."

Hernán spat into the fireplace. "I don't like him," he said with emphasis.

"I wonder who does?"

Hernán turned with a wide grin on his face. "He does!"

Later, as they lay in the huge bed and watched the firelight dance on the low ceiling, Hernán turned to look at Steve. "What will happen when we get back to Santa Fe?"

"*¿Quién sabe?* I'll catch it from Uncle Carter, and you'll have your Tio Eusebio looking for you with a wagon tongue for a switch in his hand."

Hernán shivered a little. "You are in the First New Mexico Volunteers."

Steve sighed. "I was. I don't know what Captain DeWitt will say about me."

"If you are allowed to stay in the regiment, do you think you could find a place for me there?"

Steve hesitated. "Well... I think so..."

"You do?"

Steve nodded sagely. "They said they needed burros to haul supplies. I think you ought to do nicely, *chico*." Then he ducked under the counterpane to get away from a swinging blow of Hernán's pillow.

———

IT WAS pitch dark in the big room when Steve awoke at Hernán's tug on his hair. "What is it?" he demanded.

Hernán clasped a hand over Steve's mouth, then placed his mouth close to Steve's left ear. "I went to get a drink of water," he whispered. "On the way back, I heard voices in the captain's room at the front of the house. I crept up there and could hear him talking to some man."

Steve removed Hernán's hand from his mouth. "So, what's wrong with that?"

Hernán leaned closer to Steve. "At four o'clock in the morning?"

Steve sat bolt upright, then swung his legs over the side of the bed. "Lead on," he said.

Hernán eased open the bedroom door and led the way toward the big-living room at the front of the house. They paused in the hallway. Yellow light shone through the space between the front bedroom door and the side of the doorway.

The voices were muffled, and Steve could not distinguish any words. He started into the living room, but Hernán held him back with a grip of iron.

It was well he did so, for at that instant, the door was

fully opened, and a man came into the living room, a big man wearing a slouch hat, and the lamplight glinted from the silver conches on it. The man turned as he reached the outer door, sharply outlining a hooked nose and a short, ragged beard. "Like I said, Captain, we got everything taken care of down south of here, but it's up to you to do the rest."

"Don't worry about that."

The tall man held a rifle in his left hand, and he raised it and shook it. "There's too much at stake now in New Mexico to let anything go wrong."

"I'm well aware of that."

The man grunted. He opened the door and stepped part way through it, then he stopped and looked back. "I still think my way is best. We could do it now."

Milas DeWitt shook his head. "Here... in Galisteo? Don't be a fool."

The man laughed shortly. "You don't much like blood, do you, Milas?"

"Not unnecessary blood."

"That may be so! My motto is: *Los muertos no hablan.*"

DeWitt waved a hand as though to brush the man away.

"There will be enough blood in New Mexico before long."

"Yes. To win, we have to kill. There's no other way, Milas. *Buenas Noches, amigo.*"

The man looked both ways quickly and then was gone into the dark night like some demon returning to the nether regions from whence he had come, leaving a reek of sour sweat and stale tobacco smoke behind him as the door closed softly.

Milas DeWitt stood there for a time, outlined in the lighted doorway, and then he struck a fist hard into the palm of his other hand, turned on a heel, and closed the door. In a few minutes, the light went out.

The two boys crept back toward their room, and as

they did so, they heard the soft tattoo of hoofs on the earth not far from the house as the mysterious visitor left Galisteo toward the south.

They got into bed. Hernán shivered.

"What's wrong, *amigo?*" asked Steve.

"He was like an *espectro*. A ghost. He made my blood run cold."

"Yes."

"Who was he? I wonder."

"*¿Quién sabe?*"

"You think this Capitan DeWitt is up to something?"

Steve shrugged. "Nothing was said to prove that."

"That is true. What they said could have been considered several ways. Except for one thing, *amigo*."

"Yes?"

"*Los muertos no hablan.*"

Then it was Steve's turn to shiver. *Los muertos no hablan*. The dead do not speak.

CHAPTER TEN

Steve Ames opened his eyes, and for a moment, he was not sure where he was, in his room at Mr. Albright's Academy for Boys and Young Gentlemen in New York, in a tent near Washington, D.C., after Bull Run, or in a house in Galisteo. But then the familiar sight of his own room in his father's house in Santa Fe reassured him.

It must be close to dawn, he thought. It was quiet, and yet something had awakened him. In the days since he had come back from Galisteo with Hernán Calvillo, both of them had been in disgrace, and Hernán had been hustled off by his Tio Eusebio and his Tia Rosa, while Steve had gotten the reprimand he had expected from Uncle Carter Ames.

Judge Ames had his hands and his mind full enough without worrying about Steve poking about in the Sangre de Cristo's while his father was away. The judge's eyes had seemed to spark and flash as he had reproved Steve and Hernán on their return to Santa Fe from Galisteo. Poor Hernán! Not only had he received full blame as well as Steve had from Judge Ames, but Tio Eusebio had used a thick switch, instead of the wagon tongue that Steve had predicted, wielded by a muscular muleteer's arm, on Hernán's shoulders.

Steve shifted in his bed and looked at the dull shine of the silver trumpet hanging over his bed. A lot of water had run under the bridge since the day Dacey Curtis had left the instrument in Steve's charge. There had been little enough Steve could do about using the trumpet to help anyone as Dacey had said it should be used. Now Steve was in trouble, unable to wear his uniform and unable to join his regiment. Confined at home like a little boy. *¡Ay de mi!* He'd hear about that from his messmates when he joined the First New Mexico. It was said they would soon move south to join the Federal forces at Fort Craig. He had pleaded with Uncle Carter to be allowed to join them, but the stern old man had said Steve would stay at home until his father got back from the South, and there had been no word at all from him when he would be back.

There had been one advantage in Steve's confinement. Trumpeter corporal Will Nolan, from Fort Marcy, had heard about the silver trumpet from Judge Ames and had dropped by to see it. He had become so interested in it after he had played it that he had given Steve a manual for trumpet music and had dropped by several evenings to coach Steve in the use of the instrument.

A dull, thudding noise came to Steve. He sat up in bed. Santa Fe, in the dead of night, was usually as quiet as a tomb.

The thudding noise came again from somewhere near the front of the house. Steve slid from beneath the covers and padded along the hallway to the living room; just as he opened the door into the rain-misted patio, he heard the banging on the front gate. He entered the hall and walked to the big door. He placed a hand on the cold metal of the double-barreled shotgun, which was kept in a niche beside the door for use against unwelcome visitors.

The thumping came again.

"¿Quién es?" called out Steve.

"Open up, by the powers! They's two men out here, soaked to the skin, tired, and hungry."

Steve grinned. It was the raucous voice of Luke Comfort. He lifted the bars and swung back the huge door to see two men standing beside horses in the wet street. Steve stared at the man beyond Luke. "Father!" he cried out.

Mark Ames came forward and gripped Steve by the shoulders. *"¡Ay de mí!"* he said. "Look, Luke! He is *mucho hombre* now! Much of the man!"

Steve stared unbelievingly at his father. Beneath the soaked slouch hat, his face was thin and drawn, while his poncho seemed to hang on little else than bones and muscles. "What happened to you, Father? You've lost twenty pounds!"

"Twenty-five," said Mark Ames. "Spanish beds and Spanish suppers don't keep meat on a man."

Steve grinned. A Spanish bed was to lie face downward on the harsh earth and pull your back over you for a cover, while a Spanish supper was to tighten one's belt and think of anything else but food.

"What about me?" demanded Luke.

Steve eyed the lean frame of the scout. He was all steel and whang leather, without an ounce of fat on him, and yet he ate like a poor relation at Thanksgiving time.

"Let's get inside," said Mark Ames. He shivered. "We've ridden all night from Galisteo in this drizzle."

They led the tired horses into the patio, and Steve took them to the stable. He took off the cantle and pommel packs, the sheathed rifles, and the wet saddles and placed them to one side. The horses were all side meat and bones as their masters had been. Steve ran a hand down the neck of his father's horse, and the animal whinnied softly, for he remembered Steve.

Steve rubbed them down and fed them, then carried the rifles into the house. The two men were seated in rawhide chairs, unbooted, while their wet feet, in holey socks, steamed from the heat of the crackling fire. Steve took his father's fine silver-mounted Hawken rifle from the buckskin sheath and hung it on the pegs over the fireplace. The rifle, as well as the men and the horses, had seen hard service.

"I'll get some forage," said Steve.

"Listen to the soldier," jeered Luke.

Steve grinned at Luke. The scout hadn't changed. He was as timeless as the mountains and deserts he loved. His sharp green eyes peered like those of a predatory bird from each side of his beak of a nose, which itself was slightly askew from some vicious blow in the past. His reddish hair, tinged with gray, hung low on his lean neck, and he wore a raggedly cropped beard.

"Seen enough, *chico?*" asked Luke. "Get the fodder!"

"Where's your uncle?" asked Mark Ames.

"In Taos, sir."

"You're here alone?"

"Yes, sir."

The gray eyes of Mark Ames studied Steve, and it seemed to Steve as though his father knew all about his disgrace before Steve had a chance to open his mouth.

Steve hurried to the kitchen and got food, heaping everything he could find on a tray. He carried it to the living room and placed the food in pots that could be heated beside the fire.

Luke sniffed. "Mexican strawberries," he said.

"Beans," said Steve dryly.

The two men closed their eyes and leaned back in their chairs until the food was ready on the table, and then they ate like timber wolves. When they were done, Steve poured cups of chocolate for them. It was then that

Mark Ames pointed a finger at Steve. "I heard about Galisteo," he said quietly.

"Tia Theresa?"

"Yes."

"I might have known," said Steve.

"Fill us in on the details, son."

Steve told them of the missing wagons and of how Hernán and he had trailed them.

The two men looked at each other. "Who has that rifle now?" asked Mark Ames.

"Oddly enough, sir, when Captain DeWitt returned to Santa Fe, he said someone had stolen it from the house in Galisteo."

"He kept the serial number, of course?"

"No."

The two men looked at each other again. "Do you happen to remember the serial number, Steve?" asked Mark Ames.

"No, sir."

Wood crackled in the fire. Steve began to clear the table.

"Would you know the man who visited Captain DeWitt in the middle of the night?" asked his father.

"I think so, sir."

"But you haven't seen him around Santa Fe?"

"I haven't been out of this house, sir, since I got back from Galisteo. I see."

"Those wagons never went south of the Galisteo Basin," Luke Comfort said. "They would have been seen."

"It wouldn't be easy to hide twelve big government wagons," said Steve.

"They could have taken them apart and burned them or scattered the parts."

"There were still twelve teamsters and a few troopers to deal with. They haven't been seen since the wagons were missed."

"They might have been in on the deal."

"And if they weren't?" asked Steve.

The strange green eyes seemed to bore holes into Steve. "*Los Muertos no hablan,*" said the scout quietly.

Steve refilled the chocolate cups. "What's doing down south?" he asked.

"Too much," said Luke. "Way too much."

Mark Ames sipped his hot chocolate. "After Major Lynde's disgraceful surrender at San Augustine Springs, the rebels under Colonel Baylor took possession of the lower valley area from La Mesilla down to El Paso. Rebel troops have been reported forming in San Antonio for the purpose of going on a gigantic 'buffalo hunt,' but we know they are actually three regiments of Texas Mounted Rifles, and their purpose is to join Colonel Baylor at La Mesilla and invade northern New Mexico and Arizona, too."

Luke nodded sagely. "They got some tough *hombres* leading those three regiments. And they got six mountain howitzers from what we heard."

Steve eyed the scout. "You must have heard a lot."

Mark Ames nodded. "I met Luke at Fort Craig, and we rode home together."

"Can Fort Craig hold back the rebels?" asked Steve.

"I think so. They are constructing bombproof buildings and earthworks all about the post. I doubt if the Texans can carry it by assault. But they can pass it."

"Then what happens?"

Steve's father shrugged. "They must fight in the field. Probably at or near Valverde, for it's my guess the Texans will advance up the east side of the Rio Grande and attempt to cross the river at the Valverde Fords, which are upriver from Fort Craig."

"And if the rebels win?"

Luke coughed. "You'll see the Lone Star flag flyin' over Albuquerque, Santa Fe, and maybe even Fort Union."

Mark Ames nodded. "We have the Regulars, of

course, and I doubt if the rebels can whip them, but we must also rely on militiamen and volunteers. I can't say that I think much of either type of soldier if you can even call them soldiers."

"I saw some of the Galisteo company of militia," said Steve. He shook his head.

"Supposing the rebels move up the Pecos?" asked Steve.

"Then the troops from Fort Union will have to stop them. I wonder if we'll get volunteer troops from Colorado as the governor requested?"

"Yes," said Steve. "The governor of Colorado has promised them."

"That's a relief!" Mark Ames stood up and paced back and forth. "Senor's Gonzalez and Tafolla want to recruit companies in the vicinity of Fort Craig. A Senor Perea wants to recruit a company at large. The Fourth Militia is being recruited at Fort Union and the Fifth at Albuquerque. Senor Alarid plans to form a Santa Fe Company. Senor Mora is ready to organize one at Mora."

Luke Comfort half-closed his green eyes. "With the exception of the Fourth and Fifth Militia Regiments, those are all three-month enlistments," he said quietly.

"There were quite a few three-month men at Bull Run," said Steve. He looked at his father. "Some of them started back for Washington just before the battle because their enlistments were up."

Mark Ames nodded. He eyed Steve. "What has your uncle said lately? That is, about the military situation." He grinned at Steve despite his weariness.

"A company of lancers under a Captain Dodd is supposed to be on the way to Santa Fe, *B* Company of the Second Colorado Volunteers. They're to be sent on at once to Fort Craig. The territory is entitled to recruit thirty-two companies of volunteers and militia to replace the Regulars. They wanted to take the Regulars from Canby, but he demanded promised reinforcements from

Kansas and Missouri before he'd release the Regulars. He hasn't seen hide nor hair of the Kansas and Missouri men as yet."

"They probably got their own hands full as it is," Luke remarked.

"The whole nation has its hands full," said Mark Ames dryly.

Luke shifted in his seat. "How soon do you want me to go back south, Mark?" he asked.

Steve looked quickly at the scout.

"I'll have to make my confidential report to Governor Connelly and to Canby sometime today," said Mark Ames. "As soon as I know the immediate plans of the territorial government and the military, I'll let you know what we want you to do, Luke."

Luke shrugged. "*Es Bueno*," he said.

"I'm going to get some sleep," said Steve's father. "Call me no later than eight o'clock." He slapped Steve on the shoulder and then left the room.

Luke fiddled with his chocolate cup. "I'd like to get out of here as quickly as possible."

"You just got back, Luke."

"You know how I hate walls and houses around me."

"Yes. What will you do when they send you down there?"

Luke winked. "Use my nose, ears, and eyes."

"Spying?"

Luke laughed. "That ain't nice! I'm a scout! A civilian employee, son!"

"What's the difference?"

Luke made a motion around his lean neck with a finger, then jerked a hand up while at the same time he tilted his head sideways, thrust out his tongue, and goggled his eyes.

There was no need for words. Steve shivered a little. He remembered only too well what had happened to a peddler in the military camps outside of Washington who had asked too many questions and had been in too many places where he had had no business being.

Luke studied Steve closely. "You've changed a lot," he said." Filled out. Something different about you, too. Like you suddenly stopped being a boy and are getting to be a man."

"I learned a lot at Bull Run, Luke."

The scout nodded. He leaned back in his chair." Took a heap of nerve to follow that trail through the Sangre de Cristo's, too."

"I got tired of sitting around here."

"I had a chance to talk to your *compañero...* Hernán Calvillo."

"How is he?" asked Steve eagerly.

Luke grinned." Still sore about the shoulders. His Tio Eusebio is a big, strong man. Hernán wanted to come back with us and join the army, but your father talked him out of it." The green eyes became speculative. "From what he tells me, you did a good job of tracking those wagons."

"It wasn't much, Luke."

Luke waggled a finger. "Mebbe so, mebbe not. Fact is you was the only ones who had any idea of where they went."

Steve nodded gloomily. "By now, they've vanished completely! If Captain Milas DeWitt had let us go after them, we might have learned more."

Luke nodded.

"When he came back to Santa Fe, he said nothing about the militia company of Captain Padilla going to look for them."

"Fact is, Steve, he never sent them."

Steve stared at Luke. "You're sure?"

"Positive."

"But that was loco! They were in the Galisteo Basin! Where else could they have gone?"

"Aye, indeed, where else?"

"I wonder about him sometimes."

Luke looked into the dying fire. "I wonder about a lot of so-called patriots in this territory. We've lost a number of United States Army officers to the rebels."

"Nothing really wrong with that, Luke. The rebel armies in the east are full of them. They resigned because they believed in state's rights."

Luke leaned forward." Aye! I've got nothing against *them!* But the war started last April! This is November and soon to be December! Seven months have passed since Fort Sumter was fired upon, and there are still men in the uniform of the United States Army who are rebels at heart. They're waiting to see how much damage they can do before they finally put on a gray suit! Men in high positions! Not second and first lieutenants but colonels and brigadier generals, no less!"

"Do you think Captain DeWitt is one of them?" asked Steve quietly.

Luke cut a hand sharply sideways. "I didn't say that! Milas DeWitt has worked hard for Canby. He's saved him from a lot of bother for one thing."

Steve nodded. "I know that for sure," he said dryly.

"He's a West Pointer, which don't mean too much as far as his politics go. But he knows this country and the people. He hasn't let anything stand in the way of his duty."

"No," said Steve. They really had nothing on the man. "Except for one thing, Luke, he's all right in your book."

The green eyes seemed to harden like emeralds. "So?"

"You don't like him."

Luke's tanned face suddenly changed. He laughed loudly and slapped his hands on his hard thighs. "Aye!"

Steve smiled. "Hernán Calvillo says one person likes him."

"Who?"

"*Himself.*"

"That is so! Hernán is no fool."

Steve placed more wood on the fire. "When you go south again," he asked quietly, "will you go alone?"

"I suppose so."

"But you wouldn't mind having a *compañero?*"

"No," said Luke.

"Luke, would you take me with you?"

"You'll have to have your father's permission."

"I know that."

"Ask him then. If he says, '*Estd Bueno,*' then you can ride with old Luke Comfort."

"*Gracias,* Luke. *Gracias!*"

Luke waved a hand. "It is nothing, *amigo.* I was going to ask him anyway."

Steve paced back and forth. "I know that country! I know the people! My father showed me the trails and the water holes. I can be of real help. I can see like a hawk, Luke, and shoot as good as most men. You won't be sorry. I'll do a good job."

A gentle snore interrupted Steve. The scout was already sound asleep.

CHAPTER ELEVEN

The wind blew through the quartermaster warehouse and set the lamps and candles to guttering. It moaned about the adobe walls and whispered through the cracks in the thick shutters.

Steven Ames looked up from the tall desk at which he stood, beyond the pool of yellow light from his lamp, and eyed the serried ranks of bales, bags, boxes, and heaps of equipment that almost completely filled the warehouse.

Major Donaldson was at the far end of the warehouse with his chief quartermaster clerk, and Steve could hear their voices although he could not distinguish the words. But the two men were worried.

Steve looked again at the two lists lying before him. It had been his misfortune early in his schooling to reveal that he wrote a fine copperplate hand, and when Donaldson had mentioned in Steve's father's hearing that he needed clerks at the big quartermaster warehouse, it had been sufficient for Steve to be practically sentenced to the job.

He hadn't been long at his task when he had learned that there were some serious shortages in the supplies that had been moved from Fort Union down to Santa Fe for eventual transshipment to Fort Craig. Now, for two days and part of the cold evenings, he had been at his desk while Major Donaldson and Quartermaster Sergeant Nye went carefully through the drafty warehouse, checking and re-checking, and as yet they had not been able to find the shortages.

Santa Fe was a place of thieves, and in fact, New Mexico Territory had a lot more than its share of them. The people were poor, more like slaves in many ways than free citizens of the United States. In fact, it had been said that the average Negro slave lived far better than did many of the peons of New Mexico. So, in order to live, they stole anything they could lay their hands on. But the warehouse was well guarded by Regulars from Fort Marcy. The windows were small and strongly barred. It was a hard nut for a thief to crack.

Steve shivered a little in the draft. He hunched his caped army overcoat higher on his shoulders and thought with longing of the bright fire that would be burning in the big-living room at home.

He copied a few more lines in his flowing hand, but his mind wandered off to the war. News trickled in from the East, some of it true and some of it false, and a man could digest it and come out with his own conclusions. There had been a few small engagements in Virginia. The Union forces had lost the battle of Wilson's Creek in Missouri. Lexington, Missouri, had been captured by the rebel General Price with the loss of the entire Chicago Irish Brigade. There had been a few actions in West Virginia at Cross Lanes, Gauley Mountain, and Buffalo Hill. A rebel general by the name of Robert E. Lee had done a little timid moving about Elk Water with raw troops and had accomplished absolutely nothing. General George Brinton McClellan was reorganizing the Union army in the vicinity of Washington and had promised the capture of Richmond in the spring.

In New Mexico, things had moved along. Luke Comfort had left for the south without Steve Ames. Colonel Canby had been promoted to the command of the newly formed Department of New Mexico. The rebel general Sibley, with his Texas Mounted Rifles, was said to be at Fort Bliss in Texas, ready for the invasion of New Mexico. Federal troops were being concentrated at Fort Craig to resist that invasion under Canby's command. One of his regiments was the First New Mexico Volunteer Infantry under the command of Kit Carson, and they lacked one drummer by the name of Steven Ames.

The major came back through the warehouse and stopped beside Steve's desk. "I hope you've found some discrepancies," he said.

"Nothing, sir."

Donaldson nodded glumly. "I had little faith that you would. This beats me."

"How much is missing, sir?"

The officer checked a list he held in his hand. "Not a great deal of one item, it seems. Rather, an assortment of items. Rifle caps, medicines, Enfield carbines, some sabers, a great many pistols, powder, and lead. Items we can hardly do without for this coming campaign in the south."

"Have you any idea what might have happened to them?"

Donaldson shrugged. "Those two lists you have there should check out. One of them was a list sent here from Fort Union; the other is the list made out by Captain Florian, whom I relieved some months ago." The officer looked toward the rear of the warehouse. "Florian was a poor man for quartermaster, but his records seemed to be accurate when I took over. One thing bothers me, though."

"Yes, sir?"

"Before I took over as quartermaster, there were some shipments made to the south. To a large depot in

Albuquerque and to smaller depots in Peralta, Belen, and a few others down south. I know those shipments were made, yet we have no records of all that material reaching those depots."

The candles guttered in the draft. The wind seemed to moan a little louder. Papers fluttered on the desk.

Donaldson struck his hands sharply together. "Some of that material never reached its destination."

"Like the wagons that were lost in Glorieta Pass last October?"

The major looked quickly at Steve. "Why do you say that?"

Steve shrugged. "They just seemed to vanish."

"Near Galisteo."

"Yes, sir."

Donaldson paced back and forth. "Some of the shipments we sent south went by way of Bernalillo, and others went by way of Galisteo." He rubbed his lean jaws. "Sergeant Nye!" he called out.

The quartermaster soldier came through the gloom of the warehouse. "Yes, sir?" he asked.

"Check through your records. Is there any way you can tell which of those shipments since this spring went through Bernalillo and which went via Galisteo?"

Nye took his lower lip between his teeth for a moment. Then he looked up. "By heaven, sir," he said quietly. "There's no need for me to check that at all!"

"Go on!"

Nye looked up at the low ceiling as though concentrating. "The only reason we sent shipments via Galisteo was because of a bad Indian scare near Bernalillo. I mind it well because I thought it was an old wives' tale. But it was said that Navahos in great numbers had been seen near Bernalillo, and so some shipments went via Galisteo, although the weather was bad, and the road was almost impassable in places. I remembered something odd the other day when we began to suspect that these supplies were missing. The shipments we had sent via Bernalillo all got through safely, while what we sent via Galisteo were the ones that had the missing items."

"You're sure of that?"

"Yes, sir."

"Why didn't you tell me before now?"

The sergeant looked surprised. "I didn't think it mattered that much, sir! All I knew was that the items were missing, and it didn't seem to matter whether they had been sent either way."

Donaldson nodded. "That's true, Nye. This we know: the items are not here, nor are they in any of the depots south of here; therefore, they must have disappeared on the way."

"It's possible, sir," said the noncom. "After all, they went down by civilian transport, not by army wagons."

"What's that, Nye?"

"It's quite customary, sir, as you know."

Steve nodded. "My father used to contract quite a lot to haul government goods and materials. But not at that time, Major."

Donaldson waved a hand. "Your father and his employees are above suspicion, young man." He looked at Nye. "Find out for me who contracted for those shipments and who hauled them."

"Yes, sir."

"I want a full report in the morning."

Donaldson took out his watch. "Nine o'clock!" he said with a surprised look on his face. "You're dismissed, young Ames." He looked steadily at Steve. "I think it hardly necessary to remind you that all you have heard here in the past few minutes is not to go beyond this warehouse."

"No, sir."

"Good night, then."

Steve took his forage cap and put it on. He saluted the officer then left the warehouse. The cold wind seemed to carry a warning of snow in it. He looked down the slope toward the quiet city and its twinkling yellow lights. Behind him, he could hear the call to quarters being played on the bugle at Fort Marcy, while below him was the diamond-shaped Garita with its towers, built originally for Spanish prisoners condemned to be hanged and now used by the army as a guardhouse.

He walked down the windy hill, and as he did so, he looked to the south through the darkness beyond the city. Somewhere down there, his regiment, with which he had never served, was at Fort Craig waiting for the enemy advance.

He passed through the dark, cold streets, and as he reached the vicinity of his father's house, he saw a figure seated near the outer gate, swathed in a serape and with a great steeple-crowned hat on its head. Steve hesitated. The streets of Santa Fe usually held a swarm of beggars, but no beggar would be out on a night as cold as this. Steve slid a hand inside his overcoat and gripped the butt of his navy Colt.

The figure moved. "*Hola, amigo,*" it said.

"Hernán! What are you doing here?"

Hernán's teeth violently chattered before he could speak. "Let us go inside," he said. "I am cold and hungry. The rabbits have their burros, and the birds have their nests, but Hernán Federico Telesfor Donaciano Gaspar Melchior Calvillo has no place to lay his head."

Steve glanced sideways at his friend as he unlocked the small door. Every time Hernán showed up, there was trouble, and yet life was a little empty around Santa Fe without the irrepressible apprentice muleteer.

Later, after they had eaten, the sad-eyed Hernán told Steve what had happened. "My uncle joined the militia, Steve. He was sent south to Socorro to guard the stores there with his company —Capitan Padilla's. On the way, my uncle was thrown from his mule and badly hurt. My Tia Rosa hurried at once to be with him. I stayed in the house for a week, and I got lonely for my friend Steve."

Steve refilled their chocolate cups. "I am glad you came, *amigo*," he said quietly.

Hernán eyed Steve's uniform. "Can you get me into the army?"

"Can you play a drum?"

Hernán sadly shook his head.

"Then I'll teach you."

Hernán looked at Steve. "But you, why are you not with the First New Mexico? They are at Fort Craig, waiting to fight the rebels. Are you not in a hurry to join them?"

Steve shrugged. "Certainly, I am. But I'm stuck here in Santa Fe, fighting with pen and ink instead of with powder and ball, and every time I open my mouth around my father or uncle, they tell me a soldier serves where he is ordered to serve and keeps his mouth shut no matter where else he wants to be."

Hernán nodded gloomily. "How can they expect the war to be won here in New Mexico without us?"

Steve stood up and paced back and forth. "There is something we can do."

"So?"

"Those wagons we tracked down to the Galisteo Basin were never found."

"That is so."

Steve quickly told him of what had happened in the big quartermaster warehouse that evening.

Hernán's sad eyes lighted up. "It seems as though there is a big hole in the air where wagons and stores vanish," he said thoughtfully. "Right near Galisteo."

They looked at each other, and then they both grinned. "Where is El Diablo?" asked Steve suddenly.

"Tia Rosa tried to ride him south to where my uncle is, but you know El Diablo. She came back afoot and got a burro. I haven't seen El Diablo since. I walked from Galisteo."

"We'll get a horse for you."

"Like El Diablo?"

Steve held out his hands, palms upward. "Where in the world would there be another El Diablo?"

"That is so!" Hernán emptied his chocolate cup. "But you are on duty here in Santa Fe. Remember what happened the last time you left here without permission."

Steve nodded. "Tomorrow is Sunday. I'm not expected for duty. That will give us a whole day."

"But it is twenty-three miles to Galisteo! By the time we get there, poke our noses into places to learn things, then ride back here, it would be at least Tuesday."

Steve nodded. "Still, I feel that we can do more good down there than we can here."

"Maybe we'll meet Captain DeWitt again."

"He's at Fort Union, *amigo*."

Hernán grinned. "This is a happy coincidence! When do we leave?"

"Tonight."

Hernán's face fell. "I knew it! I find a hot fire, warm food, a good bed to sleep in; then I have to leave."

Steve grinned back at Hernán. "You wanted to be a soldier, *amigo*. A soldier serves where he is ordered to serve and keeps his mouth shut no matter where else he wants to be."

Hernán rolled his eyes upwards. "*Madre mía!*" he said piously." We have here the philosopher."

"You can always stay here. I'm sure my father and uncle can find something for you to do, Hernán—such as cleaning out the stables."

Hernán nodded solemnly. "There is salt in what you say." He slapped Steve on the back. "I will get the horses. Which one shall be mine?"

"The sorrel mare."

"No stallion?"

"Not like El Diablo," said Steve sorrowfully.

Hernán shrugged. "I will lose face riding the sorrel mare, but it is true that I would not care to walk back to Galisteo tonight. *Vamanos* then!"

The wall clock softly chimed eleven strokes.

CHAPTER TWELVE

GALISTEO BASIN, NEW MEXICO TERRITORY—DECEMBER 1861

I t was dawn when Steve Ames drew rein and looked back at Hernán. They had ridden a good part of the night, resting now and then until they had bypassed sleeping Galisteo. Steve wanted to take no chances on being found out as they had been the last time they had come to the Galisteo area.

Hernán was muffled in his serape and had a blanket tied about his waist Indian style. "*¡Estd Frio!*" he said with chattering teeth.

"It is cold," said Steve. He looked ahead through broken country. In the gray distance, he could see a mountain range. He had no idea what they were looking for, but if those missing wagons had been taken to the Galisteo Basin and never seen again, there must be some trace of them left somewhere. "What's ahead, *amigo?*" he asked.

Hernán stood up in his stirrups and peered from beneath the broad brim of his battered hat. He smiled thinly. "There is a ruined adobe not far from here. When I was hunting with Tfo Eusebio one time, we stayed the night there."

They rode on with the keening wind knifing through their clothing until they saw the ruins. It had been a small adobe, probably used by simple and poverty-stricken people, but they had had a view that was priceless. To the south was a panoramic spread, still dulled by the retreating night, but with the sun up, it would be magnificent.

They led the tired horses into a rock-walled corral at the rear of the crumbling house and scattered food for them on a broad, wooden cart bed that lay there. They hung blankets over the horses, then carried their saddle-bags into the house.

The kitchen wasn't in bad repair, although there were holes in the earthen roof. Hernán worked quickly to gather dry juniper and piñon wood while Steve got out the food. In a short time, a smokeless fire was crackling in the fireplace. The boys placed a spider over the glowing coals and filled it with bacon. In a little while, they were munching bacon sandwiches and gulping thick chocolate.

While Hernán cleaned the spider and the chocolate pot, Steve walked outside and looked down into the great Basin below the house. The sun was just tipping the eastern mountains with a promise of warmth, but it was still cold in the Basin. Steve uncased his uncle's field glasses and began to scan the terrain with them. There was little to see until the sun rose higher. Hernán came up behind Steve. "Just what are we looking for, *chico?*" he asked.

"I don't really know."

Hernán rested his elbows on the wall. "If I were hiding stolen goods," he said, "I would place them in the Espectro Valley."

Steve turned. "Ghost Valley?"

"*Si.* It is a strange place. Many years ago, the Indians, Tewa's, I think, lived there, and then they left. Then the Spaniards came, and in time there was a little mission and chapel there, but the Indians fought with them, and there was a drought followed by a massacre, so the good padres did not go there again. In the years that followed, people tried to live there, but one way or another, they were driven away."

"Driven?"

Hernán shrugged. "*¿Quién sabe?* All I know is that it is not a good place. My people will not go there. There is a curse upon the place."

Steve peered through the glasses.

"But you will go?" asked Hernán uneasily.

"Yes."

"Alone."

"Do I have to?"

There was a moment's silence, and then Hernán spoke. "It is true that I am afraid, but I am more afraid that you would think I had no honor by not going with you."

Steve grinned. "I need a guide, *compañero*."

"You have one, *hombrecito*."

"Let's get some sleep then,"

Hernán shook his head. "Who can sleep thinking about going to the Espectro Valley? You sleep, *amigo*. I will stand guard."

Steve cased the glasses and handed them to his companion, then he went into the ruin, wrapped himself in his blankets and army overcoat, and closed his eyes. He was worried. He was absent without leave again, but nothing seemed to have been done about tracing down those missing wagons and the supplies that had disappeared so mysteriously some months before the wagons had vanished. He fell asleep thinking about the praise that he and his companion would get when they solved the mystery of the Galisteo Basin.

———

THE SUN WAS UP HIGH, driving some of the chill from the air, but there was still a cold wind searching through the valley. Hernán stopped leading his horse and pointed down the valley. "There is a ruin," he said. "Once, it belonged to the Casias family. There was a Jicarilla raid. None of the Casias were left. That was a long time ago."

They led the horses along the side of the valley away from the sweeping wind. Steve eyed the ground. There was a faint, rutted road through the valley, but it looked as though it had not been used for many years.

The old Casias house and buildings were nothing but heaps of crumbled adobe and rock with a straggling thatch of brush upon them.

It was a lonely place. Hernán was obviously nervous, while time and time again Steve found himself looking quickly back along the valley as though someone was following them, although there was no sign of life. Then, too, there was the constant feeling that they were being watched. There was no proof of this, for they could see no one, no movements of man or animal, and yet the feeling was still there.

———

IT WAS late afternoon when Steve halted and stared at the heights to the east of the valley.

"What is it, Steve?" asked Hernán.

"I thought I saw smoke."

"Up there? There is no smoke, for there is no one to make it." Hernán looked at the sun. "It will be dark before we leave this accursed place."

Steve looked at him. "We haven't found anything yet."

Hernán shivered a little. "If we stay here, someone will find us."

"There are other ruins east of us?"

"Yes."

"We could shelter there for the night."

"*¿Está loco?* Have you reason or mind? Men have come in here and have never been seen again. None of my people would, or would any Indian come in here and stay the night."

Steve grinned. "Only a loco Anglo like me, eh, *chico*?"

Hernán swallowed as he looked past Steve. "Look," he said hoarsely.

Steve turned and looked at the broken land to the east. A thread of smoke was rising until it met the unseen current of the wind, and then it was tattered and driven from sight. "What is it?" he asked, almost to himself. "Not Indians for certain."

They walked on until they reached a slope, which they ascended, and then they could look down into a place where the valley narrowed. Steve stared at some low-lying buildings, half concealed by brush and trees. They looked almost like features of the terrain itself. There was a tower there, with gaping windows, rising above a crumbling ruin. The place looked fearfully alone in the dying sunlight.

"It is the old mission, I think," said Hernán. He crossed himself quickly.

Steve led the way, but this time he held his carbine ready. The sun was almost gone when they reached the crumbling rock and adobe fence that enclosed the mission and the outbuildings.

The wind moaned through the bell tower and fluttered the dry trees and brush.

"No one comes here," said Hernán. "Not even the animals. It is a place of the dead."

Steve handed the reins of Zouave to his companion, then swung a leg over the fence. He crossed the littered churchyard, between the rows of ancient, sagging crosses of gray wood, until he stood at last upon the low flagstone platform at the entrance to the chapel. Yards of plaster had fallen from the old walls. Here and there seemed to be the pocks of bullets that had struck the thick walls. Brush shrouded the base of the structure.

He walked into the building and stopped as his steps echoed through the cold nave. The very silence seemed heavy in the place. There was a doorway to his right, cut through a thick wall, and he entered into a smaller room, the baptistry. There was a stairway built into the walls of the tower itself, and he ascended it, feeling with a free hand ahead of him while his boot soles crunched on fallen plaster and debris.

He stopped at the top, in the place where the bells hung.

There was only one of them left, a thick-shelled bell, green with age. He flicked a fingernail against it, and the soft sweet tone of the bell seemed to linger in the air.

Steve looked to the east, through the openings, and saw the heights still lighted with the last rays of the dying sun. For a moment, he stared. There was a yellow fleck of light against the reddened rock of the heights. He shook his head and stared again. A tendril of smoke rose from the vicinity of the light and then vanished in the wind.

Steve walked to the other side of the tower and looked down upon Hernán, who stood rooted to the exact spot where Steve had left him. Hernán Federico Telesfor Donaciano Gaspar Melchior Calvillo had courage all right. Steve wondered how many of his people would stand there in a so-called haunted valley while a friend prowled through a long-abandoned church.

Steve looked again to the east. The light had vanished. But someone had lighted a fire or a lamp over there. Who was it?

He went down the stairs and glanced toward the sanctuary, now shrouded in darkness. The stations of the cross had been defaced, and the floor of the nave was littered with filth and debris. A sad fate for a place of worship.

Steve left the echoing pile and walked across to Hernán. The sun was gone. "Come on," said Steve.

Hernán swallowed. He cast one more desperate look behind him, toward the west, where he wanted to be, then led the horses along the fence until he found an opening.

Steve found a low building that would at least keep the cold night wind from reaching them. They had cooked enough food that morning so that they might have a cold supper that night. Hernán ate silently, then wrapped himself in his serape and blankets. "There will be a moon tonight," he said at last. He peered at Steve. "Enough to see the trail to Galisteo."

Steve did not answer. He himself wanted to leave this echoing place of the dead, but something kept him there.

He felt as though the riddle of the missing wagons and supplies could be answered there. How, or when, he did not know, but he had a feeling deep within him that he was right.

———

THE MOON WAS WELL UP, bathing the quiet and rugged terrain in a silvery wash of light. The mission looked as though it were carved from alabaster in the soft light.

Hernán was sound asleep. Steve covered his companion with the blanket he himself no longer needed and padded softly from the room. There was no light on the eastern slopes of the valley. To Steve's knowledge, there were no roads up in that country and hardly any trails.

He walked past a long building that had collapsed into a heap of rubble until he reached a stout building, set back against a natural wall of rock. The door was intact. He tested it, but it would not budge. There was no lock, so the door might be wedged shut by debris. He went on toward the rear of the building to a window that was shuttered. He pried open the edge of one shutter with his sheath knife and worked his way into the building.

He stood there for quite a while until his eyes became accustomed to the dimness. The room was littered with rough broken furniture, shards of glass and pottery, partly burned faggots of wood, broken boxes, and torn sacks. The air was dead in the big room. Steve walked across to the fireplace, wishing there was a roaring fire in it, and as he did so, his foot struck something that rustled. He bent to pick up a crumpled newspaper. Taking it to the window, he saw that it was a copy of the Mesilla *Times,* a definitely pro-Southern sheet, dated late in October. The *Times* was known to flourish under the protection of Colonel Baylor, who had captured Lynde's command at San Augustine Springs.

How had that paper come to be there? He folded it and placed it inside his coat. This was an out-of-the-way place, scarcely the place to find such a newspaper. He looked about until he found a stub of candle, which he lighted.

The flickering light glinted from something in a corner, and he picked it up. It was an officer's shoulder strap with the twin silver bars of a captain's insignia on the blue material. It didn't look as though it had been there very long.

There was a door just behind the filthy fireplace. He tried the door, and it gave just a little. He threw his shoulder against it, and it gave a little more until he could get a purchase between the edge of the door and the doorway with a piece of broken timber. He walked into the room and raised the candle. He whistled softly. The room was piled with sacks and boxes from one end to the other. He took out his knife and slit the end sack. A thin trickle of flour came from it. He walked along the line of boxes. The place reminded him of the quartermaster warehouse in Santa Fe, and what was more, the bags and boxes were all stamped U.S.

He reached the end of the long room. There were barrels piled up there, and they too were stamped with the letters U.S. Beyond them was a rack of rifles. He leaned closer to the rack. New rifles. Issue .58 caliber Springfields. Behind the rack were sets of equipment, cartridge and cap boxes, sheathed bayonets, and pistol holsters.

Steve walked slowly back to the first room. There was no sign of life in that isolated valley. They had seen nothing but that mysterious thread of smoke to the east and the faint yellow light he had seen just after sunset. Yet here in this long-abandoned building was a small fortune in Government supplies. As he walked into the first room, he slid a hand inside his coat to touch the folded newspaper. The Mesilla *Times*.

Steve blew out the candle and walked to the window by which he had entered. He climbed outside and started for the building in which Hernán was sleeping.

He saw Hernán standing near the front of the church. Steve grinned. His *amigo* was still scared and probably wanted to get out of there while they had moonlight to show the way.

"Hernán!" he called.

Hernán turned and beckoned to him. The boy had his carbine in his hands.

Steve walked quickly. "I found the supplies!" he said.

Hernán turned, and the moonlight fell on his face. Steve stopped short, and ice seemed to course through his veins. Hernán seemed a foot taller than he really was, and now he had a great hooked nose and a ragged beard.

The carbine snapped up and flashed, just ten feet from Steve, and the yellow spurt of flame half-blinded him at the same instant a sledgehammer blow struck his left shoulder and drove him back against the church.

"Steve! Steve!" It was the voice of Hernán, and it seemed to come from a great distance.

Steve looked up at the bearded man, and he knew him. The man looked toward the building where Hernán had slept. There was a splash of yellow fire from the building and the slam of a slug against the church wall inches from the bearded man. He darted around to the front of the church, and a moment later came the hard tattoo of hoofs on the rocky ground.

Steve raised himself on one elbow to see Hernán running toward him, ramming home a charge in his Enfield carbine. The boy had saved his life. Steve opened his mouth. "Hernán... I..."

"I will stay with you, *amigo*! Never fear!" called out Hernán stoutly.

It was the last thing Steve remembered.

CHAPTER THIRTEEN

"Try it again, Stevie," said Trumpeter Corporal Will Nolan. He leaned back in his chair and closed his eyes.

Steve Ames eased his bandaged shoulder, hitched himself up a little in his bed, then placed the silver trumpet to his lips. The lilting notes of the charge came from the beautiful instrument. Steve half-closed his eyes. He could conjure up a picture of Dacey Curtis that day long ago at Bull Run, when the First Virginia Cavalry had smashed the Eleventh New York Volunteers into ruin. Then the silver trumpet had seemed to shriek in joy, high above the crash of the battle, like a screaming, wheeling eagle.

The silvery notes died away, and Steve came back to reality. He looked at the trumpeter.

Nolan nodded his head. "Fine," he said.

Hernán poked his head into the bedroom, "*¡Está bueno!*" he agreed. "I have soup for you, *amigo*."

Nolan stood up and put on his forage cap. "You're the best I've heard on the charge, Steve. Seems as though some trumpeters have certain calls they never master, and some they can play better than anyone else. I'll say this: I've never heard anyone play that call, the charge, like you can, Steve."

Hernán proudly smiled as he placed the tray on a table, then his smile faded as he saw the look on Steve's face.

Steve passed a chamois cloth up and down the instrument. "You weren't at Bull Run, Will," he said to the trumpeter. "No matter who plays the silver trumpet from now on, no one will ever play it like Dacey Curtis did that day."

Nolan buttoned his caped overcoat. "That's an odd story."

Steve nodded.

Nolan eyed Steve. "You'll be up and about soon, no doubt?"

"Yes."

"Good-by then."

"*Adios, amigo.*"

The soldier left the room, and a moment later, the two boys heard the outer door close. Steve eyed the soup. He was sick of being an invalid, and yet no matter how foul his humor was, it seemed he could do nothing to rile Hernán.

Hernán began to straighten up the room. "Your father and uncle are at the Governor's Palace," he said. "There is a rumor that the Texans are advancing north along the Rio Grande Valley."

Steve looked up quickly. "Do they say there will be a battle?"

"*¿Quién sabe?* Our forces cannot let them get north of Fort Craig. It is said they hope to capture the Valverde Fords."

"That figures. Listen! Go uptown and see what you can learn."

"*¡Si!*"

When Hernán was gone, Steve got out of bed. He

had been feeling fit for days, but Doctor Dunlap had kept him confined as though he was a child. Steve still suspected the good doctor had done so upon orders from Steve's father.

He dressed quickly, putting on his uniform. It was the first time he had donned it since that day, weeks ago when he and Hernán had left for Galisteo. The memory of the trip from Espectro Valley back to Galisteo under the care of Hernán was nothing but a painful blur to Steve. Luckily, there had been an army ambulance at Galisteo that had taken Steve at once to Santa Fe, with Hernán sitting up beside him all the way. That trip, too, was merely a mist in Steve's mind.

Steve put on his caped overcoat and buttoned it. The worst part of the whole escapade, as their dangerous trip had been labeled, was that absolutely nothing had come of it. In the confusion of getting Steve to Santa Fe, Hernán had garbled up the story of their findings in Espectro Valley. But it was true that Hernán had not seen the stores, and he himself had found it hard to believe Steve's story. His chief concern, laudable enough, had been to get Steve to safety. Later, when Steve had spoken about what he had found, the story was treated as delirium coupled with a desire to cover up for what was a second serious breach of discipline by Steve.

Steve brushed off his neat forage cap, with its polished brass infantry trumpet insignia pinned to the crown and placed it on his head. He put the silver trumpet inside its cloth case, then took it to its storage place in the old rosewood piano.

The only person who had listened to Steve had been Major Donaldson, and through his instigation, a cavalry detail from Fort Marcy had ridden at last to Galisteo under the command of Captain Milas DeWitt. That had been another fiasco for Steve, for DeWitt had reported that there was nothing but ruins in the valley and certainly no sign of purloined military stores. Still, Major

Donaldson, a busy man, had covered up for Steve by saying that Steve had had his permission to ride to Galisteo. He had meant to pursue the search still further, but the war had caught up with the entire Department of New Mexico by that time. Headquarters had been moved to Fort Craig, near the Valverde Fords.

There had been some lively little skirmishes down south. Captains Mink and Vidall and their commands had been captured at Canada Alamosa. The score had been evened by the capture of a captain and nine men from Baylor's Second Regiment of Texas Mounted Rifles. Both Union and Confederate forces had many fights with raiding Indians, and some had said that it would be better if the New Mexicans and Texans joined forces to wipe out the Indians so that the white men could get on with their own private war in peace and quiet.

Steve walked out onto the dark, cold patio. He hunched into the collar of his coat as he went toward the plaza. It seemed as though everything he had done since he had come home to New Mexico had been wrong. His father and uncle worked like Trojans for the territory, with little time for Steve and his problems. His father had donned the uniform of a staff officer working with the territorial government. Many officers and enlisted men whom Steve had known and seen around Santa Fe had been sent south to Fort Craig, and among them was Captain Milas DeWitt. He was due for promotion, it was said, nothing less than a colonelcy. Steve felt as though he had done the man an injustice by being so suspicious of him. Milas DeWitt had worked hard for the defense of the territory and had insisted on being assigned to Fort Craig when he, with a major's rank, could very well have stayed in Santa Fe and out of the way of rebel Minie balls.

Strength had been coming to New Mexico in dribbles and drabbles. Some Colorado Volunteers, Pike's Peaker's, had been sent to Fort Craig, while others were said to be on their way to Fort Union and thence to Santa Fe or farther south if needed.

The territorial legislature had convened in Santa Fe in January, and it soon had become evident that Union men had the majority, for one of the first acts in the Session of 1862 was to repeal an act entitled 'An Act Providing for the Protection of Slave Property in this Territory,' which had been passed by the legislature on February 3, 1859. Repeal of the law of 1859 demonstrated that New Mexico Territory had reversed itself on the slavery question and let the world know that New Mexico had firmly allied itself with the Union cause. One of the members of the legislature who had fought wholeheartedly for the repeal had been Steve's uncle, Carter Ames.

There were few people in the wind-swept plaza. Steve wandered over to the Governor's Palace to see if he could pick up some news, but the place was almost deserted. An orderly nodded to Steve. "Feeling better?" he asked.

Steve grinned ruefully. "I feel better than I did before I stopped that piece of lead."

The orderly smiled. "That was one part of your story that was proved to be true. You did get shot."

Steve flushed. He started for the door and saw a pile of luggage and boxes beside it, topped by some uniforms on hangers. "Who's moving out?" he asked.

The orderly looked up. "That's Captain DeWitt's stuff. I was told to clean out his room and send that stuff up to Fort Marcy for storage. Guess he'll be busy for a time down at Fort Craig, and they need his room."

Steve eyed the top uniform blouse. It wasn't a new one and seemed to have seen a lot of service. The lamplight shone on the brass buttons and on one of the shoulder tabs. Steve moved closer to the uniform. The right-hand shoulder tab's color was dull, the gilt faded and greenish from much exposure to the elements, but the left-hand shoulder tab was much brighter and of a slightly different pattern.

"Watch the door," said the orderly. "I'm going to get me a cup of coffee."

Steve was alone in the room. He moved the lamp to a table beside the pile of luggage and uniforms and studied the two shoulder tabs. There wasn't any doubt that the two tabs were not exact mates. He thrust a hand into his overcoat pocket and drew out the tab he had found in the building the night he had been shot. He placed it beside the older tab on the uniform. It was an exact mate in color, texture, and size.

Footsteps sounded in the hallway. Steve placed the lamp on the orderly's desk and stepped back. The orderly entered the room. "Thanks, Steve," he said. "Cold and getting colder. They say there's snow up around Raton Pass, and they expect a blizzard. Rough on the Colorado boys."

"How so?"

"The First Colorado Volunteers are on the way down here, it's said."

Steve nodded. He had hardly heard what the orderly had said. He walked out into the cold night. A shoulder tab was hardly enough to incriminate a gentleman and an officer in the crime of stealing government property, and on top of that, Steve was hardly in a position to accuse anyone of such a thing, not after the two messes he had already gotten himself into.

It was getting late. There was a spit of snow in the cold air mingled with the odors of burning piñon wood. Steve was heartily sick of being confined to his home and the city. He raised his head as he heard the steady tattoo of hoofbeats coining from the direction of the Cerrillos Road. It seemed to whisper to him of the freedom of the open country. Maybe he could get sent to his regiment down at Fort Craig.

The sound of the hoofbeats came closer and closer, and then a horseman swept into the plaza and galloped toward the Governor's Palace. The horseman drew his mount in hard, and the big horse reared and flung off. The horseman dropped to the ground. "Where's Major Donaldson, soldier?" he demanded of Steve in a familiar voice.

"Luke! Luke Comfort!" cried out Steve.

The scout bent his head and stared closely at Steve.

"Steve," he said urgently, "where's the major?"

"In the palace, Luke."

Luke brushed past Steve. "What's up, Luke?" asked Steve.

The scout turned, and the light from a window fell on his tired face." It's all over down south," he said tersely. "Three days ago, the rebels under Sibley defeated our forces at Valverde. They're advancing up the Rio Grande Valley now. I rode three horses to death gettin' up here. My orders are for all stores in the way of the rebels to be destroyed and for Santa Fe to be evacuated!" The scout passed into the palace.

It was only a matter of an hour before the whole city knew about the disaster at Valverde. Lights glowed in all the houses. Frightened citizens were attacking the hard ground with picks and spades to find hiding places for their money and treasures. Couriers galloped north and east through the cold night to alert all outlying military forces.

Something else besides Luke Comfort had come to Santa Fe. It was *fear,* and it hovered over the city like a dark cloud, whispering in the wind, and the word it whispered oftenest was *degüello. Degüello,* 'no quarter,' for it was said that the *Tejano's,* 'the Texans,' maddened by their losses at Valverde, intended to put Santa Fe to the sword and then burn it to the ground.

―――――

LUKE COMFORT EXTENDED his tired feet toward the cheery blaze in the fireplace and looked up at his little audience of Mark and Carter Ames, Steve, and Hernán. He had reported into the major and had come home with Steve's father and uncle. "The battle," he said at last, "should have been ours, but you know the luck of battles."

They all nodded, and the memory of how Bull Run had turned against the Union forces came back to Steve.

Luke stared into the fire. "We had about four thousand men at Fort Craig, and the rebels had about two thousand."

"They were afraid to attack the fort, so they crossed the Rio Grande and advanced north to Valverde. On the morning of the twenty-first, our forces left Fort Craig to defend the fords at Valverde."

"We fought back and forth a good part of the day without much result. Then we were to attack their left flank while we held our center with artillery. But, as luck would have it, they decided on practically the same thing. So, while we advanced on the south side of the battlefield, they advanced on the north side of it. The troops we had in support for our artillery were not in position, so the Texans captured our artillery and turned it against us. We had to retreat to Fort Craig. They knew it was too strong to take."

"Canby sent couriers to the north, and I was one of them. Some of the boys didn't get through. Anyway, I carried orders that all supplies at Albuquerque, Santa Fe, and Fort Lyon must be destroyed. It looks right bad, gentlemen."

Mark Ames put on his army overcoat and cap. "I'm to leave as soon as possible for Las Vegas," he said, "to rush the Colorado troops and some of the Regulars from Fort Union toward Santa Fe."

Carter Ames nodded. "I'll ride with you, Mark," he said. "The territorial government is to move to Las Vegas, and Governor Connelly wants me to go ahead to make arrangements for quarters and so forth there."

Mark Ames looked at his son. "Obviously, you're ready for duty, Steve," he said. "Major Donaldson can use you as an orderly here. If the city is evacuated, you are to accompany the troops to Las Vegas. Is that clear?"

"Yes, sir."

When the two brothers had left, Luke Comfort glanced up at Steve. "I didn't mention the fact that we had lost Captain Milas DeWitt at Valverde, Steve."

"No."

Luke stared into the fire with his strange green eyes. "I saw him at the end of the fight. He could have pulled out across the river with the rest of us, but he just stood there near our captured guns and gave his sword to the first Texan officer he saw."

Luke turned and eyed Steve. "He had plenty of time to get away, Steve. It's my opinion that Milas DeWitt is wearing a new gray uniform right now."

"Amen," said Hernán Calvillo.

CHAPTER FOURTEEN

GLORIETA PASS, NEW MEXICO TERRITORY– MARCH 1862

Steven Ames kneed Zouave to the right to pass by the trudging column of infantrymen. They were Germans of Captain Maille's Company finishing their march to Pigeon's Ranch. The smoke of bivouac fires rose in the narrow canyon to mingle with the dust. Supply wagons lined the dusty road for a long distance. It was March 28. There wasn't any doubt that the rebels would soon advance from the city through Glorieta Pass to capture Las Vegas and Fort Union.

Steve had been so busy since the news of the Union defeat at Valverde had come to Santa Fe that he had had little time to think of anything else but his duties. He had been plunged into the type of service he liked with a vengeance. He had been detailed as a courier and spent most of his time in the saddle, delivering dispatches and verbal messages as the Union forces prepared for the next passage of arms that might decide the fate of New Mexico.

There had been fighting and skirmishing in the echoing canyons. News trickled in that the rebels held Carnuel, fifteen miles east of Albuquerque, to hold back any Union force that might attempt to retake the city by way of Tijeras Canyon. Meanwhile, the rebels in Santa Fe had made probing advances toward Johnson's Ranch near Apache Canyon, the entry to Glorieta Pass.

Steve spurred Zouave once he had passed Maille's Company. There should be some units of the Fifth United States Infantry on the road from Las Vegas. Slowly but surely, Federal forces had entered Glorieta Pass to plug the hole. There were units of the Third United States Cavalry and the First Colorado Volunteer Infantry, the 'Pike's Peaker's,' who had made a heroic march of one hundred and seventy-two miles through icy winds and falling snow in five days to reach Fort Union.

Somewhere to the south of the pass, there was a command of four hundred Union cavalrymen, led by Major Chivington and guided by Lieutenant Colonel Manuel Chaves and Scout Luke Comfort. This command had turned off at San Cristobal Canyon to attempt a wide western swing that would take them to the rear of the rebels who were advancing eastward toward Glorieta Pass.

Steve delivered his message and was about to ride swiftly back to Colonel Slough's headquarters at the ranch when he heard a shrill hail behind him. "*¡Hola, amigo!*"

Steve smiled as he recognized the voice of Hernán Calvillo. Hernán galloped toward Steve on the little sorrel mare that had replaced the long-missing El Diablo. But it was a different Hernán Calvillo from the boy who had left Santa Fe with Steve. He seemed larger and far more imposing, and no wonder, for he was now in the uniform of a drummer boy of militia, with nine rows of white braid set horizontally across his chest, and on his head was a battered Kossuth hat whose wide brim flopped up and down with the motion of the horse.

Hernán drew in his horse, letting it fling off while Hernán doffed his ludicrous hat. "You see before you

Hernán Federico Telesfor Donaciano Gaspar Melchior Calvillo!"

"No!" said Steve.

"Drummer in Capitan Rafael Castaneda's Independent Company of New Mexico Provisional Militia!"

"A veteran unit," said Steve suspiciously. "Where are they?"

Hernán grinned. "It so happens, *soldado*, that Capitan Castaneda was promised a commission on the day he signed up his first company member."

Hernán brushed his hat. "*I* am that first member," he said.

"And the *Capitan* and his company?"

Hernán looked up at the canyon heights and whistled softly. "I am the *Capitan's* company," he said proudly. He eyed Steve. "It is the truth, *amigo!* I am enlisted."

"Has he heard you play the drum?"

"There was really little time, I..."

Steve leaned forward in his saddle. "Has he?"

"Well, no, that is to say, not exactly, I..."

Steve shook his head.

Hernán waved a hand. "No matter," he said grandly. "I have here the dispatch from Las Vegas for the Colonel Slough. Be so kind, *Soldado mío,* to tell me where he is."

"At Pigeon's Ranch."

"Then let us be on the way."

They rode together. Hernán glanced at the silver trumpet that hung from Steve's shoulder by its braided silken cord. "You are the trumpeter now?" he asked.

"No."

"Still carrying dispatches?"

"Yes."

They passed the toiling infantrymen. Some of them grinned and made catcalls at Hernán as he rode by in his finery.

Steve waited outside of headquarters until Hernán returned. "Are you going back?" asked Steve.

Hernán grinned. "I told the colonel I was to stay here. I said you had asked for me to help with the dispatches."

"I might have known!"

Hernán shaded his eyes with his hand and looked to the west. "You think there is the chance we will fight here?"

"Not very likely, *amigo*."

Hernán nodded. He looked about. "This is a good time for the siesta."

Steve paid no attention to his friend. He was staring toward two moraines to the west of the ranch, where a cavalry patrol had appeared. They were setting the steel to their mounts. The sun glinted on something in the trees. Dust curled upward from the pounding hoofs of the horses. Then there was a dull, roaring noise from the north moraine, and smoke puffed out into the clear mountain air. Something crashed into the trees near the ranch, and metal tinkled ominously on the hard ground.

The cavalry patrol lay low on their horses' necks as they reached the ranch. "The hills are full of rebels!" yelled the officer who led them.

Steve looked at Hernán as a bugle stuttered into life behind them. "You still going to take your siesta, *amigo*?"

Hernán's face was pale beneath the wide brim of his Kossuth hat. "I think it had better wait, *compañero*."

The next few minutes were a haze to Steve. Orders rattled out like hail on a tin roof as the rebel guns fired steadily at the ranch. But the Union forces moved swiftly into action while Steve, Hernán, and other messengers carried verbal orders to the various Union contingents.

Claflin's howitzers were drawn by galloping horses down the road, scattering yelling and gawking infantry-men. Rebel projectiles plunged through the trees and brush, and some of them exploded in cottony puffs on the rutted road. There was a continual slamming noise as the echoes of the artillery guns seemed to bound from one side of the pass to the other.

Robbin's Company of infantrymen double-timed up the road behind the howitzers while Ritter's six-pounder field guns went into battery south of the road, supported by the sweating infantrymen of Sopris' Company.

Colonel Slough stood exposed to the fire of the enemy. He lowered his field glasses and beckoned to Steve. "Tell Lieutenant Kerber of Maille's Company to take his Germans to the far right flank and try to outflank that rebel battery!"

Thick smoke drifted through the trees as Steve ran toward the Germans. Kerber coolly nodded as he listened to Steve. In a moment, he led his men to the right through the trees and then into an irrigation ditch that angled toward the moraine where the rebel battery was in action.

"Look!" yelled an excited officer.

A company of the enemy was double-timing across an enclosed field on the right flank. Steve raced through the trees until he saw Lieutenant Kerber. He yelled and pointed at the Texans.

A crashing volley came from the ditch, and some of the rebels fell while others reached the ditch with ready bayonets. A rebel officer went down. Then Kerber's men appeared at the end of the ditch, and his clear commands rang out. The Germans volleyed three times and drove the Texans back across the field in shattered disorder.

Steve made his way back to the road. Through the drifting smoke, he saw Hernán legging it toward a reserve company. Ritter's and Claflin's Batteries roared incessantly, and one of the projectiles struck a rebel caisson that blew up with a dull roar and a vivid splash of red flame and white smoke.

Some of the Coloradoans moved to the right to support Kerber. The smoke cleared a little to show the enemy moving against the left flank of the Federals. The

Lone Star flag of Texas waved above the rebels. Then volley fire met them from a line of steady Coloradoans and drove them back.

There was a continuous roaring in the air, and then came the sound of many hoofs pounding the road, and a unit of mounted Texans raced forward toward Ritter's guns.

"Tell them they must hold!" yelled Colonel Slough to Steve.

Steve darted forward until he was right in the middle of a battery in action. Even as he shouted his message to Captain Ritter, the guns belched grapeshot at point-blank range into the enemy and drove them back. The Texans re-formed and came on again. An artilleryman carrying a charge of grape to one of the six-pounders staggered and fell against Steve and then went down forever. Steve snatched up the charge and ran to the gun, and then for the next five minutes, he knew nothing else but the deadly and exciting work of a battery of field artillery in close action with a determined enemy.

The guns blasted flame and smoke; blackened swabs plunged into water buckets; the swabs rang against the metal as the bores were cleaned. Powder charges were rammed home; six-pounder grapeshot followed the charges; friction tubes were inserted in the touchholes; gunners stepped free of the wheels, holding the long lanyards in their hands.

"Fire!" yelled Captain Ritter.

The guns spouted flame and smoke, then reared back against their trails. Over and over again, until the Texans had had enough, they retreated sullenly to the moraines, leaving many dead and wounded behind.

Steve staggered back from the hot guns. His left shoulder ached intolerably. A blackened gunner sergeant looked at him. "When you get rid of that silver horn you've got there, sonny, you'd better sign up in Ritter's Battery. We can use a good artilleryman like you."

Steve walked back along the road, trying to get a breath of fresh air. Hoofs thudded against the hard earth, and Claflin's Battery came bounding down the slope, through the woods, and over the rocks, with a wild-eyed figure hanging on to a caisson with one hand and a battered Kossuth hat with the other. Hernán jumped from the caisson as it passed Steve, rolled over three or four times, and came to his feet with his hat at the correct angle. "Claflin and Ritter are to move," said Hernán.

Ritter's guns moved north of the road while Claflin's howitzers joined them. Infantrymen double-timed to support the guns. But the roar of battle had died away, and the smoke was thinning. Men limped toward the ranch houses.

The Texans were moving about in the trees to the right as they massed for another attack. Union officers and noncoms led their men into the woods, where they took up positions among the lichened rocks, and a tense pause seemed to fall over the battlefield.

The Texans came on steadily, with the sun glinting on rifles, bayonets, and swords. Then a hoarse, eerie yelling arose as they increased their pace. Muskets crashed from the Union lines. Smoke billowed out. Cartridges were bitten through and dumped into hot rifle barrels, and ramrods rang as the charges were driven home.

The Texans came on, and the Federal lines fell back toward the road. The rebels were after the supply wagons that they could see near the ranch.

Steve looked to the west and saw more of the enemy massing in the road. A bald-headed officer waved his hat atop his raised sword blade.

Ritter and Claflin opened fire, driving back the enemy, but they reformed and came on again. Again and again, the charges came only to be driven back.

Steve plunged through the woods with a message for Lieutenant Kerber. Minie balls whizzed through the trees as Steve relayed his message. Kerber nodded, then his face grew dark. He cupped his hands about his mouth. "Poys!" he roared. "Lay flat dere! Does you vant to go died!"

Steve couldn't help grinning as he went back down the slope. The Texans wiped his grin away quickly enough, for they were forming for the fourth time. Steve reached behind his back and gripped his Sharps, pulling it forward and unsnapping it from its sling. The Texans were trotting toward the guns again. One hundred yards, and still, the guns were blasting. Fifty yards and the command came to cease firing, while a hoarse yelling arose from the waiting Federal infantry supports. They plunged through the wreathing smoke toward the attacking Texans and met them with a shock.

Steve fired at a Texan color-bearer, but the man did not go down. Suddenly Steve saw that he was separated from his own comrades. A Texan raced through the smoke and fell heavily. A squad of them charged, yelling in that high-pitched tone that sent a chill along the spine.

Steve dropped back, looking for his own side, and then it was he saw a mounted rebel officer leading a desperate charge against the guns. Steve stared at him. The officer's hat blew off, and he raised the Lone Star flag that he held in his left hand while he fired his pistol with the right hand. It was Milas DeWitt.

A hard hand slammed against Steve's back. "Trumpeter!" yelled a red-faced Union officer, "blow the rally!"

Steve dropped his Sharps and reached for the silver trumpet while the battle raged about him as Texans and Federals fought savagely for the guns. He raised the trumpet to his lips, but there was no chance to blow it. Milas DeWitt had seen Steve. He yanked on the reins of his excited horse and drove it toward Steve. Steve jumped to one side and avoided a savage blow of the officer's pistol barrel. Tripping over a fallen Texan, Steve yanked his Colt from its holster.

Milas DeWitt was fighting with his panicky, rearing horse, and then it turned and raced off through the smoke, with the officer staring back at Steve, hate etched on his face until the wreathing smoke put a veil between them.

Steve raised the trumpet again, and the words of Dacey Curtis came to him above the crash of battle. "Take the silver trumpet, Steve. Don't use it against us rebels. Try to use it to help each othah." He lowered the silver instrument.

The two batteries were being withdrawn by small teams, leaving many dead horses behind them. Kerber's Germans held the raging Texans at bay. The guns went into battery again and took up the battle howl, driving the stubborn Texans back until they were at the far side of the battlefield. It was then that the word passed along the Federal lines to withdraw from the field.

Steve limped back toward the batteries. An angry officer was facing Colonel Slough. "Retreat, sir?" he cried. "We've whipped them!"

Slough's face went taut. "You heard my orders, sir!" He waved a hand toward the distant enemy. "I had no intention of making this a decisive battle. We will with-draw at once!"

The colonel rode from the field followed by hard glances from the sweating, smoke-blackened men. Captain Downing led his men along the road and was stopped by Captain Ritter. "You are the senior officer left on the field," he said." What are your orders?"

Downing spat. "Double-shot those guns and open fire! I've lost too many good men to stop fighting now!"

A mounted courier came up the road and looked at the angry officers. "Colonel Slough wants to know why his orders have not been complied with," he said.

"Limber up!" roared Ritter. He dashed his hat to the ground and walked away.

Hernán came up beside Steve. "For why do we leave?" he asked. "We have whipped them, *amigo*!"

Steve held out his dirty hands, palms upwards. "*¿Quién sabe?*" he said quietly. "Who knows?"

An ambulance came across the field of battle with a white flag flapping above it. It drew to a halt, and an officer got down from it and saluted Captain Downing. "Well, sir?" asked Downing in a sour voice.

"Colonel Scurry, my commanding officer, requests a truce and a cessation of hostilities. May I speak with your commanding officer?"

Downing glanced at Ritter. Ritter pointed along the road to the east. "Colonel Slough is on his way to Koslowski's Ranch," he said. "If you will allow yourself to be blindfolded, you will be led to him."

"That is agreeable, sir."

Downing looked at Steve and Hernán. "Show this gentleman to Colonel Slough's headquarters," he said.

And so it was. Steve and Hernán rode in the back of the ambulance, with their horses tethered behind it, leading the rebel officer to Colonel Slough.

———

KOSLOWSKI'S RANCH was a place of much activity in the darkness of the New Mexican night. Lanterns moved from place to place in the hands of medical orderlies and doctors as they took care of the wounded. Off to one side was a long row of the dead, covered by blankets. Wounded men moaned above the sound of the voices of tired men. Smoke drifted about the buildings and through the trees.

Someone shook Steve awake. He looked up into the face of Hernán Calvillo. "I have the good news for you, *amigo*," said Hernán.

"So?" Steve sat up.

"The Texans will not be back."

"You looked in a crystal ball, perhaps?"

"No. Major Chivington and his men have come back. A friend of yours was with them."

"*Si*, Stevie," a well-remembered voice said from the darkness.

It was Luke Comfort. He squatted beside Steve. "Heard you had a bit of a fracas here."

Steve nodded. "We should have run the rebels all the way back to Santa Fe and beyond."

"Might not have to, son."

Steve sat up. "What do you mean?"

Luke grinned. "I was scouting for Chivington, and we heard your artillery fire while we were on the march. When we reached a place called Rock Corral in the rear of the Texan's lines, the whole rebel supply train was there with about two hundred of their troops on guard. They opened fire on us with an artillery piece, but we came down from the mountainside in a rush and drove them all off."

"We captured seventy-three loaded wagons filled with ammunition, forage, clothing, medical supplies, and ordnance materials. We burned those wagons and killed off their whole horse and mule herd." Luke rubbed his hands in enjoyment. "I got a feeling the rebels are going to get a little hungry before long. Come to think of it; I ain't et all day long."

Hernán rummaged in his haversack and lighted a candle. He placed half a roast chicken, some hardtack, and a pot of cold beans before the lean scout. Luke squatted on a rock and began to eat while the boys watched him. When he was done, he wiped his mouth. "Delicious," he said." Well, I guess Colonel Scurry won't get much to eat in Galisteo."

Steve stared at the scout. "What do you mean, Luke?" he asked.

The scout waved a hand. "The Texans are retreating

that way. They'll have a long hungry trip to the Rio Grande."

Steve stood up. His mind raced. He well remembered that bulging storehouse in Espectro Valley, not too far from Galisteo. He remembered, too, finding that captain's shoulder strap there and matching it against the other one on Milas DeWitt's blouse in Santa Fe. Then the picture of Milas DeWitt came to him, wearing rebel gray and leading a desperate charge of Texans that very day against the Federal battery.

"What's wrong, Steve?" asked Luke in alarm.

Steve passed a hand across his eyes. He was desperately tired, and his mind couldn't seem to function, but he quickly told the scout and Hernán about seeing DeWitt that day, in enemy uniform, and of the stores concealed in Espectro Valley.

Luke stood up. "By heaven," he said in a harsh voice. "I was always a little skeptical about them stores being there, Steve, but I've never known you to lie yet."

Hernán nodded. "That is so," he said quietly.

Steve paced back and forth. "There were enough stores there to keep the rebels going for quite a while. I know they were there! Flour, beans, bacon, ammunition, medical supplies. Thousands of dollars' worth of them."

Luke leaned on his rifle. "Colonel Canby is down at Socorro, a long ways away from the rebels."

"Colonel Slough plans to retreat to Fort Union," said Hernán.

Luke slapped a hand against his thigh. "DeWitt was behind the whole thing," he said bitterly. "Now he's wearing a gray suit and leading rebel charges. It must have been him who side-tracked those supplies for just such an eventuality as this."

They could hear the wounded moaning in the darkness beyond the fires. The wind sighed through the pass.

Steve looked at Luke. "You won't get any troops out

of here to capture those supplies if they're still there, and I'll bet they are still there or close to that place."

"What do we do?"

Steve sat down and pulled on his boots. "Hernán and I know the way. The Texans are tired too. If we can get through the mountains and into the Galisteo Basin before they do, we can set afire those stores, and it could be seen for twenty miles."

"Yes!" said Hernán.

Steve buckled on his gun belt and picked up his saddle. "Get the horses, Hernán! If we can set that fire, the Texans will be sure to see it. It will be enough for them to learn something they couldn't be told on a battlefield."

"And what is that?" asked Hernán as he hurried toward the horses.

"That their invasion of New Mexico is over!"

"I'd best report into headquarters about this," Luke said.

"No time," said Steve. He looked bitterly at the distant building where headquarters was. "Besides, do you think anyone's going to let two boys try a thing like this?"

"No," said Luke. He spat. "Two boys and a man, Steve. Two boys and a man..."

They led the saddled horses to the road, then crossed it, and with Luke in the lead, riding as though he had eyes like a cat, they headed for the hulking mountains, which were shrouded in mysterious night shadows. As they rode, they heard the sighing of the wind and the distant howling of a coyote. The silver trumpet bumped gently against Steven Ames's back as he rode the big dun.

CHAPTER FIFTEEN

The moon hung low to the west of the Galisteo Basin, sharply etching the outline of each tree and patch of brush, making the shadows of the hills and peaks like great pools of ink.

"There is the tower," said Hernán in a low voice.

Luke Comfort stared at it with interest. "The place looks as though no one had been here for decades," he said.

"I know differently," said Steve Ames. He stifled a prodigious yawn.

Luke looked to the west toward the rutted track that led from Galisteo." Let's go down there," he said.

The two boys followed the lead scout. They had ridden steadily from Glorieta Pass, leading the horses ten minutes in each hour to rest them. There had been no sign of rebels ahead of them or behind them, but they knew there were rebel troops at Galisteo. If one courier got through to Galisteo to warn the troops there of the great loss of supplies at Rock Corral, the Texans would waste no time in getting to the stores at Espectro Valley if they were still stored there.

"It is a place of the dead," said Hernán suddenly.

The bright moonlight shone on the crosses of bright stones that had been set into the thick walls many years ago. It was almost as though the three people who approached the ancient ruins had left earth by some mysterious process and had blundered onto some long-forgotten and deserted planet.

Luke held up a hand and motioned Hernán to take the three horses off to the right, up a shadowed gully. Hernán swallowed hard, but he did as he had been gestured to do. He turned when he reached the mouth of the gully, and the silvery moonlight shone on the brave white stripes across his coat. Then he was gone.

Luke padded on until he reached the graveyard wall. He stood there a long time with his rifle in his hands, eying each shadow closely. He looked at Steve.

"Beyond the collapsed building," said Steve. "See, you can just make out the roof, close to that great wall of rock there."

"Don't look as though anyone's been here since the turn of the century."

Steve looked behind them, to the west. "I found a copy of an October issue of the Mesilla *Times* here, Luke."

Luke nodded. "Mesilla was secesh then. Like I told you back at Glorieta Pass, I've never known you to lie yet."

They crossed the graveyard and walked past the silent church. Steve glanced sideways as they did so. There was the place where he had fallen with the slug in his shoulder. There was the deep pockmark of Hernán's bullet.

"Lead the way, *amigo*," said Luke. He seemed to be testing the night air with all his senses.

Steve walked to the window by which he had entered the first time. He opened it as he had done so before, with a sheath knife and a little skill. He looked back at Luke. "Someone has been here since Hernán, and I left in such a hurry," he whispered. "This window was unfastened when we left."

Luke nodded. He jerked his head. "Get back," he said.

Steve shook his head. He eased the window back and put a long leg into the room, drawing his carbine in after him. In a moment, Luke was beside him. The place was cold and evil-smelling.

Steve crossed the room. There was the stub of the candle he had left.

Luke spat. "Ain't Jicarilla's that used this place anyways," he said quietly.

"How so, Luke?"

Luke picked up a battered tin plate. It was full of fish bones. "No Apache would ever eat fish, Steve. Streams are full of trout, but they don't touch them. It's taboo."

There was a movement in the corner, and Luke dropped the plate and whirled, raising his rifle. An animal scuttled for cover. Luke whistled softly and wiped his face.

Steve pried at the stout door that led into the other room. The door swung back on creaking hinges. Steve poked his carbine barrel inside the room first and then walked inside. There was no sound or sign of life. Luke came in behind Steve. Steve struck a block match and lighted the candle stub. The light flickered up, guttering in the steady draft.

Luke whistled sharply. "This gravels me!" he said.

There was a vast feeling of relief in Steve. The room was much as he had left it, but he was sure there were more stores in it now. The place was literally packed with supplies.

Luke placed a hand on Steve's shoulder. "Thank the good Lord I listened to you," he said." I only wish some of them back there in Santa Fe had done so long ago. If we hadn't come here this night, and the Texans had gotten ahead of us—"

Steve nodded." With Canby far south at Socorro and

Slough retreating to Fort Union, the rebels have a lot of country to keep under control, providing they have powder and ball."

Luke grinned. "And somethin' to eat. Well, we're here now, and we don't need these supplies." He followed Steve along the lines of sacks and boxes until he found the place where the kegs of powder were piled. He whistled softly. "Whoever planned this thing was an expert on supplies."

Steve placed the candle atop a pile of boxes, a good ten feet from the powder cache. "I think we know who planned it," he said quietly. "And he is an expert on supplies, as well as in being a traitor."

"Milas DeWitt."

"Yes."

Luke took a keg from the top of the pile and stove in the head of it with his rifle butt. He picked up the keg and began to lay a thick powder train along the passageway between the rows of supplies. The keg was empty when he reached the door. Luke looked at Steve. "When I get my hands on Milas DeWitt..." His voice trailed off.

"Just what *will* yuh do?" a harsh voice asked from behind Luke.

An icy feeling came over Steve. It was too dark down there to see what had happened, but the voice was familiar.

"Come on down here too, sonny," the voice said. "Seems to me yuh would'a learned yore lesson last December when yuh come pokin yore nose in here."

Then Steve knew who it was. The bearded, hooknosed man who had had that mysterious talk with Milas DeWitt in the middle of the night, the man who had shot Steve through the shoulder.

Steve had left his carbine atop some sacks near the door. He walked toward the door with his heart in his mouth as he felt the gritty gunpowder beneath his boot soles.

There was a strange look on Luke's face as Steve stopped beside him. The yellow light of the candle showed the fierce bearded face of the hook-nosed man, and there was no mercy in the hard eyes. A phrase he had used that night in Galisteo came back to Steve. *Los Muertos no hablan...* 'The dead do not speak.' "To win, we have to kill," he had also said.

"Outside," said the man curtly.

Steve followed Luke, but there was no chance to get at his Sharps carbine, and he knew the man would never give him a chance to get out his Colt.

"Back against the wall," came the command.

Steve stood beside Luke.

"Raise yore hands!"

They elevated their arms. The man reached inside the doorway and got Luke's rifle and Steve's carbine. He grinned widely, showing uneven yellow teeth. "Two more guns for Sibley's boys. They kin use 'em."

"They'll need them," said Luke. "You rebels can't last. Why don't you give up and go back to Texas?"

"Me? Yuh locol, I ain't no Texican! I ain't nothing but a *hombre* looking for to make a pile of *dinero* out of this war. Let 'em kill each other off. Barney Gaskil is working for profit, not for the love of country."

Steve shifted his feet. There was a chance he might get through that window. Where was Hernán?

"What's DeWitt's angle?" asked Luke.

Gaskil grinned. "Same as mine. Only he had to go and make a hero out of hisself by putting on a uniform."

"Two uniforms," said Steve.

Gaskil nodded. "DeWitt was smart enough to stay with the Federals until he saw which way the ball was rolling. He figured he'd lay in a supply of materials for the Texans. It was easy enough to do." Gaskil laughed harshly. "Man, he was right in headquarters! He switched supplies and wagon trains around until no one but him and me knew what was going on. He worked it, so the teamsters that drove the wagons were in his pay."

"And the soldiers who were with those twelve wagons last October?" asked Steve.

There was no need for Gaskil to answer. His look was enough. *Los muertos no hablan.*

"So DeWitt stays with us until the rebels win at Val Verde, then he deserts the Union and joins the Confederacy," said Luke.

Gaskil nodded. "He believed Sibley would take all of New Mexico."

"But he didn't."

Gaskil shrugged. "The rebels ain't whipped. They're men! With these supplies, they can sit tight long enough to get reinforcements. Canby is sitting down at Socorro, figuring Sibley would run out of supplies. I just come from Galisteo. Colonel Scurry knows Colonel Slough has retreated toward Fort Union. Scurry will fall back on Galisteo to get these supplies. After that, well, it looks like Milas DeWitt might'a played the right side after all. Me, I'm in it for the *dinero*." He grinned. "Let 'em all kill each other off. Makes more room for men like me."

"Men?" said Luke softly.

Steve wet his lips. Gaskil had placed the rifle and the carbine near the door to the left of Steve and Luke.

The hook-nosed man's face was set as he came closer to Luke. "You say I ain't a man, *hombre?*"

A new sound came to them above the sighing of the night wind. The steady thudding of many hoofs on the hard-packed earth and the dull rumbling of many wheels.

Gaskil spat at Luke's feet. "That'll be DeWitt," he said, "and the boys from Galisteo for these supplies."

"*¡Alto!*" a sharp voice rang out from outside of the house. The voice of Hernán.

"Good Lord!" said Luke. "The *muchacho* has gone loco. Stopping all them Texicans!"

Barney Gaskil stared at Luke, then started for the door. Steve thrust out a leg and yelled at Luke. Luke was on the big man as he fell over Steve's leg. There was no time to lose. Steve jumped over the two struggling men and ran toward the door of the supply room. He snatched the guttering candle from the mantel over the fireplace and hurled it onto the floor of the supply room. There was a hissing noise as the powder train caught fire. "Get out, Luke!" yelled Steve. He ran toward the outer door. In the flaring light from the other room, he saw that Gaskil had Luke by the throat and was on top of him.

Steve snatched up his carbine, drove the steel-shod butt against Gaskil's head, then dragged Luke to his feet as the bearded man released Luke. Luke and Steve dived through the outer door, Luke snatching up his beloved rifle as he did so.

The area beside the church was full of white tilted wagons and slouch-hatted Texans on their horses. They were but fifty yards from their much-needed supplies, and in front of them was Hernán Calvillo, with presented carbine aimed full at the chest of Milas DeWitt, who sat a gray horse at the head of the Texans.

"*Vamanos*, Hernán!" yelled Luke and Steve in chorus as they leaped the graveyard wall and dropped flat.

"What's goin on heah?" shouted a Texan.

There was a dull, thudding noise and then a tremendous crashing of sound and a huge flare of reddish-yellow light that illuminated the entire valley in a spectral glare. Debris hurtled through the air and smashed against buildings or pattered on the hard earth. Smoke and gas rushed from the explosion, and the trees and bushes bent before it.

The great echoes slammed back and forth against the valley walls as though making their way to the Galisteo Basin below.

In the silence that momentarily followed the last

sound of the explosion, there rose the sound of human voices and that of the frightened horses and mules. Mule teams broke from the control of their teamsters and raced in every direction on the valley floor, followed by yelling Texans trying to master their stampeded horses.

A figure sailed over the wall behind which Luke and Steve crouched and lighted on its skinny haunches. Luke raised his rifle to strike the grotesque figure, but Steve gripped the rifle and forced it upward. "It's Hernán!" cried Steve.

"Let's get out of here," said Luke.

They gripped Hernán under the arms and half dragged him across the graveyard while pandemonium reigned among the Texans behind them. They darted up the gully to where Hernán had left the horses. One of them was gone, the sorrel mare that had been ridden by Hernán. Luke led the horses up the gully while Steve helped Hernán up behind the mounts.

They did not stop until they were almost at the brim of the valley. Then they looked down toward the old mission. Flames leaped and danced among the buildings and the trees. Most of the white wagon tilts were ablaze too, and in the flickering lights, the raging Texans looked like fire worshippers as they leaped and postured about their precious supplies.

"You see DeWitt?" asked Luke. He raised his rifle and placed a fresh cap on the nipple. "I figure it about two hundred yards range for my old Hawken here." Luke dropped to the ground and thrust the long rifle barrel over a rock.

Hernán spoke for the first time since he had called on the Texans to halt. "Put up your *escopeta*, Luke," he said quietly. "Milas DeWitt will never betray our country again."

They looked at the blackened boy. Hernán wiped the cold sweat from his face. "The blast went over me. Part of the roof struck Capitan DeWitt."

Luke stood up. "You might say he was killed by his own deviltry."

"What do we do now?" asked Steve.

Luke stared down into the valley, and then he turned with a grin. "Nothing," he said." We did what we came to do." He placed a hand on Steve's shoulder. "Only, next time, as a favor to me, Steve, don't time your plans for destruction so closely. You know, for a minute, I didn't think we were going to make it down there."

"Neither did I," said Steve dryly.

"Look at them," said Hernán.

The Texans were rounding up the horses and mules.

But many of the mounts had escaped. Some of them were racing down the valley.

A horse snorted from the brush near the gully.

"There's a mount for you, Hernán," said Steve.

Hernán took a *reata* from Luke's saddle and trotted toward the gully. A horse appeared, etched against the moonlight. Hernán stopped. "It is El Diablo!" he said. "I would know his noble figure anywhere."

"Oh, no!" said Steve.

Hernán dropped the *reata* and ran toward the horse. "*¡Mi bravo! ¡Mi Vida! ¡Mi Querido, amigo!*" He clasped his arms about El Diablo's neck and then turned to take a few steps toward Steve and Luke. It was then that El Diablo swapped ends, laid down his ears, and neatly planted his rear hoofs against the seat of Hernán's trousers, lifting him from the ground and dropping him into a clump of cactus.

There were tears in Luke's eyes as Steve helped Hernán from the cactus. "My brave one!" he said weakly. "My dearest! My dearest friend!"

Hernán stood there in his dignity, wanting to pluck the spines from his flesh but too proud to do so. Then he stalked to his carbine, picked it up, and walked down the slope toward the south.

Luke wiped his eyes. "You told me about that hoss,"

he said to Steve, "but I would'a never believed it! You think I hurt Hernán's feelings too much?"

Steve shook his head. "I think he expected El Diablo to do that. Seems to be a form of courtesy between them. Where do we go now, Luke?"

Luke scratched his lean jaws. "Best head south. Rebels are to the north and west, between our own people and us. Canby is down south, at Socorro, but the rebels hold Carnuel, which keeps Tijeras Pass closed to us Federals. Best thing we can do, now that the rebels will have to retreat south, is to take to the hills and keep out of sight for a time."

"*Si*," agreed Steve.

The scout eyed Steve. "Thanks for saving my life down there, Steve."

Steve waved a hand. "I nearly killed both of us."

They got the three horses and led them south. Far down the slope, they could see Hernán Federico Telesfor Dona-Ciano Gaspar Melchior Calvillo limping along in cold dignity. El Diablo whinnied harshly, but Hernán did not turn his head.

Steve was bone-weary. It seemed as though he'd never get enough sleep. But they would have to keep going for a time until they saw the familiar dusty-blue of Federal uniforms somewhere along the great Rio Grande Valley. The war had come to Steve Ames with a vengeance.

The cold moonlight shone with brilliance on the silver trumpet that hung at Steve's back and swung easily at every motion of his body.

CHAPTER SIXTEEN

JORNADA DEL MUERTO, NEW MÉXICO TERRITORY—APRIL 1862

Steven Ames awoke in the darkness of the cave and lay there for some time listening to the night sounds of the Sierra Oscura, the soft sighing of the dry wind and the rustling of the brush, mingled with the dry snoring of Luke Comfort and the rustling of mice in the rear of the shallow cave. It was almost as it had been so many months ago in the Sangre de Cristo's when Hernán and he had trailed the lost wagons. He raised his head and looked toward the entrance of the cave and saw the shadowy outline of Hernán's disreputable Kossuth hat.

So much had happened in the time since he had returned to New Mexico. Now he wanted to see his father and his uncle, but that too would take time because a great part of New Mexico was still in turmoil.

The three companions had left the Galisteo Basin and had ridden south, traveling through the mountains by night and hiding by day, keeping away from the trails and roads that led toward the distant Rio Grande Valley. They had learned that the rebels were in slow retreat in the direction of the great valley, with the Union forces under Colonel Canby maneuvering about them. Here and there, detached units of both sides moved about the vast country to rejoin their comrades, and mingled with these straggling units were parties of *ladrones* who would rob either side with no compunction whatsoever.

Then there were the Apache who had taken advantage of the bitter fighting in the territory to strike, raid, loot, and kill almost on the outskirts of the bigger towns. Beyond the guns of the Texans and the Federals, the Apache held undisputed sway. The smoke of burning ranches, little towns, and wagons stained the clear spring skies every day. It was death for a white man to use the springs and water holes so necessary for life in that arid country, for the Apache watched them, and if a man was foolish enough to make his camp beside the water, it was the last camp he would ever make this side of heaven.

Luke had led Hernán and Steve to the south, waiting for a chance to get through to the Rio Grande and join Colonel Canby's forces. Time and time again, they had had to take wide detours around war parties. They had done without water when they had desperately needed it to avoid the water hole ambushes. They had done without food because they feared to discharge a weapon. It had been Hernán who had caught rabbits for the three of them by thrusting long strands of thorny brush down into the rabbit holes, then twisting the strands so that the thorns caught in the fur like a hook in a fish, to pull the struggling animals to the surface of the ground.

But now they were without food and with precious little water, and it was only a matter of time before they must strike for the Rio Grande across the northern end of the Jornada del Muerto, the dreaded waterless land that stretched for ninety miles on the eastern side of the Rio Grande, with ranges of harsh, dry mountains blocking the river from the *Jornada*.

Hernán shifted. Then he crawled into the cave and placed a hand over Luke's mouth. The boy swallowed hard. "*Los Indios!*" he said in a dry whisper. "The Apache!"

Luke and Steve threw aside their blankets and reached for their weapons. The three of them lay down and looked beyond the cave into the shallow canyon below them. It was the time of the false dawn.

For a while, they saw and heard nothing, and then there was a movement along the slope fifty yards below them. A line of mounted warriors appeared as though moved by the invisible strings of a master puppeteer. There was no sound from them, for the horses moved on rawhide boots. But there was no mistaking the thick manes of dark hair and the broad, deep chests of the Apache. Now and then, as one of them turned a little, white lines of bottom clay, painted across noses and upper cheeks could be plainly distinguished against the dark faces.

Fear seemed to float above the silent file of riding warriors, and its grayish-green scum of panic flicked into the cave onto the three whites crouching there.

Steve could feel sweat trickling down his sides and greasing his gunstock beneath his hands, which gripped it so tightly to keep from shaking. Their horses were picketed in a draw a quarter of a mile away. If the wind picked up their scent and carried it to the keen-nosed Apache or to their mounts...

Then the warriors were gone as silently and as mysteriously as they had appeared, and it would have been hard to believe they had been there at all if Steve hadn't known better.

Hernán rested his head on his hands." I saw the first one fifteen minutes ago," he whispered shakily. "I must have dozed off because one minute he was not there, and the next minute it seemed as though I could reach out and touch him." The boy drew in a deep breath.

The canyon was as quiet as the grave again.

"When he left," continued Hernán, "I was sure it was a dream until three more of them came along. It was then I woke you."

Luke wet his lips. "No matter how many times you see 'em like that, you never get used to them. I counted thirty of 'em."

"Thirty-two," said Steve.

It was getting lighter. Steve looked past Hernán, and he made a quick sign for silence with his free hand.

Another party of warriors was angling down the slope toward the floor of the canyon. There were at least fifteen of them in this party.

"Look!" hissed Luke.

On the far side of the canyon, in the graying light, they could see more warriors dismounting from their horses. The horses were led off and concealed somewhere on the jumbled slope of the canyon wall.

"*¡Dios en Cielo!*" said Hernán. "What do they do here? There is no water and no food."

Luke rubbed his bristly jaws. "There is a spring some miles from here, and this canyon is the only way to get there." Luke's strange green eyes looked at the boys. "It's my guess these warriors are preparing an ambush for somebody."

"But who?" asked Hernán.

"What difference does it make? We couldn't do anything about it. Matter of fact, *amigos*, we ain't in such a good situation ourselves. How much water we got, Steve?"

"Why talk about it, Luke?"

"That's what I figured."

"What do we do now, Luke?" asked Hernán.

Luke laughed dryly. "We set, and we sweat."

And so it was. They sat, and they sweated as the sun came up.

But the Apache had wasted no time. Those who were at the bottom of the canyon had dug holes along each side of the faintly rutted road. Most of them had crawled into the holes while the rest had covered the holes with blankets and the blankets with earth so that when the tracks had been erased by dragged brush and the horses had been led off and hidden, there was no sign on that canyon floor that even a lizard had a hole there.

It was the same along the far side of the canyon and to the east end of the canyon. Where before there had been many warriors, now there was nothing but rocks, beginning to change color with the coming of the light and the thorny brush still in the windless air.

The sun rose higher and began to flood the silent canyon with its light, but there was still no sign of the Apache. They had the patience of spiders.

"Listen," said Hernán suddenly.

The other two raised their heads. Faintly they heard a familiar sound. The thudding of hoofs and the rumbling of wheels mingled with the popping of whips. A wreath of dust rose up from the east side of the canyon and hung in the still air.

"Now we know," said Luke quietly.

A lone horseman had topped the rise at the eastern entrance to the canyon. He surveyed the seemingly empty place, then raised an arm and pumped it up and down. He rode down toward the canyon floor, and in a little while, there came a squad of slow riding cavalrymen, wearing slouch hats and gray shell jackets.

"Rebels!" said Luke. "Rebels!"

Half a dozen wagons appeared, with rickety wheels, drawn by weary mules who staggered in their harnesses. Infantrymen slogged alongside the slowly rolling wagons, while behind the last wagon rode another party of cavalrymen, some of them mounted on mules.

Steve took out his uncle's fine German field glasses

and focused them on the approaching party. The Texans were thin-faced from lack of food. He scanned the line of wagons and saw men lying in them, with the canvas sides rolled up a little for air. There was no doubt that the men in the wagons were sick and wounded.

"Trying to reach the Rio Grande," said Luke quietly.

"They're in a bad way," said Steve softly. "Those mules hauling the wagons *might* make the river." He raised the glasses again. "About half of those men have no rifles or pistols."

"Maybe *we* had something to do with *that,*" Luke said.

"But the Apache!" said Hernán. He looked at Steve with wide eyes. "They will swarm down on them once they are in the middle of the canyon! They will be slaughtered!"

"What do you want us to do?" demanded Luke.

Hernán's face was a mask of horror.

The Texans had no chance whatsoever. They were outnumbered and had the disadvantage of the sick and wounded with them. The Apache had the vital element of surprise.

There was nothing the three watchers in the cave could do... nothing at all.

Steve turned away. It was only a matter of ten or fifteen minutes before those wagons reached the place where the Apache lay hidden on each side of the road. No one would ever think of looking for them there. When they struck, the warriors on the far canyon wall would also strike. The warriors at the eastern end of the canyon would close in to stopper the bottle.

There was nothing they could do. Steve shifted his carbine, and it struck something that seemed to chime like a faint chapel bell. He looked down at the cased silver trumpet.

Luke and Hernán were staring fascinatedly at the approaching Texans.

Steve stripped the cover from the trumpet.

The wind came on a little, carrying with it the steady popping of the whips, the thudding of hoofs and feet, the rumbling and squealing of the ungreased wheels.

Steve stood up. "Luke," he said quickly.

Luke turned. "What's up, Steve?"

"We've got to help them."

"They're rebels!"

"They're human beings, and half of them are sick and wounded."

"He is right," said Hernán. His face was a dirty white.

Luke rubbed his jaw. "All right," he snapped. "But what can we do?"

Steve held out the trumpet. "I'm going to play a concert for those red devils."

"You loco?"

Steve buckled on his gun belt and put on his forage cap. "You and Hernán have a job to do too."

"So?"

"We'll have to get the horses first."

They got their weapons and followed Steve from the cave. It wasn't easy, for they could have been seen by the warriors on the far side of the canyon and the splintered rock and thorny growths played havoc with flesh and clothing, but at last, they reached the horses.

Steve swung up on Zouave and looked down at Luke and Hernán. "I'm riding to the west end of the canyon. When you hear me play my first call, I want you to start riding toward the western entrance dragging bundles of brush behind you."

"He is *muy loco!*" said Hernán.

"No," said Luke. He slapped Steve on the leg. "It might work." He looked up at Steve. "If it doesn't, Hernán and I might have a chance to get away."

"I hope you do, Luke."

The scout looked away. "But you won't, Steve."

Steve kneed the dun away from them. He rode swiftly down the slope, angling toward the western end of the small canyon. There was no time for fear. The only fear he had now was that he might not be able to fool the Apache in time.

He could see the hazy *Jornada* to the west as he turned around a great shoulder of rock and looked toward the jagged mouth of the canyon. He drew rein and swung the silver trumpet from his back to his hand. He blew gently into it to warm it, then flourished it. A second later, the striking notes of 'A Foragers' rang out on the still air and seemed to bounce from the rocky heights above him.

He glanced behind him. Dust was rising high from the broken ground. In a moment, it would be seen within the canyon. He spurred the dun forward and lipped into the charge. Again and again, he played it as the dust rose higher and thicker, and it seemed to Steven Ames that he was back in Virginia on a blazing July day, listening to a brave Southern boy playing his heart and blood out on the silver trumpet.

The beautiful instrument sounded like a silver bell, like the shrieking of a fierce bird of prey, like the howling of the winter wind among the heights of the Sangre de Crista. The bright sunlight flashed from the silver trumpet as Steve flourished it, then lipped again into the charge. The silvery notes seemed to lance through the clear air and into the canyon.

Then Steve saw dust rising near the western entrance to the canyon, coming from within the canyon. He slung the trumpet over his shoulder and drew his Sharps forward. He set spurs to Zouave and raced toward where he knew Luke and Hernán would be waiting. The dust was rising higher and faster as he plunged the big dun into a draw.

"Take it easy!" yelled Luke.

Luke and Hernán stood by their sweating horses.

Their faces were masks of dust, and Steve couldn't help laughing in vast relief.

"Look!" said Hernán.

Steve slid from his sweating dun and raised his carbine.

"No," said Hernán quietly.

The canyon entrance was filled with galloping horses and mules, rumbling wagons, and thick dust. The Texans came tearing down the slope, covered by a handful of their cavalrymen.

There was more dust rising from within the canyon. Toward the eastern entrance, it seemed to move faster and faster until, at last, it faded away in the rising wind of morning.

The Texans drew to a halt fifty yards from the draw. They stared about them in surprise. "Where are they?" asked a lanky infantryman as he clambered down from a wagon.

None of the Texans spoke for a long time as they looked to the west and then to the north and south. There was nothing of human life to see, nothing but the hazy expanse of the Jornada del Muerto, stippled by the fast-moving shadows of high clouds. The mountains were already enveloped in a purple haze.

An officer shoved back his hat and looked at the canyon entrance. "They had us cold in theah," he said. "You men see them devils come up outah thet ground like snakes?"

A big sergeant nodded his head. "We was trapped in theah, suh. They was up on the canyon walls and behind us. They must'a let us walk into thet ambush as neat as yuh please. But wheah is the cavalry we heard out heah?"

"It wouldn't matter if they were our own people or the Yankees," said a red-faced teamster. "Anything is better'n them Apache."

They sat their horses and looked about them, and then the officer shook his head. "This beats me," he said.

He seemed to shiver. "I never did like this country. Always thought it was haunted anyways." He pumped his arm up and down. "No use asking Providence how it saved us. The fact is that it did save us. On to the Rio Grande!"

The column moved out, and in time it was nothing but a coil of dust rising from the *Jornada,* with now and then the sparkling of metal as the sun struck it.

"What now?" asked Hernán as he mopped the dust from his face.

"I'm thirsty," said Luke.

They led their horses from the draw and mounted them. They rode toward the *Jornada,* following the distant Texans.

Twenty minutes passed before Luke spoke. "Why did you do that back there, Steve?"

Steve glanced back toward the low mountains behind them. There was no sign of Apache. "I made a promise to someone in Virginia last July," he said quietly.

The green eyes were puzzled. "I don't get it, Steve."

"I'll tell you the whole story someday, Luke."

"Yeah."

Hernán smiled. "It is a surety that Steve and I will be of great value to the army now. Myself as a drummer, of course, and Steve with that beautiful trumpet which sounds like a meadowlark beside the canal."

"No," said Steve. "The trumpet will never be played in war again."

"But you are loco!" said Hernán.

Steve shook his head. "It is said that it has magic in it; Jeb Stuart said it would turn a coward into a hero."

Luke nodded. "I believe it."

They rode on, and Steve remembered Dacey Curtis. The boy had said war was madness. "*Today, you and me fought against each othah, and tonight you tried to help me. Take the silver trumpet, Steve. Don't use it against us rebels. Try to use it to help each othah. I don't know how, but I know you'll find a way."*

The silver trumpet would hang on the wall of Steve's home in Santa Fe, near his father's Hawken rifle and above his mother's rosewood piano. Each of them had a story to tell, but the story of the silver trumpet would be the strangest and best of all.

ACKNOWLEDGMENTS

Special thanks must be given to Miss Leslie Murphey of the School of American Research, the Museum of New Mexico, for the information she forwarded to me during the years of World War II when I attempted to keep up the research on one war while engaged in another. Her help and encouragement were of inestimable value.

Nothing was of more value in the eventual construction of *The Rebel Trumpet* than the constant help and belief of my wife, Alice, that this book would someday appear in print.

SOURCES

Steven Ames, his father, Mark, and his uncle, Carter, Hernán Calvillo, Captain Milas DeWitt, Luke Comfort, Steve's comrades in the Eleventh New York Volunteers, as well as many other characters in this story, are fictitious. The boy Dacey Curtis was not a trumpeter with the famed Jeb Stuart, but Jeb Stuart did lead the First Virginia Cavalry at the Battle of Bull Run, or First Manassas, as it was later called by the Confederates. The Civil War custom was for the Union forces to name a battle after the nearest geographical feature, while the Confederates usually named the battle after the nearest town, although by no means was this a strict rule.

The research for *The Rebel Trumpet* was a long and winding trail through many books, letters, and accounts. *Battles and Leaders of the Civil War* (Century, 1887), reprinted by Thomas Yoseloff, Inc., Publisher, in 1957, furnished material about the Battle of Bull Run, the organization of both contending armies at that time, as well as material on the New Mexican Campaign of 1862. *Reveille in Washington,* by Margaret Leech (Harper & Brothers, 1941), gave much interesting information on Washington of early war days and of the various volunteer organizations that thronged to its defense in the stirring spring of 1861.

Turmoil in New Mexico, 1846-1868, by William A. Keleher (Rydal Press, Inc., 1952), gave a wealth of information on the causes and events of the New Mexico Campaign of 1862. *New Mexico,* American Guide Series (Hastings House, Publishers, Inc., revised edition, 1953), was invaluable for its material on the state of New Mexico, its historical information, and the geographical descriptions of portions of the state that appear in *The*

Rebel Trumpet. Texas C.S.A., by James Farber (The Jackson Company, 1947), gave much insight into the point of view of the brave Texans who formed Sibley's Brigade in the invasion of New Mexico.

The Look of the Old West, by Foster-Harris, (The Viking Press, Inc., 1955), as always, is invaluable for descriptions of uniforms and other equipment of Civil War times. *New Mexico Historical Review,* published quarterly by the Historical Society of New Mexico and the University of New Mexico (The University Press), contained various articles in many volumes of the series, which were of great value as background material.

Colorado Volunteers in the Civil War, The New Mexico Campaign of 1862, by William Clarke Whitford, D.D., printed by the State Historical and Natural History Society, Denver, Colorado, 1906, provided what is probably the best-written descriptions of the battles of Valverde and Glorieta Pass, as well as activities of the Colorado Volunteers and other troops who fought in New Mexico in 1862.

As always, *Official Records of the Union and Confederate Armies* yielded battle and campaign accounts, correspondence of the historical figures who appear in the story, and other excellent background materials. Other books too numerous to mention went into the making of *The Rebel Trumpet.*

A great deal of research was done over a period of ten or twelve years in the Chicago Public Library, the Newberry Library of Chicago, the library of the Chicago Historical Society, the Los Angeles Public Library, and the Enoch Pratt Free Library of Baltimore, Maryland. The author also traveled through the state of New Mexico a number of times, following the routes of the contending forces visiting the battlefields and other historical places mentioned in the novel.

THE MOSQUITO FLEET

To Ruth Canton, in deepest appreciation

CHAPTER ONE

The United States Light Draft Ship Dart

A fine needle-like rain was sifting down through the thick foliage of the trees that bordered the sluggish river. A ragged, drifting mist obscured the opposite bank, but the sound of men's voices carried through the opaqueness with a ghostly tone. There was a continuous dripping noise, mingled with the soft, soughing rush of the wind through the swamp.

It was cold, and it was damp, and it was a long way from fresh salt air and clean salt water. The thought was Greg Hollister's as he eased his damp sea bag from his shoulder and glanced back toward the road to where the seven other sailors of the draft had huddled together under a sagging shed roof.

"You see anything, matie?" called out Gunner's Mate Ab Cory.

Greg shivered in the damp air. If there was a United States Naval Ship on that silty stream, it certainly wasn't in sight, yet he could still hear those distant and mysterious voices mingled with the thudding of a hammer and the occasional clanging of metal.

Greg stared through the mist. Something was taking shape in the grayness, and then he saw a square bowed skiff being slowly poled down the middle of the river by a boy about his own age. "Ahoy!" called out Greg.

The boy stopped poling and looked at Greg.

"I'm looking for the United States Light Draft Ship *Dart*!" yelled Greg.

"You come to the right place then, bub."

"Well, where is it?"

The boy jerked a thumb over his shoulder. "Over there," he said laconically. He poled the skiff a little closer to the muddy bank. "Where you come from, bub?"

Greg straightened up. He had been in the navy since '61, shortly after President Lincoln had called for volunteers, and now in the first part of 1863 he had more than a year and a half of service completed before his sixteenth birthday due in May. He didn't like this civvie kid and his downright lack of respect for the uniform of the United States Navy.

"Philadelphia," said Greg coldly.

"Do tell! Philadelphia where?"

"Pennsylvania!"

"Long ways from the osheaan, ain't it, bub?"

"What's going on over there?" called out Ab Cory.

Greg crooked a finger at the boy in the skiff. "Come here, *bub,*" he said softly, itching to get his hands on him.

The kid leaned nonchalantly on his pole. "Nope," he said.

"Why?"

"These swamps is full of Mississippians who can thread a needle with a minie ball al two hunnert yards. How do I know you ain't one of them?"

Greg looked down at his wet pea coat and wide-bottomed blue trousers. He slapped a hand atop his soggy flat hat. "Do I *look* like a rebel?" he demanded. "Do I *talk* like one?"

The kid grinned. "Nope."

"Then come on to shore."

"What's in it for me?"

Greg doubled up a fist and waved it gently, but the kid seemed unperturbed. "I've got an extra Barlow knife," said Greg.

"Toss it over."

"It's in my sea bag."

"Hollister!" yelled Ab Cory.

Greg could hear the soaked men of the draft mumbling back at the shed. They had been on the way for days. First by train, then by steamer, then by army wagon to this swamp in Mississippi. They had had no mess since evening of the day before with the exception of army hardtack and coffee strong enough to peel the paint from the turret of the *Monitor*.

To top it off, they were all seagoing men who had been taken from their beautiful and fast blockader, the steam sloop *Yantic,* for a draft to the river war along the Mississippi, and this place of mist, mosquitoes and fever was no place for deepwater men of the United States Navy.

The kid cased the skiff to shore and lightly hopped to the bank. He wore dark blue trousers with a light blue stripe down the seams, and a thick huck shirt. A battered forage cap hung at the side of his head, and pinned to it was the brass hunting-horn insignia of the infantry. Some "bummer," thought Greg contemptuously, who had stolen parts of a uniform.

"What kin I do for you?" asked the kid. He eyed Greg closely with a pair of the sharpest blue eyes Greg had ever seen. "You must be the new draft for the *Dart.*"

"You guessed it, bub," said Greg.

The kid grinned widely, revealing even white teeth, and for some reason or another Greg seemed to forget his animosity.

"You want to go aboard the *Dart?*" asked the kid.

"That's the general idea."

The kid stuck out a hand and Greg gripped it, and

the strength in it surprised Greg. "I'll take you there. I work aboard her. Name of Zelah Powers."

Greg grinned this time. "Zelah?"

The smiling face seemed to change quickly. "Yup, bub! Zelah! You don't like it?"

"Sure. Sure," said Greg placatingly. "I'm Greg Hollister."

"Greg for *Gregory?*" Zelah grinned again.

"You don't like it?"

"Sure! I'll call you Greg. O.K.?"

"O.K., Zelah."

"Folks mostly call me Chip." Zelah touched his straw-colored thatch of hair. "On account of my hair looks like wood chips. Silly, ain't it?"

"I like it better than Zelah."

"So do I!" Chip looked through the woods toward the road. "How many men you got with you, Greg?"

"Seven. Eight counting me."

Chip nodded. "I'll pole you over. Take two trips."

Ab Cory came through the dripping woods. His square-cut, mahogany-tanned face was grim. "Any luck?" he asked Greg.

"Aye, mate," said Greg. "This is Chip Powers. He's from the *Dart*. Said he'd take us aboard."

Cory eyed Chip, then looked out toward the misty river, then through the wet woods. "So?" he said softly. His hard, gray eyes studied Chip. "Who might you be?"

"Chip Powers."

"I know that! But who are you?"

"I'm a 'cub' on the *Dart*."

"Cub?"

Chip straightened up. He was almost as tall as Greg but not so heavy or so well built, but there was a sugges-tion of wiriness and rawhide strength in him. "Yup," said Chip. "My uncle Tobias Powers is chief pilot aboard the *Dart*. Uncle Toby has been teaching me the river."

Ab Cory eased back his damp pea coat and placed his

hand on the butt of the Navy Colt he wore holstered at his waist. "That might be so, young'un, but any funny business out of you and you won't know *any* river. Understand?"

Greg hoisted his sea bag to his shoulder. The rest of the men squelched through the mud. The army teamster who had dropped them off at that place had told them the swamps were full of guerillas and partisans, experts at the unseen and deadly ambush.

Ab Cory heaved his bag into the skiff and sat down in the stern sheets with his hand still on the butt of his issue Colt. Greg got in, followed by Taffy Hayes, Perry Shepherd and Tom Bruce. The skiff was pretty low in the water as Chip shoved off and began to pole his way through the clinging mist. It was then that Greg saw the bright-barreled carbine resting on a thwart. Chip nodded. "I'm on patrol," he said.

Taffy Hayes eyed the dull surface of the river. "Here?" he asked in his Irish brogue. "What are ye patrolling for, lad?"

Chip leaned hard on his pole and shoved the skiff on toward the far shore. "Swamp rats," he said quietly.

"Rats, lad?"

The boy nodded. "Mississippi rebels. They know this country like no one else does. Every creek and stream, path and road. I'll swear they have webfeet, the way they get around."

"Some war," said big Tom Bruce in disgust. "A seaman could die of fever in this country and never hear a shot fired."

The blue eyes of Chip Powers glanced at the big gunner. "'You'll hear some shooting, sailor," he promised.

"That'll be the day!"

The noise of voices and the thudding of hammers against metal seemed to drift closer in the swirling mist. There was something hulking up through the tenuous shadows of the far shore. Greg stared at it as- it grew in outline and he began to distinguish its features. It was a small steamer with a stern wheel and towering twin stacks each surmounted by an elaborate ironwork crown. The square-shaped pilothouse was placed abaft the stacks, and instead of windows it had mere slits for observation at eye level. The sides of the steamer had been plated with iron through which gun ports had been cut. On the foredeck the iron slanted down, somewhat like the bow armor of the *Merrimac,* and three-gun ports had been cut into the plating. Rowboats were slung from davits on the promenade deck of the craft. She was an ugly, ungainly-looking sort of thing.

Ab Cory shook his head. "What in tunket is that thing?" he growled. "Looks like a seagoing barn."

Chip Powers poled closer to the steamer. "That's the *Dart,*" he said calmly.

The seamen stared at the kid. "Stop the joshing, boy," said Tom Bruce. "I ain't in any mood for funning after that trip out here to nowheres."

"We're assigned aboard the U.S.S. Light Draft *Dart,*" said Ab ominously. "Not that hulking barge!"

Chip whistled softly. 'That's her," he said. "Only we don't call them Light Drafts."

"What *do* ye call 'em?" demanded Taffy Hayes.

"Tinclads. That's the *Dart* all right, mates."

"For the love of heaven," exclaimed Perry Shepherd.

"*This,* after the *Yantic,*" said Greg. He groaned as he thought of the sprightly *Yantic*, under full sail, over-hauling a blockade-runner off the Cape Fear River.

"And will ye look at the number av her?" said Taffy in a hollow voice.

The number was emblazoned on the gray side of the pilothouse in tall black figures. Number 13.

"Halt!" rang out a crisp challenge from the upper deck of the *Dart*. A sentry leveled his rifle. "Who goes there?"

"Chip Powers, Sam."

"Who's that with you?"

"Sailors," said Chip with a sly grin. "Real salty boys from the osheaan, Sam!"

Tom Bruce turned a little to eye Chip. The big gunner spat on a knotted fist. "Keep it up, matie," he said quietly, "and I'll douse the glims in those purty big blue eyes of yours!"

Greg eyed the slab-sided river craft, and a sickening feeling came over him. He glanced at the pole in Chip's hands and watched it dip down into the silty water. It hardly wet a few feet of its length. They were so close to the *Dart* that the water could hardly be deeper under her fiat bottom.

Chip nodded at Greg. "*Dart* draws only twenty-four inches," he said proudly. "She kin run on a heavy dew and sometimes where the ground is just a little damp."

Taffy Hayes groaned hollowly.

"What's that contraption at the bow?" asked Perry Shepherd, jerking a thumb toward something that looked like a huge hay rake.

The skiff bumped alongside the scarred rubbing strake of the steamer. "That's a torpedo rake," said Chip. He gripped a line tossed to him by the sentry. "The rebs fill these rivers with torpedoes. We lost a couple of good boats that way."

"So now you just scoop 'em up with that rake," said Greg dryly.

"That's the general idea, bub," said Chip.

The seamen tumbled out of the skiff and entered a metal-sheathed door set into the plated side of the *Dart*. Ab Cory glanced at the plating and whistled softly. "How thick is this stuff, Chip?" he asked in a curious voice.

"That's boiler iron. Three-quarters of an inch thick. Farther astern, near the boilers we got railroad iron, maybe a *Utile* thicker."

"That stuff won't stop solid shot," said Tom Bruce.

Chip shoved off. "It ain't supposed to. Just minie balls

and the like. Now you know why we call them tinclads,'"
he said cheerfully. He poled off into the drifting mist.

Greg looked about. They had entered into the
lightly plated superstructure forward of the engine
room and boilers. Dim lanterns hung from the deck
above them. Despite the dampness outside and the
chilling mist, it was almost uncomfortably warm inside
the *boat*, as Chip had called it. "I wonder what it's like
inside one of these tin cans on a hot summer's day," he
said thoughtfully.

"Aye," said Taffy gloomily. "Wid the guns going and
all."

Tom Bruce spat through the doorway into the turbid
river. "Wid the guns going and all," he mimicked. "Fat
chance we'll ever have of seeing any action on this mud
creeper of a *boat*!"

Greg peered through the mist. He could hear the soft
voices of the men on the far shore. It was a ghostly place,
with Spanish moss trailing from dead-looking trees.

"The skipper wants to see all of you," a broad-shoul-
dered man called out of the dimness behind the seamen.

"There are three still coming, mate," said Ab Cory.

The big man stared at Ab. "Ab Cory!" he cried out.
"You salty son of a sea cook! It's Webb Downey!"

The gunner stared at the man and then glanced down
at the sleeves of the blouse the other man wore.
"Boatswain now, Webb! You finally made it!"

They gripped hands. Ab turned with a wide grin and
his gingery chin whiskers seemed to wriggle with plea-
sure. "Mates, this is Webb Downey. We were messmates
on the old *Wabash* before the war. Webb, these lads are
Tom Bruce, Perry Shepherd, Taffy Hayes and Greg
Hollister, all good men and top gunners."

The huge boatswain shook each of them by the hand
and eyed Greg. "How old are you, mate?" he asked.

Greg straightened up. He was as tall as Perry Shepherd and taller by half a head than the little Irishman

Taffy Hayes. "Seventeen, going on eighteen, Bos'n," he said.

"So?" Downey half-closed one eye. "I was seventeen going on eighteen when I reported aboard my first ship."

Ab Cory placed a hand on Greg's shoulder. "The lad is a good seaman and a first-class gunner, Webb."

"I can see that." The big man eyed the others. "Let's hope you are all the same."

"We can take care of ourselves," growled Tom Bruce sourly. He was tired and he was hungry.

The eyes of the boatswain seemed to harden and glint in the dim light. "See that you do," he said quietly. "This is a good ship and a tight one and we brook no malingerers aboard the *Dart.*"

Chip was getting close to the *Dart* with his second load. The three sailors were hunched on the thwarts, gloomily eying the slab-sided *Dart.* The wind had shifted and the mist was being tattered and driven westerly, toward the distant Mississippi.

"You figure there *might* be a war here," said Bruce.

Webb Downey nodded. "There is a war here, sure enough. A war such as you have never seen, sailor."

"I'll believe it when I see it," said the big gunner sarcastically. "Buried out here in the mud aboard a leaky old hay barge, hundreds of miles from salt water and a good honest sea fight. I knew we was getting a raw deal when we was drafted from the good old *Yantic.* A war, sure enough? You make me laugh, Bos'n."

There was the sound of a dry stick being snapped, over in the wet woods across the river. It seemed as though a bright, orange-red blossom, petaled in soft whitish gray, suddenly sprouted amidst the dreary vegetation. The sharp report of a rifle seemed to slam back and forth between the trees that appeared to wall in the river.

One of the seamen hunched in the skiff had jerked a little at the sound of the rifle shot. Now he slumped over and fell face downward into the mud and dirty water sloshing around in the bottom of the skiff. One of his mates lifted the stricken man's head and then eased it down. He looked up at the men staring at him from the doorway. "He's dead," the mate said in a strange, small voice.

"Get aboard!" snapped Webb Downey.

The two seamen tumbled aboard, followed by Chip Powers. The boy held the painter of the skiff in one hand and his carbine in the other. He darted to one side as Webb slammed shut the door. An instant later a slug rapped smartly against the metal sheathing of the door.

Chip looked at Greg.

The boy's words came swiftly back to Greg. *"These swamps is full of Mississippians who can thread a needle with a minie ball at two hunnert yards."*

"You believe there is a war here now, Bruce?" asked Webb Downey.

The big gunner nodded. There was a strange look on his face. "Jim Haslett, the lad who was killed, was from Rhode Island, same as me."

"He'll be buried in Mississippi, a long ways from Providence," said Perry Shepherd.

"I'll wait until the mist comes down again, Bos'n," said Chip quietly, "then I'll get some of the boys to help me get him out of the skiff."

"Follow me," said Webb Downey.

The draft shouldered their sea bags and followed the boson to a large compartment hung with hammocks. "Dump your sea bags here," he said, "and we'll go and see the Old Man."

Greg looked back as he trailed after the rest of them. Chip was peering through a slotted loophole and his carbine was ready in his hands. A cold feeling came over Greg and it wasn't from his damp clothing. It was from the chill of death as he had seen it come from the dripping swamp to kill a young man from Rhode Island hardly older than Greg himself.

CHAPTER TWO

The River War

Lieutenant Donald Currie was a medium-sized man, with sandy reddish hair and clear gray eyes. His uniform was neat and clean, surprisingly so in the middle of a Mississippi swamp. He was a Regular. Any seaman could spot him as such almost instantaneously. He stood behind his paper-littered desk and eyed the new draft of men for his vessel.

"They are all gunners, sir," said Webb Downey. He allowed a faint smile to pass across his face. "And good *seamen*, too, sir, according to Gunner's Mate Cory here."

The officer nodded. "We need good gunners, although you navy men may find the guns a little different to what you are accustomed. As far as being seamen, I am afraid you will not find much use for sea lore here, men, but the hard discipline of a man-of-war's man will not be amiss aboard the *Dart*." He studied their faces. "I know what you are thinking," he continued. "You are sailors, used to a heaving deck and sharp salt air. The feel of a good ship in a lively sea. Marble-hard canvas, and a kicking wheel against the palms of your hands."

Greg thought of the slim-hulled *Yantic*. The officer sounded like a poet.

Currie paced back and forth. "These tinclads may look like a seaman's nightmare but they have done yeoman service here on the western rivers. There never has been a war quite like this one in the history of the world. Navy men have fought river vessels from the battles of Forts Henry and Donelson, through gunnery support at Shiloh, the capturing of Island Number Ten, and the hard fighting off Memphis in June of 1862. We are practically fighting an amphibious war here in the bayous and winding rivers of the Mississippi Valley, and I say without reservation that the Army, God bless them, could hardly exist in this country without naval support."

"Amen,'" said the irrepressible Taffy Hayes.

Currie smiled. "General U.S. Grant is trying to capture Vicksburg, the Gibraltar of the Mississippi, and it is our job to help him. You will find yourselves in strange and weird places, fighting a mad sort of war on water that is half land, and the change may be hard on you, *but*..." The steady eyes traveled from the tanned face of one man to the other. "We fight on these waters as men of the United States Navy, and never forget that fact! Your discipline, training, and above all, your courage, may help to decide whether or not we take Vicksburg."

Currie came forward and shook each man by the hand. "Welcome to the Mosquito Fleet," he said with a smile. It was then that Greg Hollister knew he would follow this quiet, smiling man right up to the ramparts of Vicksburg any time he was asked to do so.

Currie glanced at Webb Downey. "Boatswain! Burial service in half an hour! Dismissed!"

They filed out of the room and walked aft to their quarters. "I like the cut of his jib," said Ab Cory at last

Webb Downey nodded. "He is a *man*, Ab."

THEY BURIED Jimmy Haslett on the low muddy island to which the *Dart* was moored. Part of the crew of the *Dart* attended the service, under the guns of the tinclad. The mist drifted through the moss-draped trees as Mister Currie read the burial service and his mates lowered the canvas-wrapped body into the grave and then quickly filled it in.

Greg had seen other shipmates buried after a sharp action on the Atlantic, wrapped in canvas, with a solid shot at their feet, dropped over the side to plunge downward into the clean salt water, as a sailor should be buried. This was different. It *was* a different kind of war.

They filed back aboard the steamer. It was getting dark outside. The mist still boiled up from the surface of the river. A smell of rotting vegetation seeped aboard the boat. Something shrieked in the distance, and the echo seemed like the crying of a lost soul; *maybe that of Jimmy Haslett.*

Greg looked at Chip Powers, who squatted on an overturned water bucket, diving a fork into his stew. "Catamount be like," said Chip. "Gives a man the shivers to hear him."

"This is a crazy country," said Greg as he sat down on a box near Chip and began to eat his thick stew. "Too many big rivers, and the land is hardly land at all."

"You get to like it," said the boy.

Greg eyed him. "You *like* the rivers?"

"Yup. I was born and raised at Mound City, Illinois, up near Cairo. Mound City is the Western Naval Base of the Union Navy. My pappy is a shipwright up there. Ten acres of shipyard." Chip grinned. "Sometimes under water, too!"

"Seems odd, having a naval base on an inland river."

"Lotsa odd things out here. We Westerners don't fight wars like you Easterners do."

Greg eyed the boy. "I'm from Manitowoc, Wisconsin, Chip."

The kid stared at him. "Do tell! How come you end up in the seagoing navy?"

"My father had a schooner on the Great Lakes. They needed seamen for the blockade. He had been an officer in the navy. He went back." Greg's voice trailed off.

Chip eyed Greg. "So?" he asked softly.

Greg looked away. "They needed every ship they could get for blockade duty. My father was given command of a leaky old ferryboat and was ordered south. The ferryboat was lost with all hands-off Cape Hatteras."

"I'm sorry, Greg."

Greg put down his plate and stood up. "I worked as a hand on a lake schooner to Buffalo, New York, jumped ship and hiked to New York City where I was enlisted as a powder boy."

"Pretty young, weren't you?"

"My family had to have someone righting in the war. Besides, you're no older than I am."

Chip stood up. "Nope. So why worry about it?" He grinned. "This is a crazy war in the first place and especially out here, bub. The original ironclads were contracted for by the Army and built at Carondelet, Missouri, and Mound City, Illinois, but commanded by naval officers. My Uncle Tobias was a civilian pilot under contract to the Army, until the Navy took over command of the River Fleet in October of '62, then they made him a master's mate in the Navy. Sergeant Ellis and his sharpshooters aboard the *Dart* are from the Army of the Tennessee, and some of the gun crews are artillerymen from the Army of the Cumberland. Some of the River Fleet even have *Marines* aboard 'em!"

"I've seen the elephant now," said Greg dryly. "Marines on mud scows in the Mississippi River Valley!"

"Better not let some of the old-timers hear you call the *Dart* a mud scow! She's one of the best, and there ain't a better crew on any of the *other* boats in the fleet!"

Later, after they had cleaned their mess gear. Chip

showed Greg over the *Dart*. It was a great deal different from the *Yantic*. The engine room sat on the lower deck, and the engine and the boilers were practically exposed to enemy cannon fire but they had been protected to a certain extent by a thick cribbing of wooden timbers beyond which were the wooden sides of the superstructure plated with railroad iron. "Most of the tinclads are stern wheelers," said Chip as he showed Greg the greasy, warm engine room. "Jonce Tolliver is our chief engineer, and what he don't know about these engines ain't worth knowing. Them's the pilot's signal bells over there." Chip pointed out various parts of the mechanism. "Reversing gear, steam drum, cam-gear rod, poppet valve and the relief or safety valve." The boy grinned. "Sometimes we put extry weights on the safety valves when we want to move in a hurry. I don't know when I get more scairt, when the rebels are trying to cut us off or when the safety valves are weighted down."

"I can see what you mean, Chip."

"These type engines are mostly built in Cincinnati. Boilers carry pressure up to about 250 pounds to the square inch. We can make about eight or nine miles per hour upriver and about twelve miles per hour downstream. The *Dart* is known as a racer. She can run like a scairt cat when she has a mind to. We got a shot through the engine room here about three days ago. That's when the mud drum blew up. Hot steam and water filled this old room then, I tell you! Luckily there was only two men in here."

"What happened to them?"

Chip looked away. "They're buried out on the island, close beside your mate, Greg." He brightened. "Won't be long 'til we get out of this slough and go down to the Mississippi. J once hasn't got much more to do to fix the damage."

They walked aft to where they could see the big stern wheel exposed to the enemy without a shred of protection. "The ironclads have their wheels covered in," said Chip. "Some of them, the side-wheelers, have big humps on the sides to cover in the wheels. Sure, looks crazy. But we can't carry the weight of all that armor anyways. We have four rudders on the *Dart*." He glanced sideways at Greg.

"*Four?*"

"Yup! Two to a side, just forward of the wheel." Chip pointed to the exposed rear deck. "You can see the steering ropes there. Kinda dangerous if they're shot away and have to be replaced."

"I can imagine," said Greg dryly.

They walked forward past the engine room and boilers. "We carry howitzers aboard the *Dart*," said Chip. "Six 24-pounders."

"Why army artillery on a navy ship...*boat?*"

"Naval guns are far too heavy to carry. The howitzers are much lighter. Besides, the rebs usually have 6-pounders or 12-pounders at the heaviest. So we can give 'em billy blue blazes with our 24-pounders. But Mister Currie managed to *requisition* a naval gun and it's his pride and joy. That's why he was so glad to see you navy gunners today."

They walked along past the two howitzers of the port broadside. "We carry two howitzers in each broadside," said Chip, "and two forward."

"I saw three-gun ports when we came up on the *Dart*."

"Yup! But Mister Currie is going to do some shifting around. Up forward we had two 24-pounders, but since we got the navy gun, we aim to move both of the howitzers aft, one to each broadside, and leave the naval gun up there. That will probably be your gun, bub."

"Yup."

The forward ports had been closed but in the dim light from a battle lantern Greg could see the three forward guns. The howitzers were one on each side of the naval gun. Greg whistled softly as he saw the familiar bottle-shape of the big gun. "It's a Dahlgren," he said.

"Yup!" said Chip proudly. "A 32-pounder. We sure can do some heavy sharpshooting with that fat baby!"

Greg looked about. He may have been on a river steamboat, lightly plated with boiler and railroad iron, squatting almost on the muddy bottom of some unnamed river in Mississippi, but he knew a navy man had placed that gun there. Racks contained battle-axes, shot tongs, shell bearers, priming wires, gunlocks, fuse wrenches, spongers, cups and rammers. There were extra training tackles, breeching and preventer gear. Everything had a place and everything was in its place. Chocks, pouches, tampions, vent covers, elevating bars, rollers and handspikes. To port and starboard of the three heavy guns were other racks containing navy issue cutlasses, bayoneted rifles, boarding pikes and grenades.

Chip jerked a thumb toward the last items. "Times it gets pretty hot up and down these rivers and the rebels try to come aboard, so we have to chase 'em off."

"Repel boarders."

"Yup! One lime on the *Cricket* they hooked up the hoses and fed steam through 'em to chase off some reb cavalry that was trying to come aboard."

"Cavalry? On a navy ship?"

Chip grinned. "Well, when you figure these tinclads draw between twenty-two and twenty-four inches for the most part, they kin get pretty close to shore and them rebel troopers, particularly them Kentucky Bluegrass boys, will ride a horse just about anywheres!"

Chip led the way to a ladder and went up it like a tin monkey on a string. Greg followed him up into the cramped pilothouse which was dominated by the huge six-foot wheel. The only light came in through narrow eye slits sloped up at a 45-degree angle. "Deflects shot and musket balls that way," said Chip, passing a hand along one of the slits. He looked about him proudly. 'This is the post of honor, Greg."

"So?"

"Yup! Many a good pilot has been lost in these shebangs. The rebs know how valuable pilots are, so they always try to pick them off."

Feet grated on the ladder and a tall bearded man came into the pilothouse. "I've been looking for you, Chip," he said.

"I've been showing Greg here, my new shipmate, around the *Dart,* Uncle Toby."

The pilot held out a big hand to Greg. "Pleased to have you aboard, lad. You'll be good company for Chip here. Maybe you can tame him down a mite. He's always trying to win the war by himself, and if I don't bring him home safe, his paw and maw will thrash me good. Your name?"

"Hollister, sir. Gregory Hollister, U.S.N."

"You don't have to *sir* me, son."

Greg glanced at the plain naval uniform the pilot wore. It was that of a master's mate, and these were not commissioned.

Tobias Powers smiled. "I used to be an Army contract pilot, and I wore shoulder straps with no insignia then, being a civilian subject to Army discipline."

"On a navy ship."

The man grinned just like Chip. "You're getting the idea, son. This is a wildcat navy out here."

"Uncle Toby hasn't missed a fight on the rivers yet," said Chip proudly.

The pilot waved a deprecating hand.

"Yup! Forts Henry and Donelson, Island Number Ten, Memphis... I could go on and on."

"Well, *don't*..." said Tobias Powers dryly.

Greg peered through one of the eye slits and was instantly jerked back 'by the pilot. Seconds later a bullet spat hard against the plating of the pilothouse, followed by the distant crack of the rifle. Greg wiped the cold sweat from his face with a shaking hand.

"They watch us like hawks," said the pilot quietly. "Stay away from the eye slits, son. Sometimes they can see a movement behind them and they fire on a chance of getting someone."

Greg leaned against the great steering wheel. "What about when you are up here conning the boat during a fight?"

"I *said* it was the post of honor," said Chip quietly.

"Best get below," said the pilot. "They know we are in here."

They followed him down to the lower deck. Some of the crew were playing checkers. Others were busy washing clothing, cleaning weapons or quietly talking over thick graniteware cups of coffee. There was a miscellany of uniforms. Some of them wore the wide-bottomed trousers, loose blouses and flat hats of the navy; others had on army trousers and dark blue blouses, with forage caps on their heads. To the caps were attached the brass hunting-horn insignia of the infantry, although Greg saw one long-legged corporal who had crossed sabers on his cap. A blouse and cap hung from a hook, and on the cap were the crossed cannon barrels of the artillery arm.

"Infantry are sharpshooters," said Chip. "We have artillerymen for some of the howitzers. Cavalry Corporal Sturgis was wounded at the Yazoo, taken aboard, served as a gunner and sharpshooter in a couple of fights and became one of the crew. No one knows how. He's a good man."

They climbed a ladder up to the upper deck and into the cabin used by Tobias Powers. He sat down in a rocking-chair and filled a great calabash pipe with rough shag tobacco. He lighted it and leaned back in the chair. "It's an odd sort of war," he said thoughtfully. 'These western rivers are technically under Army jurisdiction. The early crews of these boats were civilians and army men who knew the river. Then the Navy came in and brought seamen and gunners. We have ironclads, tinclads and timber clads, transports, hospital ships and supply ships. I daresay we have more craft on these rivers than the Navy has at sea, Greg."

"That's a little hard to believe, sir."

"You'll see when we get back to the Mississippi," promised Chip.

The pilot puffed at his pipe and watched the bluish smoke drift toward the half-open door. 'The rebels depend on river transportation and so of course, they try to hold the key points on the main rivers. An army can contain itself for a time for some distance from the rivers, but they can't undertake a real campaign without support from us of the Mosquito Fleet."

"Yup," said Chip. "We go everywhere! On patrols and expeditions on the Mississippi, Tennessee, Cumberland, White, Arkansas, and Yazoo."

"We're a sort of floating wing of the Army," said Tobias Powers. "In this half-drowned country, they can hardly get along without us."

"And all the time I thought we'd never see any action out here," said Greg soberly.

"You'll fight plenty of scraps without names, son. Fights that will never enter the history books. It can get pretty hot at times. I wish Chip would go home and get work with his father."

"I'm your cub," said Chip stubbornly.

The man nodded.

The door-swung open and Lieutenant Currie appeared. Greg and Chip jumped to their feet.

"At ease," said Mister Currie. He looked at Tobias Powers. "The river is rising, Tobias. I want to get out of here at the first light of dawn. I wouldn't put it past the rebels to float torpedoes down on us tonight or tomorrow."

The pilot nodded. "Jonce says the engine is O.K. First light of dawn then."

"Aye. Can you conn us out?"

"Yes."

Currie nodded. "You young men better get some sleep. You both might have work to do tomorrow."

Chip and Greg left the pilot's room after the officer had gone to his quarters. They quietly got into their hammocks. Greg had slung his beside Chip's. He lay there staring up at the low deck just over him. He could hear the soft rushing of water along the sides of the tinclad. Then something bumped at the stern and scraped along the side. Greg sat up.

"Driftwood," said Chip sleepily. "You'll get used to it in time."

Greg lay down again.

Chip yawned. "Funny thing," he said. "Driftwood sounds just like a torpedo bumping along the side. You never know the difference until the explosion comes."

"Thanks, *oh*, *thanks*," said Greg sarcastically.

CHAPTER THREE

Battle Stations

"All hands to battle stations!" The harsh voice of Boatswain Webb Downey roused Greg out of a sound sleep. He had his feet on the damp deck and his legs into his trousers before he had his eyes fully open. He could hear the men grumbling *sotto voce* as they pulled on their damp clothing. It was dark in the quarters except for a shaded battle lantern in one corner. The soft pattering of rain sounded against the sides of the tinclad. Now and then, Greg heard the scraping of a scoop shovel on the plating as coal was fed to the fires.

"Still dark outside," said Chip. He slapped Greg on the shoulder. "Got to get to my post."

"Piloting?"

"Nope. Uncle Toby handles it. I'm letting *him* get some experience. He ain't a *close-fit* pilot like Old Chip, but he ain't *too* bad." The towhead disappeared into the dimness.

"Listen to him," snorted Tom Bruce.

"He carries messages from Mister Currie," said an army artilleryman. "The kid is fast and smart."

There was a quiet hustle-bustle inside the tinclad as the crew moved to battle stations. Gunners stood to their guns behind closed ports. Greg took his position as powder monkey at a quiet word from Ab Cory. The Dahlgren had been turned over to the new draft, as it was the type of gun to which they were accustomed, as compared to the army-type howitzers manned mostly by the artillerymen and rivermen.

"Load!" said Ab Cory.

First Loader Taffy Hayes thrust the silk-encased powder charge into the grinning maw of the gun. Second Loader Perry Shepherd slammed the charge home with a mighty heave of the copper-capped rammer. The wad was inserted, then Shot Man Tom Bruce heaved up a shell and dropped it into the bore to be rammed home and followed by another wad.

The artillerymen and mixed naval ratings on the other guns were watching the new gun crew.

Lieutenant Currie stood to one side. "Trice up the port when you are ready, Gunner," he said.

"Aye, aye, sir!"

"Open port!" snapped Ab Cory.

The tackles whined as the port was triced up, revealing the flat surface of the river boiling with thick white mist and pocked by raindrops. It was the false dawn.

A young officer came from aft and stood beside Ab Cory. "This is Mister Luscombe," said Lieutenant Currie. "In charge of the First Division, Gunner."

Cory knuckled his forehead.

Mister Luscombe was hardly more than twenty years of age. An ensign with shiny braid, hardly out of the Academy, from all indications. Currie walked toward the ladder that led up to the pilothouse. He glanced back at the gun crew. Luscombe eyed the expressionless faces of the crew. "You men must remember that if shot and powder are not fully driven home, the charge might explode at the weakest part of the barrel," said Mister Luscombe.

The thick silence was embarrassing.

Greg glanced at Ab Cory. Ab had once sighted a Parrott rifle at a speeding blockade-runner in a wild sea and had placed a 70-pound shell squarely in her boilers at half a mile range. "Aye, aye, sir," said Ab.

Luscombe eyed Greg. "How old are you, sailor?"

"Seventeen, going on eighteen, sir."

"So? Do you know your duties?"

"Yes, sir."

"A powder boy is an essential part of the gun crew. In time you will learn other duties on the gun, so keep alert and watch well."

"Aye, aye, sir."

"Listen to the squirt," said Joe Bell, one of the new drafts, in a low voice to Tom Bruce.

Mister Luscombe did not hear Joe, but Ab Cory did, and his eyes seemed to strike Joe Bell like the lash of a cat-o'-nine-tails.

"We'll be casting off soon," said Pleasant Landers to Greg. He had been in the skiff when Jim Haslett had been killed. He peered through the mist on the river. "Them rebs sure can shoot."

"Listen!" said Tom Bruce.

Somewhere down the river they could hear noises.

"Sounds like waggins," said a seaman.

"Artillery, most likely," said an army gunner.

"Ours?"

"*Theirs*."

"I thought *our* Army held this country," said Ab Cory.

The artilleryman shrugged. "It does and it doesn't. The rebs shoot out flying columns of cavalry and horse artillery. They go into position along these rivers and snipe at tinclads and transports. It's one of our jobs to clean 'em out." He leaned against his howitzer. "Their gunnery don't scare me near as much as their sharpshooting. One thing you navy boys better get used to is watching for shells and solid shot ricocheting off the water. We all go down at the command of the gun captain when he sees them."

"And if you don't?"

The gunner grinned. He passed a hand sideways across his throat and tilted his head to one side. "You might be walking around with no head on your shoulders, sailor."

The *Dart* was ready to move down the river. "Cast off!" came the command.

Bells rang in the engine room and the *Dart* moved forward as the great stern wheel thrashed into life. The water began to pull back from the low bow of the craft. The rasping and clanging of shovels and the metallic banging of the fire doors became louder and steadier. The noise of hissing steam began to sound above the sound of the shovels. The pistons were thrusting harder now and the *frash-frash-frash* of the paddles increased.

The *Dart* edged out into midstream.

Greg peered over the shoulders of the tackle men trying to pierce the cottony mist with his eyes. He wondered how Tobias Powers knew what he was doing up there in the lofty pilothouse.

Tackles whined as the port and starboard broadside batteries triced up their gun-port covers.

"How far to the Mississippi?" asked Tom Bruce suddenly.

"Ten or twelve miles," said a seaman.

"Like this all the way?"

"Like this, mate."

Bruce whistled softly. It was like plowing through a bale of cotton.

Greg figured the pilothouse men might have vision above the layers of shifting mist; or at least he hoped they did. He had been in fogs off Cape Hatteras but never when going into a possible fight.

The banks were no longer visible. The gunners shifted uneasily on their bare feet, and calloused hands gripped rammer, training tackle or handspike just a little tighter.

Greg hefted a powder charge from one hand to another until Ab Cory placed a firm hand on Greg's left shoulder and squeezed hard.

The heat from the thudding engine room became more noticeable. Men began to spread a layer of wet sand on the decks near the engine and boiler rooms after the acrid smell of scorched wood had begun to trickle through the tinclad's interior.

Then the mist began to thin. The *Dart* heeled a little as she veered toward slack water along the starboard shore.

Then Greg saw a thin, dark line against the water to port. It was a spit of land, hardly higher than the water itself, and there was something on it. The mist was clearing now ahead of the fresh dawn wind.

Bare feet slapped on a ladder. Chip Powers approached Mister Luscombe. "The cap'n says you can fire at will, sir," he said smartly.

"At *what?*" growled Ab Cory.

They didn't have long to wait. There was a puff of smoke centered with orange-red and a sudden rushing noise in the air. It came from the mud spit, and just as the shell struck the water ten feet from the port bow of the *Dart*, Greg saw the dim figures of the rebel artillerymen as they swiftly reloaded their brass piece. A shower of mud and water cascaded against the tinclad and poured in through the closest gun port, deluging the crew.

Ab Cory didn't hesitate. 'Train left!" he commanded. He stooped to sight over the thick breech of the Dahlgren, then twirled the elevating screw. "Stand clear!" he snapped. He jerked the gunlock lanyard and the gun reared back roaring in anger, driving a thick ball of cottony smoke ahead of the swiftly moving *Dart*, obscuring the vision of the gunners. But there was no time for them to gape at the view. The gun had stopped its recoil hard against the manila breechings.

"Sponge!" rapped out Ab Cory.

The sponge end of the heavy rammer disappeared deeply into the smoking maw of the gun, to quickly reappear, blackened and steaming.

"Load!"

Taffy Hayes took the powder charge from Greg, shoved it into the muzzle, followed it by a wad, then stepped aside as the copper-clad end of the rammer drove them home. Tom Bruce slid the heavy shell into the muzzle and a wad was crammed in after it. Once again, the rammer thudded hard against the wad, seating charge, shell and wads firmly against the Gomer seat of the breech interior.

The gunlock had been recocked and reprimed. "Run out!" came the command. Ab checked his sighting, now that the smoke had dissipated. He adjusted the elevation. 'Train left!" he called out. He jumped back as the gun moved. "Stand clear!" he called sharply, jerking the lanyard an instant later. The Dahlgren spat smoke and flame, and an instant later the shell burst thickly in the mud, hurling a mass of it against the rebel gun.

The Dahlgren smashed back against the breechings. "Run in!" yelled the gun captain. "Sponge!" Then the detailed routine of loading began again, and in hardly more time than it takes to tell, the Dahlgren grinned from the port and roared happily as it hurled a third shell into the scattered rebels.

In the instant's silence that followed they clearly heard the three sharp taps on the signal bell that alerted the engineer, then the signal was three short taps and two ringing clangs. *Feed the fuel!*

Greg heard the sharp rattling of musketry from the upper decks of the *Dart* as Sergeant Ellis opened up with his sharpshooters. The port-bow howitzer had been deluged with water and could not fire, but the two port broadside howitzers slammed quickly in succession, then were reloaded and fired again, as the swift *Dart* came abreast of the mud spit. The rebels scattered into the dripping woods but rifle fire opened up on the tinclad and rattled against her plated sides as she surged past the spit with a bone in her teeth.

The *Dart* rounded a bend, slipping into slack water, then out again, as the paddles thrashed steadily against the chocolate-colored water.

"Down ports!" came the command from Mister Luscombe.

The tackles whined as the port lids came down at a run and were dogged shut. The sweating gunners grinned at each other.

The young officer came up to Ab Cory. "Gunner," he said quietly, "I've seen a few gun crews in action but nothing like this one. Regulars every one of them!"

"Thanks, sir."

The officer smiled a little shamefacedly. "I'd like to work out with you. Seems as though you can teach me a thing or two."

"I'll be happy to, sir."

Lieutenant Currie came down to the smoke-filled gun deck and looked at the men. "Fine work," he said. He looked at the gun crew of the Dahlgren. "I think we can consider the new gun crew as part of us now. What do you say, men?"

Ab Cory's face was brick red as cheers broke out.

"Act like they never seen *real* gunners in action afore," growled Tom Bruce, but there was a satisfied look on his broad face just the same.

They reloaded the hot guns. Half of the crews stayed with their guns while the others messed. Word was passed around that there had been no casualties, but that the port stack looked like a sieve near the base from musket bullets.

The crew stayed on the alert as the *Dart* swiftly

plowed down the rising river toward the Mississippi. Now and then gusts of wind-swept rain against the plated sides, but the mist had cleared. Greg peered through a loophole at the tangled shore line. It was always the same. Half-drowned trees, dark water, thick underbrush and dripping moss. Driftwood flowed past both sides of the snub bow of the tinclad and bumped steadily along the sides. The torpedo rake was still slung up. Greg asked a seaman why they did not lower it.

"We've too shallow a draft to be bothered by their torpedoes," he said. "We usually go ahead of the ironclads and transports to rake up the torpedoes."

"Nice work," said Greg soberly.

"Aye, but we on the tinclads are a little bit of everything. Vedettes, convoy escorts, raiders, patrols and general handymen. I like it. It's better than slogging up and down on the Atlantic Blockade for my money."

Greg watched him walk aft. It was all in the way a man looked at it. Greg had hated to leave the blockaders because of the clean life of it, but on the other hand there had been days and days of storms when they had ridden under bare poles and with dragging anchors off the mouth of the Cape Fear River while food ran low and bedding was soaked, and there was nothing to do but stand watch and watch hour after hour and wish you had never been mad enough to leave Manitowoc, Wisconsin.

The engine thudded steadily. The gunners cleaned up about their heavy charges. Mister Luscombe was busy with tape and pad figuring out where to cut through the gun ports on each side of the tinclad for the two 24-pound howitzers that would be moved back to form additional broadside guns. That left the gunner's post of honor, the bow, under the care of the new draft from the *Yantic*, bolstered a bit by other members of the crew.

Ab Cory slapped the breech of the Dahlgren. "A good gun," he said quietly. "True as they come."

"She'll likely need a name," said Taffy Hayes as he

wiped burnt powder from the muzzle. He scrubbed hard. "And a bit av red paint on the muzzle will let the rebels know it is a man-o'-war's gun crew they are dealin' with, and that's a fact!"

Perry Shepherd nodded. 'The first shot was for the Devil, the second was for God, and the third shot was for Old Abe."

Tom Bruce grinned. "Call the gun 'Old Abe,'" he said. "Can you think of a better name for a gun that will help bring the rebels back into the fold?"

Ab Cory folded his thick arms across his chest. He looked at his gun crew. "Well?" he asked.

They all nodded.

Ab took up a dipper and filled it with the powder-blackened water from the sponge bucket. He dribbled it over the thick breech of the gun. "I christen thee 'Old Abe,' and may you bring home the wisdom of unity to our erring southern sister states," he said sonorously.

Chip Powers came down the ladder. "The Mississippi is just ahead!" he called out.

"Trice up the gun ports! Secure guns!" commanded Mister Luscombe.

Tackles whined again as the gun ports rose slowly. Ahead of the *Dart* was a lighter flow of water, and it was so wide that the farther shore was hardly visible through the slanting rain and faint mist. It was the Father of Waters, but it still did not mow unvexed to the sea. The thought was Greg Hollister's as he stared out of the port, heedless of the cool rain that struck his heated face. But that was why *he* was there, and Ab Cory, Chip Powers, Webb Downey and all the others on the little *Dart*, stanch fighter of the Mosquito Fleet.

CHAPTER FOUR

The Pact

The *Dart* angled across the broad river, and as it did so a string of signal flags crept up the mast of a low-lying craft moored beside a huge side-wheel steamer. "That's the *Benton*," said Webb Downey, pointing at the ironclad. "Most powerful fighting craft on the river."

"Slowest and ugliest, too," said Chip Powers. "She's been a flagship all along," said the boatswain.

"She was Foote's flagship at Island Number Ten and Davis' in the fighting at Memphis."

Greg eyed the battle-scarred veteran of the river. She had a rectangular superstructure raised above the lowest deck. The superstructure was heavily armored and pierced with gun ports. Twin stacks stood just aft of a rounded sort of pilothouse that was also armored. The huge wheel that drove the big craft was encased in an armored drum that rose part way above the flat top of the superstructure.

"She's one of the original Eads' boats," said Webb. "Used to be a twin-hulled snag boat named *Submarine 7* at Saint Looie, until Eads rebuilt her by bridging over the two hulls and forming one bow. One thousand tons burden, three-and-a-half-inch armor, sixteen guns."

Lieutenant Currie approached them. "I'm to report aboard the *Benton* at once, Bos'n."

"Aye, aye, sir! I'll have a boat ready in a jiffy!"

Currie eyed the big ironclad. "She's the toughest customer on the Mississippi," he said thoughtfully, "and yet if it hadn't been for a real patriot, we might never have had her at all."

"How was that, sir?" asked Greg.

"The Quartermaster-General advertised for proposals to construct a number of ironclad gunboats for service on the Mississippi. Captain James B. Eads got the bid and promised to have seven gunboats ready for armaments and crews in sixty-five days. It was a tough proposition to meet. Wood had to be gotten from Minnesota, plate armor from Pittsburgh, cannon from Youngstown, shipwrights from the East, and machinery from Cincinnati, Pittsburgh or Saint Louis. It took a little longer than was anticipated to get the seven boats done, and at first they were refused by the government, but Captain Eads continued the work on them at his own expense and then turned them over to the government. He built the *Benton* after he had built the original seven vessels at either Carondelet, Missouri or Mound City, Illinois. They were the *Carondelet*, *Saint Louis*, *Louisville*, *Pittsburgh*, *Mound City*, *Cincinnati*, and *Cairo*.

"It's entirely possible that we *might* have been able to conquer the Lower Mississippi as early as the fall of 1861 if we had had those vessels ready for action at that time. As it is, we now have to fight for every foot of the way."

When the officer had left, Greg and Chip climbed up to the top deck of the *Dart*. The rain had stopped and a watery sun had appeared. Chip had borrowed his uncle's powerful telescope and as he pointed out various vessels of the river fleet, Greg trained the glass on them.

"The long funny-looking ironclad at the far end of the line is the *Choctaw*," said Chip. "She's a sort of development of the earlier Eads' type of gunboat. She's practical and powerful but she sure is ugly, ain't she?"

Greg nodded. The huge paddle boxes thrust themselves up near the stern, and just forward of them was a tall armored pilothouse sitting on a sort of armored knoll. The deck then slanted down and leveled off. Two tall stacks were just abaft of a low turret, or rather casemate, which had sloping sides. The armored foredeck was almost level with the water.

"She's a side-wheeler," said Chip, "and each wheel acts independently of the other so as to make it easier to turn in narrow channels. She carries three 9-inch smoothbore guns and a rifled 100-pounder in the forward casemate. The casemate forward of the wheel has two 24-pounder howitzers and a third casemate abaft the wheel contains two 30-pounder Parrott rifled guns.

"Her sister ships are the *Tuscumbia*, *Indianola*, *Lafayette*, and the *Chillicothe*."

As long as the sun remained out, Chip pointed out the strange-looking but efficient vessels of the Mississippi squadron. The sprightly tinclads, such as the *Dart*, the *Rattler*, *Silver Lake*, *Marmora*, *Nymph*, *Cricket*, *Forest City*, and others. The huge hospital steamboat *Red Rover*. The transports *Black Hawk*, *Benefit*, *Warner*, and many others. The timber clads, armored only by thick timbers and walls, such as the *Tyler*, *Lexington*, and *Conestoga*. The supply ships *Palestine*, *Reveille*, *Irene*, *Belle Peoria*, *Rob Roy*, *Mercury*, and *Lizzie Martin*. There were signal boats, patrol boats, towboats and tugboats.

Chip held out a hand. "Raining again," he said laconically. "Ain't good to get wet unless you can't help it. Brings on the ague."

"What are those steamers in a group near the *Benton*? They don't look like they're armed."

"They ain't. Those are the Ellet rams. They took some old steamers and rebuilt them. The pilothouse is lightly armored. The bows were filled and strengthened with huge timbers and the boilers are surrounded with a double tier of oak timbers twenty-four inches thick."

"Do they work?" asked Greg incredulously.

"Do they *work*, bub? *Aieeee!*" Chip slapped the side of his head. "At Memphis they tore into the rebel River Defense Fleet like bulls after a red flag! The rams were led by Colonel Charles Ellet, who had thought of the idea of using them. He went into the fight on the hurricane deck of the *Queen of the West*, followed by the *Monarch*. When the fighting was over, they had sunk the *General Lovell*, the *General Price*, and damaged and captured the *Beauregard* and the *Little Rebel*. The rest of the rebel fleet was either burned by themselves or escaped.

"Colonel Ellet died of a wound he received in the fight. But his brother and his son are still in charge of the rams. They're the scrappiest bunch you ever saw on the river, bub."

"I can imagine."

The rain was coming down harder. They started to leave the hurricane deck when a big steamer appeared in the mist, driving upstream through the slanting rain.

Chip's face sobered. "That's the hospital transport *Imperial*," he said quietly. "She's loaded to the guards with sick and wounded men. Every week either she or the *Empress* takes a load up north."

Greg eyed the big steamer. He could see men lying on the decks. "I didn't know there were any big battles going on, Chip."

"There aren't. But it's the fevers and the agues, dysentery and typhoid. Then there's the constant little fights going on in the bayous and swamps. A dozen men here and fifty men there. It all adds up, and Old Useless Grant ain't any closer to Vicksburg than he was months ago, and ain't likely to get there at the pace he's going."

They descended to the next deck and then down to the gun deck. "He's a pretty good man from what we heard in the East," said Greg quietly.

Chip peered into the galley. "Let's mug up," he said.

They filled huge graniteware cups with strong issue coffee. "It ain't that I don't *think* he's a good man," said Chip earnestly, "but when you see boats like the *Empress* and the *Imperial* plowing upstream like that, loaded with sick and wounded men, and see the graves lining the levee tops so close you can hardly walk between 'em, you begin to wonder if well ever take Vicksburg."

"What makes it so hard to capture? We've got the men and the ships, haven't we?"

Chip nodded. "Yup! But you got to take in consideration where the place is. They don't call it the Gibraltar of the Mississippi for nothing! There's high ground behind it, but the trick is to *get* there. You can't take it any other way but from the high ground. Then they have heavy guns, and plenty of 'em in the river batteries to keep the boats from passing the town to carry troops below there, so's they can circle around to the east and come in on the high ground I told you about."

"What about coming down the east side of the river and trying to get around the town that way?"

Chip gloomily shook his head. "No go! The country is about half under water with all kinds of bayous, streams and rivers tangled up. The Big Sunflower, the Yazoo, Deer Creek, Steele's Bayou, the Tallahatchie and the Yallabusha. Enough to give an alligator the headache trying to thread his way through "era. They say the rebs have forts at key points in the mess. I've heard tell the Army has cut some of the levees farther north to flood more water into the mess so that" some of our boats can float through toward Vicksburg. I'm glad we won't be one of them."

Webb Downey appeared and blew his boatswain's whistle. "Coal up!" he roared. "Coal barge and tug will be alongside in a few minutes! Coal up! Coal up!"

Chip sighed and put down his cup. "Just when I was

getting ready for a nice long nap. Tis a hard life we lead, bub."

"Aye! That it is!"

It was almost dusk when the empty coal barge was towed away from the side of the tinclad. Seamen in bare feet and with rolled-up trousers washed down the dirty decks. Coal dust still floated in the air and glinted in the light of the lanterns.

The captain's gig appeared from the darkness, was challenged by a sentry and then allowed to come alongside. No sooner had the boat bumped against the rubbing strake when Mister Currie was out of it. "Messenger!" he snapped out, "notify all officers, warrant officers and senior ratings to report to my cabin at once!"

"Aye, aye, sir!" said Chip. He placed his hands against the small of his back and groaned a little, then scurried off to carry out Mister Currie's orders.

"Something's up," said Hank Schultz, one of the engineers, as he rubbed his hands with waste.

Greg eyed him. "What do you mean?"

"The Old Man always acts like that when something is up. I know. Don't make any plans for shore leave, bub."

Greg peered through a gun port at the dim and flooded shore. "I'm not so sure Td *want* shore leave, Hank."

The crew quietly went about their duties. Driftwood bumped against the hull and the tinclad rolled a little uneasily in the strong current of the great river. The rain had begun again and it pattered steadily on the rust-streaked plating. Now and then a man would look up toward the promenade deck where Currie had his cabin. Something was up, as Hank Schultz had said.

"Ammunition supply boat coming alongside," said a sentry.

The men groaned. They'd be sore the next day. Coaling and replenishing the ammunition supply in one day was a rough go. They were unloading shot and shell, grape and canister, powder charges and wads, when a small boat came alongside and several shipwrights and metal workers came aboard. They set to work cutting new ports in the places indicated by Mister Luscombe's chalk marks. They finished their work when the last of the ammunition was on board.

Ab Cory came aft to his gun crew as they ate evening mess. "We've got to move those two 24-pounder bow howitzers back to the broadside batteries," he said.

"Who wouldn't sell a farm and go to sea?" growled Tom Bruce.

"You can always join the Army, Tom," said Perry Shepherd.

"Ahhh!"

"Grumble you can but go you must," said Joe Bell, wiping the sweat from his face.

They set to with a will, detaching the temporary breechings of the guns, then rolling them back to the new ports, and attaching the tackles again. The racks for their gear were taken down and placed near them in their new positions. Then the two extra bow ports were closed and sealed, leaving the one port for the powerful Dahlgren gun to fire from.

It was a weary lot of men and boys who dropped to the decks for coffee just as Lieutenant Currie came down the ladder from the promenade deck. "Stay as you are, men," he said with a smile. He surveyed them for a full moment. "I know you have been working hard but there is a reason for it." He paused. "General Grant has caused the levees to be cut farther north at Yazoo Pass. That's a somewhat *winding* bayou, ten miles long, eighty feet wide, and thirty feet deep. It used to be a passage into the Yazoo many years ago and it will be used again.

"The Yazoo River is actually one river with three names: Yallabusha, Tallahatchie and Coldwater, and their combined length is over five hundred miles. The expedition will consist of five or six thousand soldiers on transports, perhaps more, I am not quite sure about that. The naval forces will consist of the ironclads, *DeKalb* and *Chillicothe*, and two steam rams, the *Fulton* and *Lioness.* Naturally, there will be some tinclads going, too..."

The men all eyed the officer closely.

"*Rattler*, *Forest Rose*, *Romeo*, *Marmora*, *Signal*, *Petrel*, and last, but certainly not least, the *Dart*!"

The men cheered until the noise within the super- structure was deafening.

"Now you know why we have had to coal up, replenish the ammunition stores and move the two bow howitzers. This might be the move that will find the key to the defenses of Vicksburg, and I, for one, am happy that the *Dart* will go along!"

"We all are, sir!" shouted big Webb Downey.

The officer folded his arms across his chest. "You might call it an 'overland cruise,' men, for that's just about what it will be, from what I can gather. The rebels will know we are coming soon enough when they see the smoke from our stacks and hear the crashing noise of our progress. We have information that they have fortified certain points, but we do not know exactly where these are located.

"We will fight not only the enemy but the country as well. Each of you men has a job to do. The crew of a ship must work in close harmony as a team. One weak member of that crew might cause the loss of the ship itself. No matter how humble your job is aboard the *Dart*, you must do the best you can to carry it out.

"I deem it an honor and a privilege for the *Dart* to have been chosen as one of the naval vessels to escort the troops on this expedition. Let us all make sure we prove to our commanding officer, and to the Army, that we merit that same honor!"

Later, when the tired boys were in their hammocks, Greg thought of Currie's words. A little chill crept through him. Supposing he turned out to be the "weak" member that might cause the loss of the *Dart*?

"Chip?"

"Yes, Greg?"

"Let's make a pact, mate."

"So?"

The boy was silent for a moment, and then he spoke quietly. "Let's promise to stick together, to help each other out, and if one of us weakens, the other is to straighten him out in a hurry, the hard way!"

"Aye, Greg."

They gripped hands in the darkness.

CHAPTER FIVE

The Inland Cruise

"*W are sharpshooters!*" The shrill cry echoed through the interior of the *Dart*. Gun ports slammed down and doors were shut. Lead tattooed loudly on the metal sheathing of the vessel. Somewhere on the hurricane deck a branch scraped against metal. There was a snapping sound and then something struck the slowly turning paddle wheel. Guns coughed thickly upwind, and the sound was mingled with that of the steady rattling fire of enemy musketry.

Abner Cory wiped the sweat from his face as he crouched by the bow gun of the tinclad. "Ye'd never know it was winter, would ye now?" he asked no one in particular.

Greg Hollister jerked his head as a slug slapped hard against the metal plating just behind him. He ruefully rubbed his skull.

Tom Bruce grinned. "Lucky for you it wasn't a solid shot, mate," he said. "I've heard of men having their skulls crushed that way."

"Not *his*," said Chip Powers, peering through the rungs of the ladder that led up to the next deck.

"How does it look up there?" asked Pleasant Landers,

Chip shook his towhead. "That noise you heard a little while ago was the galley stack being carried away."

"Pretty hot up there, ain't it?" asked Joe Bell.

The boy nodded. "Dan Gregg is piloting. A little while ago Mac Duncan got hit by a bullet. Creased his skull and he fell away from the wheel. The skipper took over. It's like being in one of them booths at a fair where you pay your money and heave balls at a head stickin' out of a cloth. Only them rebels ain't using rubber balls. They're using minie balls!"

"How much farther do we go up this river?" asked Tom Bruce.

The boy slid down to the bottom of the ladder. "We're not too far from where the Tallahatchie meets the Yallabusha."

"Oh, great!" said the big man sarcastically. "And where docs that put us in the sovereign state of Mississippi?"

Chip grinned widely. "Right near the Yazoo, sailor."

Greg wiped the sweat from his face. It wasn't warm outside, but inside the metal-sheathed superstructure, with the engine laboring and the boilers having full heads of steam, the place was like a Turkish bath.

"*Ware sharpshooters!*" came the strident cry.

Greg got up and walked over to Chip. "This is a mess," he said quietly.

"Yup."

Driftwood thudded against the hull and men's eyes widened as they waited. One vessel had struck a drifting torpedo and had been badly damaged just the day before.

"You think the rebels have a fort around here?"

"Yup."

"Then they'll have a lot of torpedoes in the river to stop us from getting close enough to shoot."

"Yup."

"Greg bit his lip. The tension was getting almost unbearable. "Is that all you can say?"

"Yup!"

"Oh..."

The boy slid an arm about Greg's shoulders. "Come on to the hurricane deck. There's a place there where you won't get hit by sharpshooters. At least you can see what's going on."

Greg looked at Abner Cory. The big gunner nodded. "Ain't likely we'll be doing much shooting until we reach a rebel fort, Greg," he said. "But you come arunnin' if we need you."

"Aye, aye!"

The two boys climbed the ladder and paused for a moment at the base of the ladder that led up into the armored pilothouse.

"Larboard a mite, sir," said Dan Gregg.

They heard the wheel chains rattle as the officer turned the great wheel.

"Dead ahead, sir."

Tree branches scraped and grated along the topsides of the tinclad as she veritably forced her way through the swampy land.

"*'Ware sharpshooters!*"

A howitzer boomed from one of the other vessels, and the sounds of the discharge and subsequent explosion of the shell somewhere in the swamp echoed back and forth amongst the thick growths of trees.

Chip climbed a ladder, swiftly slid back a hatch cover, then bellied out onto the hurricane deck of the craft. Greg followed him. Upper deck structures shielded them as they worked their way aft until they were almost above the turning stern wheel. It was dangerous, more so from the trees that scraped the decks and sides of the tinclad than from rebel sharpshooters who infested these swamps, for they could hardly hit a man lying flat on the hurricane deck unless they could look down upon him.

Greg eyed the terrain. The trees covered the land for miles, with hardly an elevation visible. There was no wind to speak of, and a thick mingled smoke of smokestacks and guns hung in layers above the trees. The river here twisted and turned on itself so that Greg could see the four vessels, or at least their upper works and stacks, that were following the *Dart,* and each of them pointed in a different direction. Yet they hardly covered half a mile in distance. It was a nightmare country and hardly the place for a combined army-navy operation.

There had been nothing but trouble since the vessels had started out on the expedition. The enemy's right flank rested on the Yazoo Valley, a vast oval tract of partly overflowed country, two hundred miles long and interlaced with innumerable bayous and streams. The oval area was bounded on the west by the Mississippi River, and on the north, east and south by what was in reality one long river, known in its successive parts as the Coldwater, Tallahatchie and Yazoo rivers. The bounding rivers made the Yazoo Valley almost an island, the only break in the continuity being at the northern end of the Valley, at Yazoo Pass, a bayou which had formerly joined the Coldwater with the Mississippi, but which had been closed off by a levee. The greater part of the Yazoo Valley was impassable for troops, and the streams themselves were hardly passable for river craft. But the district was a vast storehouse of Confederate supplies, which could be carried in small vessels through obscure channels and passages to Yazoo City and thence to Vicksburg. At Yazoo City was a large inland navy yard, protected by torpedoes in the river and by rebel forts at Haynes's Bluff. Several rebel gunboats were said to be in construction at Yazoo City.

Admiral Porter had thought of the plan to cut the levee at Yazoo Pass, to restore the entrance to the Coldwater and raise the level of the rivers. Then the Federal gunboats and transports could attack Yazoo City. But it involved a vast circuit of two hundred miles through tributary streams in the heart of the enemy country. It was audacious, original, a fine piece of inland naval strategy but also so delicately balanced that it could easily fail.

The *Dart* slowed down, hesitated, then took to the soft mud of the bottom easily and gently.

Chip Powers groaned. "Not *again!*"

The bells jangled in the engine room and the great wheel reversed itself, spinning the silty waters into chocolate-colored foam. The frame and superstructure of the tinclad shuddered with vibration.

"Look!" said Greg.

Another tinclad had rounded the bend behind them and was coming on too fast. Only the upper works and twin stacks of the *Dart* could be visible in the pilothouse of the oncoming craft.

"It's the *Forest Rose*," said Chip.

They could hear the clanging of the coal scoops in the interior of the *Dart* as the stokers kept up a full head of steam. The wheel slowed down, stopped, then slowly went forward, driving hard against the water. It was no use. Bells jangled once more. The wheel went into reverse and the craft moved a little.

They could hear Boatswain Downey yelling down below, and then the *Dart* began to sway slowly from side to side as the crew raced from starboard to larboard and back again to break the bottom suction.

"The *Forest Rose* is coming on!" said Chip, excitement sharpening his voice.

The fast-moving tinclad was laying down a dense cloud of smoke that drifted through the thick woods. The *Dart* was slowly moving backward right into the path of the *Forest Rose*.

Greg glanced toward the pilothouse of the *Dart*. Didn't they see the oncoming vessel?

The wheel of the *Dart* was at full reverse speed now, spinning like a great top, sending thick waves rolling toward the low banks of the Tallahatchie.

Chip looked at Greg. "We got to do something!"

The hurricane deck was bare and exposed except where they were lying. Shadowy figures flitted through the half-drowned lands on either side of the river. Mississippians who were swamp hunters. Deadly sharpshooters. The type of marksmen that formed Barksdale's Mississippi Brigade in the Army of Northern Virginia. The men who had almost stopped the building of the pontoon bridges across the Rappahannock at Fredericksburg, Virginia, the December before, when General Burnside had his Army of the Potomac poised for the assault.

Greg slapped Chip on the shoulder. "Get up," he said quickly. "Wave your shirt! Get the attention of the pilot on the *Forest Rose!*"

"Oh, sure... With them rebels waiting to plant a minie ball in my head!"

"Get up and wave!" yelled Greg. He leaped to his feet and raced along the sooty hurricane deck toward the slab-sided pilothouse of the *Dart*. He hunched his shoulders and slapped his calloused bare feet hard on the deck. He hurdled a rope rack and something cracked against the side of the rack. It was a bullet. He crashed into the rear of the pilothouse and beat upon it with his fists, yelling with all his might up at the narrow eye slit. "Tinclad comin' up astern and acomin' fast!"

He glanced over his shoulder. Chip Powers was dancing about like a teetotum on the after-hurricane deck just above the stern wheel, waving his huck shirt and yelling at the top of his voice. The *Forest Rose* was coming on with her plume of smoke pouring thickly from her twin stacks.

Cottony puffs of smoke seemed to sprout amongst the trees and brush along the shore lines. Greg clearly saw a sharpshooter aim at Chip, but the boy was moving about too fast and too erratically for anyone to get a good bead on him.

"Who's yelling out there!" demanded a harsh voice from the rear eye slit of the pilothouse.

"Greg Hollister! Look astern! Tinclad comin' up like billy blue blazes!"

"For the love of heaven!"

An instant later the big whistle of the *Dart* broke into strident life, cascading hot steam droplets down upon Greg. The whistle blasted away. Then the *Forest Rose* gave voice, too, and the hoarse bellowing of the great whistles echoed and re-echoed across the swamp. The *Forest Rose* went into reverse, but her forward motion was still strong and the great wheel thrashed thickly sending up great gouts of foam and mud.

Bullets pattered against the sides of the *Dart* and slapped crisply through her twin stacks. But her stern wheel had slowed down and now went into forward motion to drive the boat across the mud bank into deeper water.

The whistle of the *Forest Rose* was blasting steadily. She came up at a full clip, although the stern wheel was fighting to slow her down, stop her and then go into reverse.

Chip was still dancing about.

"Down!" screamed Greg as he raced aft.

The sharpshooters were having a field day aiming at the kid. But Chip was too excited to get down. Greg tackled him and drove him to the deck just as the *Forest Rose* drew up close, missed the stern wheel of the *Dart* by inches, then veered off to paddle toward the center of the stream.

"You mud hens!" yelled an irate voice from the pilot-house of the *Forest Rose*. "Can't you stay off the bottom!"

"Where's your mule!" yelled Chip angrily.

"Go boil your shirt!" echoed Greg hoarsely.

Then the *Dart* surged forward as her bottom broke free and she floated out into deeper water just as the *Forest Rose* struck hard and shuddered to a halt. The *Dart* surged past, beating up a storm with her paddles.

"You mud hens!" screamed Chip at the *Forest Rose*.

"Can't you stay off the bottom!" yelled Greg. His voice broke as he finished, and both boys rolled about on the dirty deck convulsed in laughter.

"Get below, ye scuts!"

The voice came from the hatchway, and they could see the mahogany face of Bos'n Webb Downey glaring at them, while his chin whiskers seemed to snap and crackle in anger.

They crawled toward the hatchway and down the ladder to meet Webb Downey at the bottom of it.

"Are ye mad to stay up there!" he roared.

"If we hadn't been up there, we would have been rammed," said Chip easily.

"Look!" snapped Downey.

Two men were leading another man aft from the ladder that came down from the pilothouse. His hands were clasped across his eyes and blood streamed down them from between his fingers.

"Who is it?" asked Chip quietly.

"Assistant Pilot Dan Gregg. Got a ball through both eyes. Dead-eyes they are now; he'll never see the light of day again, poor fellow."

Tobias Powers hurried toward the pilothouse ladder, pausing to tap Gregg sympathetically on the shoulder. He went swiftly up the ladder.

"The post of honor," said Greg.

"Aye," said Webb.

Greg looked at Chip. In less than an hour a wheelsman had been creased by a bullet and a pilot had been blinded for life, yet Tobias Powers had quietly gone up that ladder into the deadly pilothouse to do his duty.

The commanding officer of the *Dart* came aft along the deck. He stopped as he saw the two boys. "I don't know what you were doing up on the hurricane deck a little while ago," he said quietly, "but it was a good thing that you *were* there. If we had been rammed by the *Forest Rose...*"

"Aye, sir," said the boatswain.

"'*Ware sharpshooters!*" came the cry from below.

Port tackles whined shrilly. A moment later one of the 24-pound howitzers bellowed angrily. Greg glanced toward a partly open port on the larboard side. The shell exploded in the swamp. He heard the faint yelling of the sharpshooters.

"It's a dirty war," said Mister Currie.

"Aye," said Webb Downey.

The two boys scuttled below to the smoke-filled gun deck. Now and then a gun port would be triced up and a howitzer would swiftly be run out, aimed, fired, then withdrawn before the echo of the shot died away, while slugs would beat an angry tattoo on the closed port.

The big bow Dahlgren wasn't used for such work. It was too heavy and cumbersome to be run out so swiftly and then be withdrawn. They had tried it a few days before, and one crew member had been killed and another wounded by sharpshooters. The big Dahlgren was patiently awaiting a better test of its strength and accuracy. Say a rebel 12-pounder or a riverbank fort. Then Old Abe would roar and hit hard.

"We're making slow time," said Ab Cory gloomily, as he leaned against Old Abe with folded arms.

"Aye," said Pleasant Landers.

"We could have pushed on," said Tom Bruce. He inspected a hole in his blouse. "What's holding us back anyway, Ab?"

The gunner's mate shrugged. "I've heard tell that Lieutenant-Commander Watson Smith is in ill health."

"Fine man to command such an expedition," said Joe Bell.

"We need a goer," agreed Pleasant Landers. "By now the rebels will have plenty waiting for us. They've had time enough to get heavy guns through these eternal swamps. And when we run into 'em..."

Taffy Hayes grinned. He carefully wiped the thick

breech of Old Abe with a cloth. "We'll be ready, that we will, eh, Abe?"

Greg busied himself about the gun. Following behind the ironclads, rams and tinclads were the transports, loaded to the guards with the tough infantrymen of Brigadier-General L. F. Ross's division. The army detachment consisted of about four thousand men who had come by boat from Helena, Arkansas, to join the naval forces on the Coldwater. There had been nothing but delay after delay in the expedition. The soldiers had arrived late due to lack of transportation. The Confederates had already blocked the way to the Coldwater by felling hundreds of trees into the streams, making an almost impenetrable tangle which the army engineers had to cut through. That had taken two weeks of hard, unremitting labor to accomplish.

After the Coldwater had been passed through, they had reached the Tallahatchie on the 6th of March, and Commander Smith had not pressed on as he should have. He was a sick man and the immense difficulties of the operation had done nothing to make him feel better.

But the ironclads, tinclads and rams had moved on, followed by the deeply laden transports, and all the while the sharpshooters had hung on to the flanks of the expedition like gnats and mosquitoes, stinging and hovering only to sting again.

There was already a feeling of failure amongst the men as they moved slowly through the tangled labyrinth. They were damaging boats and losing others. Many men had been wounded or killed by the sharpshooters.

"It isn't as though we were in a battle," said Ab Cory suddenly. He wiped the sweat from his face. "A man does not mind the loss of mates so much then because he knows it is war and losses are part of victory. But here..." His voice trailed off.

No one spoke. They all felt the same way. Greg thought of Pilot Dan Gregg with his sight gone forever, lost because of a Mississippi swamp hunter wearing a gray uniform, who was just as determined to stop the passage of the boats as the crews of the boats were to get them through.

A port slammed down on the starboard side at a quiet command from Mister Luscombe. The howitzer was run out. As is spat flame and smoke, a bullet sang into the opening and spun a crew man about to drop him dead on the sandy deck. The port slammed down.

"*'Ware sharpshooters!*" came the mournful and monotonous cry from the upper deck.

CHAPTER SIX

Dangerous Reconnaissance

The *Dart* swung uneasily at anchor in the center of the Tallahatchie and the night was alive with mysterious noises. The dim shore line was a tangled mess of willows, and eerie splashing sounds came from there. The thick smell of smoke, mingled with that of silty water and rotting vegetation, hung over the anchored tinclad. Driftwood bumped gentry against the sides in the fast-running current of the river. The bow of the tinclad dipped steadily up and down, scooping up water and driftwood which piled up on the low deck just ahead of the plated superstructure.

Greg Hollister flattened himself against the metal-sheathed side of the *Dart* and looked aft from where he stood on the narrow ledge-like deck just above the rushing waters-He had a grease bucket in one hand and a heavy brush in the other. He could hear the heavy breathing of Joe Bell as he swabbed the deck and the side of the tinclad as high as he could reach with the grease. Any attempt at boarding by the enemy would give them a precarious slippery footing. It was almost midnight but there was little rest on any of the vessels of the expedition. The Mississippians in the swamps did not rest either. They prowled about, shooting at chinks of light or the sounds of voices which carried clearly across the water. Gun-crew members stayed beside their charges, waiting for warning of boarding boats. Sharpshooters lay flat on the hurricane decks waiting for the flashes of enemy guns at which they shot instantly.

"A dirty-war," said Joe Bell softly as he stopped beside Greg.

Greg nodded. There was a spit of rain in the damp air. Far to the west was a faint, flickering light.

"Gunfire," said Joe Bell.

"More probably lightning, Joe."

"Aye."

They worked their way forward to the low rounded triangle of the forward deck. Shadowy figures were at work there sliding muddy snags and tangled brush from the low deck into the water. Chip Powers came around from the starboard side of the boat and came close to Greg. "Sta'bd side all greasy-o, mates," he said cheerfully. "If we get a good sun tomorrow, we kin fry wheat cakes on the metal."

"Shut up!" snapped a sailor. "You want to get a slug in the head!"

Taffy Hayes was on his knees at the very bow. He stared into the tattered mist that hung over the water. "What's that?" he said curiously.

Chip looked over his shoulder. A hoarse cry broke from his throat and he dropped bucket and brush as he bellied down on the deck and stretched out his hands. Greg dropped beside him. He didn't know what Chip had seen, but he knew without asking that it was something dangerous to the boat. His hands struck cold, rounded metal, and something stabbed into his left bicep, causing him to wince with pain. He reached over with his right hand to free the sharp point from his flesh.

"*Don't...shove...down...on...that,*" said Chip breathlessly.

It was a pronged metal rod attached to the rounded

metal object to which they now both clung, and it was heavy and long. "Give us a hand!" gasped Chip.

The sailors knelt on the deck and gripped the slippery cylinder and heaved it gently up on the deck.

"What is it now, Chip?" asked Taffy Hayes.

"Torpedo."

Taffy gulped. "For the love av heaven," he said.

The bow port was open and they carried the dangerous thing into the interior of the superstructure. The port was let down and someone turned up a battle lantern and opened its hood. The yellow light revealed a sheet-iron cylinder about five and a half feet long and a foot in diameter. It was pointed at both ends, and near one end was an iron rod about three and a half feet long, sharply pronged at the upper end while the lower end was set in a sort of hinged arrangement. Two plates had been attached to the side opposite the rod, and holes had been drilled through them to which were attached lengths of greased rope.

"An odd-looking contraption," said Ab Cory with Yankee interest.

"Quite effective, too," a quiet voice said behind the men.

They turned to see their commanding officer. "How does it work, sir?" asked Greg.

"Chip can tell you."

The boy nodded. "I knew what it was as soon as I saw it."

"And a good thing you did, boy."

Chip wiped the grease from his hands. "I seen one of these in the Tennessee."

"*Saw*," said Tobias Powers.

Chip grinned. "I saw one of these in the Tennessee. When I *seen* it, it was lying on the shore. Come adrift it did."

"Oh, Lord," breathed his uncle, raising his eyes upward.

The boy squatted by the cylinder. "Inside of this gadget is a canvas bag with about sixty-seventy pounds of powder in it. There's a gunlock inside the casing, just about even with the bottom of this iron rod here. The gunlock is cocked and capped.

"The torpedo is anchored by these lines you see here." He indicated the greased ropes. 'There are two anchors, and they hold the torpedo in such a way that this prong sticks up, allowing boats going downstream to slide over it but boats coming upstream would strike this rod, ramming the sharp prongs into the bottom and driving down the rod. The rod actuates the lever and the lever triggers the gunlock inside, exploding the powder charge. Neat, eh, mates?"

Taffy Hayes nodded. "Aye, but we weren't moving either way, Chip. And, underway, we've been going downstream toward the Yazoo, lad."

The boy nodded. "Sure, that's why they went upstream and let it drift down. If it had hit one of those loaded troop transports..."

Tom Bruce whistled softly.

"What do we do with it, sir?" asked Webb Downey.

"Why, we disarm it, Bos'n."

The whites of the men's eyes showed in the dimness as they glanced at the officer, at each other and then down at the deadly cylinder on the deck at their feet.

"I'll do it," said Mister Currie.

"You'll need help, sir," said the bos'n.

Greg stepped forward. "I'll help you, sir."

"Me, too," said Chip.

"There he goes *again*," breathed Tobias Powers.

"Have it carried up onto the hurricane deck," said the officer. "If it does blow it won't hurt the guns, hull or engines."

"Yup," said Chip softly. "Only *us*!"

It was eerie on that open deck as the three of them crouched beside the cylinder in the dimness lighted now and then by the ghostly lightning. The officer worked quickly and steadily to detach the rod from the hinge. When that was done, they all breathed easier. If the removal of the rod had tripped the gunlock...

Mister Currie placed a cold chisel against the place where the base of a nose cone was attached to the cylinder itself. He looked at the boys. "Can those rebel sharpshooters shoot by sound, lads?"

Chip nodded. "Sound, sight, feeling and any other way."

"Can't be helped," said the officer laconically. "Here goes nothing!" He lapped hard, and again and again until the bolt sheared off.

A rifle cracked from the bank and instantly one of the *Dart*'s sharpshooters fired at the flash. There was a wild howl from the bank. "Blasted Yank! Yuh creased me!"

"Sorry, Johnny! I'll shoot lower next time!" yelled back the rifleman.

It took half an hour to peel back the rusted edge of the metal and remove the cone. The officer gently slid in his hand, looking at the two boys all the time but his mind was on what was inside that dark cylinder. Then he withdrew his hand and held it out toward Greg. He placed the copper cap in Greg's hand. "You boys can breathe easier now," he said quietly. He reached in again and let down the hammer of the gunlock, then gripped the heavy canvas bag and drew it out of the cylinder. Something fluttered to the deck and Chip picked it up. It was a piece of paper. He held *it* close to his eyes and grinned.

"What is it?" asked Mister Currie.

Chip grinned again. "Note from the rebel who made this contraption," he said. "Says: 'Have a nice trip onward and *upward*, Yankees!'"

The officer smiled. He hefted the bag. "Well, we'll just load this into one of our guns and send it back to them with the compliments of the United States Light Draft Ship *Dart*."

They dropped the cylinder and its parts over the side, then went down below.

They heard a sentry hailing someone from the fore-deck. A sailor came up to Mister Currie and knuckled his forehead. "Sir, it's a boat from *Rattler*, with a message from the commanding officer." He handed the message to Mister Currie. The officer held it close to the battle lantern and read it. He looked at the sailor. "Tell the boat commander that I have read the message and that it is understood. Tell him also that it will be obeyed and to convey my compliments to Lieutenant-Commander Smith."

After the small boat had left, Mister Currie assembled the crew on the gun deck. 'The commanding officer wants me to make a small boat reconnaissance down the river before dawn in order to see if there are any obstructions. I will make the reconnaissance myself. I'll need a coxswain, four oarsmen and several riflemen for our protection."

"I'll go as cox'n, sir," said Webb Downey.

"No, I can't afford to have you off the *Dart*."

"What about the lieutenant himself, sir? We can ill afford to lose you."

Currie waved a hand.

Ab Cory came forward. "I'll go as cox'n, sir."

"Good!"

One man after another raised his hand to go. Greg and Chip pushed forward. The officer looked at them and shook his head.

"I can see like an owl, sir," said Chip.

"I have ears like a bobcat," said Greg quickly.

"And big noses like a parrot for trouble," growled Webb Downey.

"I'll need fine swimmers," said Currie. "No telling whether or not we'll have to swim back."

'Two fishes, sir!" said Chip, grabbing Greg's hand and raising it aloft with his own hand.

The officer eyed them. They were two good sailors, those boys, and Chip knew the river country as well as any man aboard. "All right," he said.

Tom Bruce shook his head. "I learned one thing in the Navy when I was a lad," he said.

"What was that, Tom?" asked Greg.

"Keep your eyes open, your mouth shut, be first in the mess line and the pay line and *never* volunteer for anything."

The boys grinned as they hurried to get ready.

The wherry was brought alongside. The crew got quietly into it. They carried Sharps carbines and Navy Colts, and each man had his clasp knife slung from a lanyard about his neck. Webb Downey squatted on the narrow deck and watched them as Mister Currie got into the boat. "We'll need a hail and an answer, sir," he said.

"Jefferson Davis," said Mister Currie with a grin.

"Countersign Abe Lincoln, sir!"

"Aye, aye!" Currie looked at Ab Cory. "Cast off!"

There were to be no commands except by signal. The oarsmen were Greg and Chip, Pleasant Landers and a seaman named Bob Mead. Ab Cory had the tiller and two army riflemen squatted in the bow of the wherry.

They pulled easily and steadily. The rowlocks had been wrapped in rags to muffle them. The current was running fast and they bad Utile rowing to do. They were half a mile from the *Dart* when Currie signaled to the coxswain. Ab steered in toward the west bank and signaled for "oars." The blades were lifted dripping from the water. A moment later one of the riflemen in the bow fended off from a great log that floated in the water.

There was an eerie nickering of deer horn lightning in the west. "Look, sir!" said Ab Cory.

The river was a vast tangle of logs and driftwood. Trees had been felled so as to lie across each other, and their heavy branches had been chopped off to about five or six feet. The branches had then been interlaced with each other, and the current of the river had forced them tightly against each other. Driftwood had piled up and over the tangled mess.

The men pulled the boat into a thick covering of overhanging willows. They could hear a faint spattering of rain on the river now. Now and then a rifle shot cracked out upstream.

"We'll never get the *Dart* through that, sir," said Ab Cory.

The officer was standing up, studying the tangle in the pale flashes of lightning. 'There are torpedoes in there, too," he said quietly.

The men looked at each other. There wasn't a one of them who didn't know that the expedition had been too slow in its advance. The Confederates had had time and time enough to bring up heavy guns through the swamps and to place them at strategic points. By the time the boats got through this mess in the Tallahatchie, the rebels would have time to make the river impassable by other tangles, field artillery and forts farther down the river.

Currie pointed to the right. The boat moved slowly across a strange area. It was flooded land and tree stumps; trees and brush stippled the dark waters. Now and then an oar caught on something and dumped an oarsman back into the muddy bottom of the wherry. On and on they went while the lightning darted through the gloomy skies, and Greg began to wonder if they'd ever find their way back to the Tallahatchie.

The rain pattered down steadily. It was a curse in one sense and a blessing in another, for at least it would keep the rivers high enough for the pass to navigate, if such a word could be used in the middle of a Mississippi swamp, half water and half land and covered with tangled woods.

The boat came to a halt beside a lightning-shattered

tree. Lieutenant Currie stood up again. Then he held a hand down for complete silence. Greg looked back over his shoulder. For a moment he could see little, then as the lightning lanced across the streaming sky, he saw something that wasn't a part of the natural features of the swamp. It was low and humped. Here and there something thrust itself up, and as Greg watched he saw a movement.

The officer squatted down in the boat. "That does it," he said. "That's a cotton-bale fort there, on that spit. They have some fairly heavy guns there—24-pounders at least. They can fire right across that tangle in the river."

Chip shoved his forage cap back on his head. He looked to his left. "If you can't take 'em head on, you kin always go the long way 'round, sir."

The officer nodded. They moved softly along, hardly daring to breathe until they were two hundred yards from the fort. They tested the depth of the water with their oars. "It's a channel hereabouts," said Chip wisely.

"How can you tell?" snapped Ab Cory.

"I was born around these rivers. Tm half horse and half alligator."

"And all wind," said Pleasant Landers.

"Quiet!" snapped Currie. He leaned close to Chip.

"You're sure this is a channel?"

"Aye, sir!" The boy stood up. "Half close your eyes and wait for the next flash of lightning. Look in that direction."

They waited in the gently bobbing boat. Every man jack had his eyes half closed. When the lightning flashed Greg saw something. The trees seemed to form irregular lines to the southwest almost as though walling in a channel. They pulled the boat ahead. Pleasant Landers tested for bottom and looked at the officer. "Beyond the oar tip, sir."

Chip reached for a lead line, stood up, twirled it dexterously over his head and then heaved it out, letting the line run through his fingers. "By the mark one and a half, sir," he said softly.

Nine feet of water. More than enough for the heaviest boat in the expedition.

"Keep sounding, pilot," said the officer.

Chip moved up forward and as the boat moved out into the channel, he cast the lead steadily. "By the mark twain! By the mark quarter-twain!"

Twelve feet of water deepening to about thirteen and a half feet.

They moved on until the fort, unseen in the drifting rain and swirling mist, was a beam of them.

A rifle flashed in the swamp and the slug sent up a spurt of water.

"By the mark quarter-twain!"

They were well past the fort now, west of it and shielded by the thick tangle of trees and brush.

The rifle cracked again and a splinter flew from the side of the boat inches from the boy who stood in the bow casting the lead.

"By the mark twain!"

Currie nodded. The channel was fine. Now if it only led back to the Tallahatchie!

There was no use for secrecy now. The sharpshooters had seen them. Mister Currie nodded to Ab Cory. "Give her ten!" rapped out the coxswain.

The oarsmen pulled as hard as they could for ten strokes, and the wherry moved quickly out of range.

"By the mark quarter-twain!"

Greg glanced back over his shoulder as the lightning flashed. The channel they were in was opening onto a bigger channel. The way was clear.

"The Tallahatchie!" cried out Chip. He cast the lead. "By the mark three!"

"Come about, Cox'n," said Mister Currie.

"Hold water!" came the command. "Back water port! Pull hard starboard!"

The wherry slowly swung about.

"Give way together!"

The wherry surged against the current. It was dark now and the rain slanted down in long cold sheets. They reached the channel of the Tallahatchie through the thick woods. A way would have to be cut through them by the army engineers for the boats to get through into the back channel which led around the fort.

The *Dart* loomed up in the dimness.

"Halt! Who goes there?" rang out the challenge.

Ab Cory cupped a hand about his mouth. "*Dart!*" he called out, the proper answer when the commander of a ship was aboard a small boat.

"Jefferson Davis!"

"Abe Lincoln!" called out Ab.

"Come aboard!" There was a moment's pause. "Is it wet out *there*, too, boys?"

The men in the boat grinned. They pulled alongside and made the wherry fast, then got aboard the *Dart*. Mister Currie turned to Ab. "I'll write out a report. Get some coffee and by the time you are through I'll have you take the message to Commander Smith. We'll need a saw boat to get through into the other channel."

"Aye, aye, sir!"

Greg sat down on a bucket and felt the water run down his cold body. It had been a long hard day.

"Who wouldn't sell a farm and go to sea?" asked Pleasant Landers.

The rain pattered steadily against the sides of the tinclad.

CHAPTER SEVEN

Failure on the Tallahatchie

In the cold watery light of the predawn the *Dart* moved upstream to take the pull from her anchors, then she weighed anchor, let the current swing her about and steamed down toward the thick tangle that blocked the river. Behind the tinclad came a light-draft steamer carrying members of the Engineering Regiment of the West. Lashed alongside the steamer was the saw boat, or more properly, saw raft. Greg peered from an open gun port at the odd contraption.

Chip hurried by, then came back. "That's quite a gadget, Greg. They used 'em at Island Number Ten to saw out the channel."

"How does it work. Chip?"

It was a long raft with an upright post about ten feet high set on the deck. A crossarm was hung on a thick bolt that protruded from the post, and there was a frame arrangement depending from the crossarm.

"You see that frame? Well, a long flexible saw is attached to the bottoms of the vertical arms you see. The ends come up through holes at each end of the raft. Two sawyers get aholt of each handle. The raft is set against a tree that sticks up out 'a the water, the sawyers pull back and forth, thus cutting the tree off under the water, about six feet down."

"Pretty sharp," said Greg. He grinned at his unintended pun.

"Battle stations!" yelled Webb Downey.

Someone set off a man-o'-war rattle and the strident noise filled the interior of the tinclad as she surged down toward the log tangle. Her job was to keep the fort busy while the channel was opened.

The gun ports were triced up. "Run out!" came the commands from seven-gun captains almost at once.

"Stand clear!" called out Ab Cory. He jerked the lanyard and Abe Lincoln spat out a mouthful of shell and thick white smoke. The shell rushed low across the misty waters and struck just below the rampart of the fort throwing up mud and water. "Run in!" he commanded.

The *Dart* turned to present her starboard side, and one after the other the stubby 24-pounders cracked flatly, then the tinclad surged upstream past the *Rattler*. *Rattler* plastered the cotton-bale fort in her turn. The Confederate gunners set a shell through one of her tall stacks and it crumpled to the hurricane deck as she turned to follow the *Dart*, while *Forest Rose* churned up and fired blindly through the smoke and mist to keep the rebels busy.

The transport *Chippewa* nudged close to the east bank and her derrick swung out a landing stage over which trotted a detachment of infantrymen from Ross's division. They vanished into the thick swamp, and a few minutes later the sounds of crackling rifles sounded like grease frying in a gigantic skillet as the skirmishers met the Mississippians in the gloomy woods.

The *Dart* plowed upstream as the guns were reloaded, then fell into line behind the big ironclad *Chillicothe*. The ugly but seemingly efficient craft moved ponderously down toward the pitiful little fort. Her forward casemate belched thunderously as three 9-inch smoothbores and a rifled 100-pounder fired at the fort.

The *Dart* was close to the place where the sawyers were at work. A string of signal flags crept up *Rattler*'s mast—the signal to cease firing. The fort had been practically knocked out of business for the time being.

Greg peered through the drifting smoke and mist. The saw boat was hard at work. The sawyers moved back and forth in rhythm until the tall tree stump fell over into the water and drifted away. Ahead of the raft were other boats whose crews were topping the trees for the saw boat. Other engineers were snagging the drifting logs and pulling them from the channel. A powerful little tug was working on the smaller trees and other obstructions by attaching cables to them and winching them loose from the thick mud of the bottom. Far ahead a boat was taking soundings, the calling out of the leadsman carrying back faintly in the quiet intervals. "By the mark twain! By the mark twain and shoaling!"

"Busy, busy, busy," said Chip Powers as he hurried past.

Greg nodded. It *was* busy, busy, busy... Guns roaring and rifles cracking. Paddles thrashing and steam exhausts crackling. Saws whirring and winches droning.

It was close to noon when the channel was declared open for the tinclads. *Dart* led the way and surged downstream toward the Tallahatchie with her gun ports open and the guns run out, laying down a thick plume of smoke from her stacks. The way was open now, but to what? What lay ahead in the thick mysterious swamps that seemed to fight as hard against the invading Yankees as did the Mississippi sharpshooters?

Tobias Powers was conning the *Dart* now. He eased her into the slack water, deftly rounded a point, missing overhanging branches by a few feet, and had her out on the Tallahatchie safe and sound. Not so with some of the others. The tinclad *Romeo* was close astern of the *Dart* but she did not clear the trees so neatly as the *Dart* had done. A thick branch struck the tall twin stacks just below the bracings and they crumpled back over the pilothouse with a cracking, snapping noise while thick smoke gushed up from the split seams and through the holes in the stacks.

Greg watched the procession of vessels from an after port. Some of them missed trees and stumps by inches. The mortar boat *Petrel* ran aground and was nudged back into the deeper water by the, *Chillicothe*. The smoke was thick in the woods and now and then the sparkling of gun flashes could be seen. The *Chippewa* had picked up her infantrymen by now. Most of them were soaked to the waist in mud and water. Some of them had been wounded and the white of the bandages was stained with red. Some of them did not come back.

The way to the south was clear, or so it seemed, but every man in the fleet knew that the advance had been too slow. There had been time enough for the enemy to make preparations.

Greg hurried back to his gun. It was March 11, he noted on the calendar that hung from a bulkhead. They had been a long time on the way.

The *Signal*, another tinclad, forged up astern of the *Dart*. It was her turn to make the reconnaissance. It was always a dangerous task, not only because of the torpedoes and sharpshooters in the way, but because it was entirely possible that the rebels had planted a heavy gun or two in ambush along the winding watercourses. One heavy shot through a steam drum or into a powder magazine and a tinclad would be a total wreck. But that was the work of the little steamers. Better that a tinclad be lost than one of the valuable ironclads, or more important still, one of the transports filled with troops.

The gun ports were still open and the crews at the alert. The *Signal* vanished around a sharp right-hand bend. Her smoke rose tall above the trees. She seemed to be moving at a course almost at right angles to that of the *Dart*, which was leading the advance of the main body.

"Listen!" said Pleasant Landers.

A dull thud had been heard, followed by a roaring noise and then another thud.

Ensign Luscombe paled a little. "That was a heavy gun," he said quietly. "A lot heavier than anything the *Signal* has in her battery."

They all looked at one another. The *Dart* slowed down a little, and each vessel behind her reduced speed in turn.

The dull, thudding noise came again.

"Run out!" said Mister Luscombe.

Abe Lincoln slid forward and grinned down-river.

The *Dart* moved slowly around the curve in the river. Ahead the smoke was thicker, with swirls of white mixed in with the blacker smoke. The white smoke was gunpowder smoke.

"I see the stacks of the *Signal*!" said Tom Bruce.

The tall stacks were moving back as though the tinclad were in reverse. The thudding noises were steadier now and soon the *Signal* appeared around a bend, easing into a backwater, to turn slowly and then forge upstream.

"Look at her!" said Joe Bell.

There was a gaping hole in the thin plating of the tinclad. She came upstream abreast of the *Dart*. Her commanding officer hailed Lieutenant Currie. "It's no use going down there, Currie! They've got a fort and they've sunk a steamer to block the river! They have some heavy guns in the fort."

"What happened to you?"

"A shell went right through us, didn't touch a man, and it didn't explode either! Defective fuse probably! Lucky for us!" The *Signal* passed on toward the flagship *Rattler*.

"Lucky for them is right," said Ab Cory grimly.

"We won't go down there for sure," said Pleasant Landers.

"Oh, no?" said Webb Downey. "You don't know the Old Man!"

He was right. The *Dart* moved downstream at half speed. Lieutenant Currie had to see for himself.

Greg Hollister felt the cold sweat begin to run down his face. Those had been big guns they had heard. The *Signal* was living on borrowed time after that shot that had gone right through her. This was different than trading shots with a 6-pounder or 12-pounder rebel field artillery piece or in shelling the woods to drive away sharpshooters.

None of the men spoke. The thudding of the engine and the *frash-frash-frash* of the paddles sounded loudly within the thin metal shell of the tinclad.

Greg felt as though he wanted to scream or jump about. To do anything other than to just stand there with a powder bag in his hands, bound by the iron discipline of a man-o'-war's man, waiting for that dull thudding noise and the eerie whistling rush of shell or solid shot as it came toward the thinly armored steamer.

"There's the sunken steamer," said Taffy Hayes.

Only the superstructure and the paddle boxes showed above the muddy waters. "Looks familiar somehow," said Ab Cory. He stared at the steamer. "Couldn't be though. Not *here*."

"Couldn't be what?" asked Tom Bruce.

Ab peered through the smoke. "The *Star of the West*! I saw her before she left for Fort Sumter back in April of '61."

Pleasant Landers laughed. 'This swamp has addled your brains, Ab."

Mister Luscombe raised a pair of field glasses and studied the sunken vessel. There was a strange look on his face as he lowered the glasses. "It's her, all right," he said quietly.

Greg peered at the famous vessel. It was a mystery how she had gotten there.

"Last I heard of her," said Webb Downey, "she had been seized by the rebels at Indianola, Texas, in the latter part of April '61."

It was the *Star of the West* all right, but there was little time to speculate how she had gotten there. Right now, there were more important things to do, such as attracting the fire of heavy rebel guns.

The *Dart* moved on, at lower speed now, and then the men saw the fort. It crowned a low mound on a neck of land and was built of earth and cotton bales. Guns protruded from embrasures and infantrymen lined the ramparts.

"Ain't such a much," said Joe Bell inelegantly.

It suddenly seemed quieter, even with the steady thrashing of the paddle wheel and the hiss of escaping steam.

The Confederate flag rippled in the damp breeze, the one bright spot in the drab surroundings.

"We'll have to capture it," said Mister Luscombe as he placed his field glasses into their case. "We can't get around it and we can't pass it. This will be a tough nut to crack, boys."

"Aye," said Ab Cory gloomily.

Then a rebel gun roared, a big one, and a patch of brilliant orange-red matched the bright color of the flag. A perfect ring of smoke floated toward the tinclad.

"Down!" roared Ab Cory.

The solid shot struck the water and skipped along the surface like a stone cast by a boy. At the last second, as Greg looked up from the deck, he saw the black ball leap high into the air and miss the vessel.

Bells jangled in the engine room and the *Dart* slowed and then her wheel went into reverse. Two more rebel guns coughed thickly. One projectile screamed past the tinclad while the other plowed neatly through the superstructure like a needle through two folds of cloth, and the interior of the boat rang like a bell.

The *Dart* was close to the sunken *Star of the West* and not even the agile tinclad could get past that obstruction.

"Fire," said Mister Luscombe quietly.

"Stand clear!" rapped out Ab Cory. He pulled the lanyard and Old Abe spat flame and smoke. There was a sudden upsurge of earth, smoke and cotton bales from the rampart as the shell struck.

"Run in! Sponge! Load!"

The crew moved like automatons serving their big iron master.

"Run out! Stand clear!"

Old Abe roared and another spout of earth and cotton billowed upward.

But the rebels could load fast, too, and all three guns thudded almost together. One ball skipped across the water and hopped into the woods. A second seemed to scrape along the starboard side of the *Dart*. The third slammed directly through the open port of the bow Dahlgren an instant after Ab Cory had screamed, "*Down!*"

Greg seemed to indent the sandy deck beneath him as the horrible sphere charged into the smoke-filled interior of the tinclad. It hit the deck and seemed literally to bounce over the barricade in front of the boilers, skipped over the steam drum, struck the deck beams above it, bounced down again, struck metal, then bounded back to the engine room as yelling men scattered in all directions. The deadly globe spun about on the sandy deck as though looking about for prey. An engineer thrust out a foot to stop it He was hurled hard against a bulwark and then collapsed to the deck screaming incoherently with the frightful pain of a shattered leg.

Greg opened his mouth to scream, too.

"Run in!" commanded Ab Cory sharply. "Sponge! Load!"

The gun team worked swiftly under the quick lash of the gun captain's steady voice. Greg handed the powder charge to Taffy Hayes, who in turn thrust it into the steaming muzzle. He slid a wad in after the charge and stepped aside as Second Loader Perry Shepherd slammed wad and charge home with the rammer. Shot Man Tom Bruce swung up the projectile and slid it into the bore.

The rebel guns crashed. Water spouted up from in front of the *Dart* and cascaded in through the open port, washing Taffy Hayes to one side. Perry Shepherd rammed home the projectile, and almost as though nothing had happened, First Loader Taffy Hayes was on his feet and was placing another wad into Old Abe.

Ab Cory had recocked the gunlock, capped it, then stepped aside. "Run out! Stand clear!"

Old Abe spat flame and smoke and reared back solidly against his breechings. The *Dart* turned slowly to larboard and exposed the thinly plated side.

"Fire in rotation from bow to stern!" commanded Mister Luscombe.

One howitzer after the other spat angrily, and when the last one had tired, the *Dart* turned upstream to plow against the current as shot after shot sent water leaping up about her. Then a solid shot crashed through the larboard quarter sending a thick spray of wood splinters flying through the air like great needles. It struck the after-larboard howitzer and smashed it to pieces, scattering death and destruction to the crew and the men who stood near it

Greg stared at the havoc. His throat tasted sour. He wanted to scream, to run, but there was no place to go. There are no places to hide on a naval ship in action.

"Load!" came the implacable voice of Ab Cory, and the crew attended to Old Abe. It was their job; their duty; *nothing* except disabling wounds or death itself must stop that.

The *Dart* had been hurt. Not enough to put her out

of the fight, but she had been badly mauled. As she plowed upstream through the swirling smoke of guns and stacks, a huge bulk showed up in the dimness. "The *Chillicothe*!" cried out a seaman.

The ugly and majestic ironclad was coming downstream to hand the rebel fort a little of the medicine it had been ladling out to the tinclads. Close behind the *Chillicothe* was the ironclad *DeKalb*. The *Dart* passed them and the *Dart*'s crew could hear the faint, muffled cheering of the crews of both ironclads, for the gallant but futile fight the tinclad had fought against great odds.

Behind the two implacable ironclads came the mortar boat *Petrel*. The two ironclads anchored, bows pointing downstream, and opened fire with their heavy guns, while the *Petrel*'s mortars hurled heavy shell high up over them in an effort to land them inside the stubborn little cotton-bale fort.

Chip Powers came down from the pilothouse when the *Dart* anchored upriver from the fight. He shook his head as he saw Greg. "We tooken a mauling," he said gloomily. Then he brightened. "But the *Chillicothe* and the *DeKalb* will give them what for."

Greg nodded. The *DeKalb* was one of the original Eads' gunboats, originally named the *Saint Louis,* and she carried two 10-inch, two 9-inch, six 32-pounders, and two 30-pounder guns. She was a veteran of many battles. The *Chillicothe* was another matter. She was armed with two 11-inch guns and one 12-pounder, and had been built the October before in Cincinnati to the ideas of a contractor named Joseph Brown. She had been designed to get rid of the objection to other ironclads by having a casemate forward containing the two 11-inch rifled guns, working on pivots so that they could fire through ports over the bows, abeam, or at an angle aft. She had three-inch armor and powerful engines. The *Chillicothe* was new, and green, for she had never been in a real battle as yet.

The guns thudded angrily and the smoke of stack and

gun hung thickly over the tangled woods. There was a tenseness aboard all the vessels as they waited for the ironclads to beat the fort into submission.

The crew of the *Dart* were kept busy. It was better so. The dead and wounded were taken away. The decks were swabbed and re-sanded. The guns were cleaned and then loaded.

The flagship *Rattler* had anchored near the *Dart*. Shortly after the fighting started, a string of flags crept up her signal mast, and a little while later the *Chillicothe* came slowly upriver and anchored beside the *Dart*.

Lieutenant Currie came down to the gun deck of the *Dart* and peered through an open port. Lieutenant Commander Foster, commanding officer of the *Chillicothe*, came to a port on his vessel. "What's wrong?" asked Mister Currie.

The other officer shrugged. "I don't know. We were recalled, but *DeKalb* is still fighting it out. Maybe it's just as well we *were* recalled."

"Why, sir?"

Foster cut a hand sideways in anger. "This craft is almost useless," he snapped. "Whoever built this thing should have been shot! The gun ports were cut five inches too high and then patched in. The first shots from the enemy jammed the forward port-gun shutters. In order to fight her I have to anchor, because I can't handle her while the guns are firing. Fine thing! Anchor a ship to fight it!"

"For the love av heaven!" said Taffy Hayes.

"This craft is so badly put together that my gun deck sagged down five inches when we opened fire," said Foster. He waved a hand and disappeared inside his miserable command.

The faces of the *Dart*'s crew grew long. The *DeKalb* and the *Petrel* fought on while the big *Chillicothe* squatted idly beside the *Dart*. Shortly after her return, the *DeKalb* and *Petrel* were also ordered back to anchor with the rest of the vessels. It was then that an ugly and persistent rumor crept throughout the fleet. Lieutenant-Commander Watson Smith, worn out physically, had collapsed mentally as well. It was his last order that confirmed the suspicions of his staff officers. He lay now in his cabin with his mind a complete blank.

But Foster of the *Chillicothe* was not through. Later on in the afternoon he again took his command downstream to renew the fight. Someone had to beat that stubborn little fort into submission. The guns thundered and roared again for a time. Then the big ironclad came slowly back up the river to anchor. Another rumor flew through the fleet, and it was confirmed quickly enough. The battering of the rebel guns had proved Foster's contention that his command was almost useless. The three-inch armor plating was attached to the wooden framing by four-inch bolts, and when the solid shot struck the armor the bolts flew from the framing like bullets, to kill four and wound fifteen of her own crew.

Despair came to roost in the sagging trees that overhung the dark waters of the Tallahatchie as dusk fell over the Yazoo Valley. A cold and mournful wind crept over the dismal drowned land and seemed to mock the crews of the vessels and the sullen troops packed on the transports. The days and weeks of struggle to get thus far seemed to have been of little profit.

CHAPTER EIGHT

Missing in Action

"This is like the doldrums," said Tom Bruce. He wiped the sweat from his broad face and then slapped viciously at a mosquito.

"What are doldrums?" asked Sergeant Ellis as he cleaned his long-range Sharps rifle.

"No wind. Hot. The ship rolls uneasily. The sun melts the pitch in the deck seams. The canvas flaps back and forth. The rigging slaps about. Everybody gets short-tempered. Food tastes like paste. There ain't a blessed thing to do, and you wouldn't want to do anything anyway."

Ab Cory wiped his naked upper body with a dirty towel. "Aye," he agreed. "Ye wait and pray for a breeze day after day."

Greg Hollister stood by the forward port looking out onto the dark river. Now and then a rifle cracked flatly somewhere in the tangled swamp. All along the river the ironclads, tinclads, transports and other vessels swung uneasily at their anchors. One Utile fort, armed with three guns, about a thousand rebels, and a one-armed general, was holding up the entire Yazoo Pass Expedition, the "Inland Cruise."

It was dawn of another day. In the days previous there

had been nothing but failure and disappointment for the Federals. Nothing had gone right. The *Chillicothe* had gone in the second day of the attack and had done little but run out of ammunition. The *DeKalb* had done a little better by silencing the rebel guns, but there had been no suitable place to land Ross's troops for an assault. The bottom lands had been flooded by the incessant spring rains and the opening of the levee at far-off Yazoo Pass.

They *had* to get past the *Star of the West*. An attempt to blow her up had failed. Finally, by one means or another, they had managed to clear a passage past the hulk, and the *Chillicothe* and the *DeKalb* had wriggled past to open a raking fire on the fort. The *Dart* and several other tin-clads had gone into action, too, to silence that pestiferous fort. The fort still held out. It was a crazy conglomeration of mud, earth, cotton bales, logs and anything else that could be piled together. The guns were fired from rickety log platforms that sank lower into the mud with each shot.

Behind the gunboats the transports had felt along the river and the bayous for a landing place for the troops. They could not find anything suitable in that overgrown swamp hung with Spanish moss and clinging vines that interlaced themselves between canes, willow thickets and cypresses. There were places that were a little firm, but when the troops landed on them, they often found themselves on an island surrounded by impassable mud and water.

There was a heavy toll of another sort as well as from the musketry and artillery fire from the fort. Sickness crept into the gunboats and the transports. Chills and fevers, dysentery and other ills plagued the expedition. There were reinforcements somewhere away back along the winding, tortuous way they had come. Then, too, the rebels were busy *behind* the fleet, blocking the channels, planting torpedoes, sharpshooting constantly at any Federal vessels they saw.

Small boats probed constantly into the mysterious dark waterways of the great swamp, hung with eerie-looking mosses, trying to find a way to circumvent the fort or to find a place that was firm enough for a land attack. *Failure*!

The gun firing went on most of the day, with sweating gun crews relieved every so often by the crews of other guns not in action because of the narrow field of fire. Ironclads and tinclads had suffered from gunfire. The ram *Lioness* had lost a smokestack and had to plug a gaping hole at her water line. The *Rattler* had taken Lieutenant-Commander Watson Smith back to Yazoo Pass and the Mississippi, and the officer was on the very verge of death.

A faint tinge of gray light showed in the eastern sky. The restless quiet would soon be broken by the crashing of guns.

Lieutenant Currie came down from his cabin. He looked about the shadowy gun deck at his sweating, pale-faced men. "It seems as though the gunboats can't reduce Fort Pemberton alone," he said quietly, "and the infantry can't find a place to land."

"We'll stick it out, sir!" said Tom Bruce.

Currie nodded. 'That I know. But we're running low on ammunition. The sick list is getting longer every day. General Ross's command has been hard hit, and General Quinby's command is still back on the Mississippi. We don't know when they'll get here."

Scoops rattled on the floor plates of the fireroom as the stokers got ready to build up steam pressure. Coal was getting low, too.

"We're going to try it again today," said the officer. "If we don't silence that fort, or get past it, we will return to the Mississippi."

The men looked at each other. Sick, tired and disappointed, they still would not admit defeat.

"Orders are orders," said Lieutenant Currie, almost as

though he could read their minds. He wiped the sweat from his face with a shaking hand. He had fever but would not admit it. "Once the attack starts, we are to probe along the west bank and look for a small detachment of infantrymen from Ross's command. They made a reconnaissance yesterday and did not show at the point of rendezvous. It is our job to find them. It will be dangerous. We'll be within good range of the fort. The ironclads will try to protect us."

The officer looked about at the men. "Any questions?"

There was no response.

"Carry on," he said and walked toward the ladder that led up to his post of command.

"He doesn't like this no more than we do," said Joe Bell sourly.

Ab Cory nodded. He looked about at his crew. "You've done your duty well," he said quietly. "The last day or two some of you have been a little slow in obeying orders. It is the heat and the mosquitoes, and one thing or another. I'll forget that, mates. *But*...today it will be hard going. We'll be under fire from that pesky little fort and I'll want you to snap to it, do your duty, and forget to grouse."

It was getting lighter.

"Run out!" snapped Ab Cory.

They heaved the heavy gun forward, and anyone could see that their drill did not have the snap and precision of other times. Gun ports were triced up to the noise of whining tackles. Coal scoops rattled constantly in the fireroom, and the heat from the boilers became hotter and thicker. Hissing steam worked on everyone's nerves. Feet grated on the sandy decks. There were quite a few men missing from the gun crews. Men that Greg Hollister had grown to know and like-They had gone upriver in the *Rattler* or had been buried in the stinking ooze along the shores of the Tallahatchie.

The signal for attack was the coughing roar of the big

mortar on the *Petrel*. The shell arced upward with its sputtering fuse describing a thin red line through the graying sky. It dropped swiftly and then the heavy explosion came. The *DeKalb* churned past and opened fire, and soon the river was blanketed in smoke and mist, dotted by the bright flashes of the guns and the quick pinpoints of light from rebel muskets.

Birds rose from the swamps and departed in clouds as the guns' reports slammed back and forth. The *Chillicothe* joined battle, too. Geysers of mud and water spouted here and there. The gunboats fired low and their shells and solid shot skipped across the water surface and slammed into the patchwork fort. The light was brighter now and the red and blue of the rebel flag could be seen.

Bells jingled in the engine room of the *Dart* and she moved downstream through the swirling smoke. The gun crews were at their battle stations. The tinclad eased along the west bank. Shot spouted water against her rusty sides and sluiced it in through the ports. All eyes were on the messy tangle of willows, cypresses, vines, canes and mud, looking for muddy blue uniforms.

Now the fort could get a clear shot at them, although the two ironclads and the mortar boat were still blasting away. The tinclad edged past the *Star of the West*.

A solid shot slammed through both sides of the tinclad just above the breechings, the joint that held the stack bases to the furnaces. The *Dart* turned inshore, still probing and looking through the thick smoke.

Something crashed above the gun deck and a moment later a shell plowed through a hole and struck hard on the gundeck. The men stared at it but it did not go off. Tom Bruce wiped cold sweat from his face and bent to look at the deadly thing. He grinned wanly. 'That reb gunner was in a right smart hurry," he said shakily. "He forgot to remove the lead patch from the fuse."

Greg felt a little sick. He was near his station and he could hear the thudding of driftwood against the side of the tinclad as she audaciously scouted along the tangled bank. If there were any torpedoes in that mess they were plowing into...

"Open fire!" called out Mister Luscombe.

The larboard howitzers opened up, cracking flatly, then rolling back against their tackles.

"Stand clear!" commanded Ab Cory. He jerked the lanyard and Abe Lincoln went to work, skipping a solid shot across the water. "Run in!"

Greg worked swiftly, handing the charge to Taffy, spinning about to get another charge as the gun was loaded, standing aside as the big Dahlgren roared, then handing Taffy a fresh charge. The sweat broke out on his naked upper body and soaked through the scarf that he had bound about his hair. The thick smoke billowed back from the gun muzzles and filled the hot steamy interior of the tinclad as she poked along the shore line looking for those lost men in blue.

The gun stopped firing as the *Dart* shifted her course. Greg stood there waiting for the next command, holding the heavy powder charge in his sweat-greasy hands. He saw Chip Powers standing near an empty port staring at the close-by shore line. Then the towhead swung up a leg over the edge of the port and slid outside onto the narrow deck. Greg could see him standing there staring at the shore line.

The gun crew were peering through the low-lying smoke and mist-on the river. Greg stepped back a little and looked out of the port. The rebel guns were cracking steadily. A gout of mud and water spouted up and gushed through a port. Two of the *Dart*'s howitzers answered the fire. Then somewhere aft there was a tremendous crashing noise and splinters flew through the interior of the tinclad in a deadly rain.

"Fire!" yelled a crewman.

"Fire-fighting detail aft!" called out Webb Downey.

The tinclad shook again as she was struck. The

howitzers roared defiance. Greg looked out at Chip. The boy was casting loose a small gig that had been towed alongside the tinclad. His mind was on something, but what it was Greg didn't know.

"Man the pumps! We're taking water fast!" came the harsh order.

The *Dart* was nosing into a thick tangle of driftwood and moving toward the shore. Bells jingled in the engine room and the great paddle wheels went into reverse, but the tinclad still had way on her and she kept on moving. It was then that Greg knew what Chip Powers was doing. He was standing in the gig, frantically shoving driftwood aside as he tried to get near a heavy-looking box that floated even with the surface of the water. A thick wire stretched from the box to the bank, where it was attached to a tree stump, and near the tree stump were furtive figures in the butternut uniforms of the Confederacy.

"Man the pumps!" came the cry again.

Greg was a pumpman. He dropped the powder charge and turned to report to his pumping station. Chip was dragging the gig closer and closer to the floating box. It was some sort of torpedo, of that Greg was sure, and the *Dart* was getting closer and closer to it. Chip dropped on his knees in the boat and gripped the wire. A bullet sang from the shore, and the boy grabbed at the gunwale of the gig, then fell slowly over the side into the driftwood.

Greg stepped through the port. He looked back. The pump parties and fire-control parties had raced aft to fight leaks and fires. It was his duty to join them. But Chip was in the water, and the *Dart* was getting closer and closer to the torpedo.

Greg raced forward on the narrow side deck until he reached the bows. He couldn't reach that torpedo by swimming. He took a chance and leaped onto a thick log. He leaped from it to a tangle of flotsam, felt it sink beneath his feet, then reached a second log. He ran the whole length of it, with his bare feet slipping and sliding on the slime that coated it.

The guns were still roaring and crashing. The smoke was thicker than ever and the sound of the panting engines of the boats was under all the noise. Greg glanced back over his shoulder and saw that the *Dart* was still moving toward the torpedo. He leaped desperately for the gig, felt it wallow precariously beneath him as he landed it, then ran forward toward the torpedo. There was no time to examine it. He shoved at it, got it in front of the gig, then gripped the oars. He rowed hard, driving the sluggish box ahead of him as the *Dart* began to tower over him. Bullets sang about his ears.

Slowly but surely, he forced the torpedo toward the shore. He could see the rebels standing there aiming at him. A slug whipped through the wooden side of the gig.

Now the snub nose of the *Dart* was just astern. It struck the gig and drove it aside. There was a splintering of wood. But the torpedo was out of the way of the tinclad at last. The side of the *Dart* raked and grated past the gig. The great sternwheel was thrashing in reverse and her forward way was almost gone now. Slowly, ever so slowly, the tin-clad moved back, safe from the deadly torpedo.

The gig was sinking. Greg saw Chip lying across a tangle of wood and brush and he was close to the beating paddles of the tinclad. Greg stepped from the sinking gig, ran lightly across the driftwood and flotsam and then plunged down into the water close by the side of Chip. He gripped the towheaded boy by his thick thatch and forced his way through the tangle, not daring to look back at those great paddles beating up a frothy storm so close behind them.

The waves from the paddles swung both boys up and down and then cast them on a mudbank. The *Dart* was in full reverse now, a good fifty yards from the torpedo. It was then that one of the rebels jerked the wire in savage frustration. The torpedo exploded with a tremendous crash, sending up a muddy plume of water high into the air, higher than the top of the tinclad's pilothouse. The explosion struck the rebels on the bank, and when the water cascaded down, Greg saw that they had been killed or desperately wounded by the explosion.

The *Dart* rocked wildly in the blast but she was safe now. She was going astern at full speed, fighting the current of the river, while smoke poured from her after ports. She looked badly mauled.

"Ahoy, *Dart!*" screamed Greg.

Chip moved a little and moaned. His face was fish-belly white and a thin trickle of watery blood coursed down it.

"Ahoy, the *Dart!*" yelled Greg hoarsely.

It was no use. The guns were still roaring and the paddles thrashing, and amidst the hissing of steam and the crackling of the exhausts no voice could have been heard.

The tinclad turned slowly and then her wheel drove her forward, upstream, through the drifting smoke and mist, brushing aside trailing Spanish moss from-the trees at the river's brink.

Greg gripped Chip by the shoulders and dragged him farther up the muddy shore. He crouched beside him in a dank nest of driftwood and vines, staring woefully out at the river, as the guns crashed on and on.

Then one by one the Federal vessels moved upstream, until only the *DeKalb* was in sight, firing steadily. Then she, too, was gone. Fort Pemberton was still there and not taken, and the Federal fleet would go back to Yazoo Pass, mission not accomplished, while two boys from the United States Light Draft *Dart* would be listed as missing in action.

CHAPTER NINE

The Swamp Fugitives

The afternoon sun was slanting down through the tangled treetops when Greg returned to the place where he had left Chip. Greg was wet to his armpits, scratched and lacerated by vines and brush, and hungry as a fledgling. Time and time again he had been forced to retrace his steps when he had found himself sinking into the morass.

The Federal vessels were long gone. For a time, earlier in the afternoon, he had seen their thick black smoke hanging over the trees to the north. He knew they were Federal vessels because of the black coal smoke, for almost all of the rebel vessels were wood burners.

The swamps were comparatively quiet now that the guns no longer blasted away at each other. The wind had shifted, and it had become a little cooler and there seemed to be the promise of rain in the damp air. Mist still boiled up from the sluggish waters and dripped from the leaves.

Greg panted heavily as he neared the Tallahatchie. The rebels were still in the fort, as he could hear their voices carried to him by the wind. Now and then, as he had looked about the swamp he had heard the progress of men through the dripping tangle. Rebels for sure.

Maybe they were patrolling. Maybe they were looking for Yankees. Maybe they were looking for Chip and Greg.

He bent low as he neared the riverbank. The fort was hardly visible through the drifting mist but sound carried well. Greg whistled softly and heard Chip's return whistle. Greg crawled into the hole Chip had burrowed into the driftwood tangle. "How does it go?" he asked anxiously.

Chip patted the dirty bandage he had around his head. "You can't kill a Powers by hittin' 'em on the head. What'd you find out?"

Greg shrugged. "There's more water, more cypresses, more vines and more smell every way you go."

"That's what I figured."

Greg rubbed his tired eyes. "You see any of our boys?"

"Only one and he wasn't any help. He floated by an hour ago."

Greg nodded. He had seen other bodies in the swamp. Yank and Johnny Reb alike. "We can't get anywhere without a boat, mate."

Chip grinned. "The gig drifted ashore a couple of hours ago. I patched her up after I emptied her out."

"Great! Now that we got transportation, where do we go?"

Chip leaned back. "We can always cross the Tallahatchie and give ourselves up. Wait!" he said quickly, as he saw the look in Greg's eyes. "I was only kiddin', mate!"

"You better be," threatened Greg.

Chip reached down behind him. "Found these, too. The rebels who were going to set off the torpedo under the *Dart* left 'em behind when they got blowed up." He held up a Navy Colt revolver, complete with gun belt, ammunition, and cap pouches. He patted the stock of a short-barreled carbine which he had taken out with the revolver.

Greg grinned. They both had their sheath knives as well as the two guns. The gig would get them afloat. But where would they go? "Which way do we go, Chip?" he asked.

The boy rubbed his jaws. "We could head back upriver, but it would be hard going and we'd never catch up with the fleet."

"No."

"Downriver we'd have to pass through rebel country."

"Yup."

Chip looked toward the setting sun. "That's the only way left."

Greg looked at the thick tangle beyond them and shivered a little. A man could get lost in there and never be found. "What's between us and the Mississippi?" he asked.

"I looked at a map in the pilothouse the other day. First comes the Big Sunflower River, then the Bogue Phalia, and after that Deer Creek."

"Ho," said Greg dryly, "is that *all*?"

Chip shook his head. "Those are the *big* ones, bub. The Lord alone knows how many *little* ones there are."

A cold, searching wind crept through the swamp. The muted sound of oars creaking in rowlocks, and the splashing of the oars themselves.

"Small boat," said Chip quickly.

"And it's a cinch it isn't one of ours!"

Greg crawled from the hide-out and saw the gig drawn partway up the bank of a small stream that fed into the Tallahatchie. He beckoned Chip on, then crawled toward the gig. The noise from the approaching boat was louder now. The boys crawled into the gig and Greg shoved it -ill with an oar. It drifted out into the stream.

"Yuh say yuh saw a Yankee snoopin' around heah, Jim?" a soft voice said out of the mist.

The oars had stopped.

"Yeh," said another voice. "Looked like a young lad. Weren't one of ouah boys, I don't think."

The oars splashed again.

Greg gripped a vine and drew the gig into a willow thicket. Chip closed a hard hand on Greg's arm.

Through the mist they could see the vague outline of a big rowboat and the silhouettes of men wearing slouch hats, seated in it. Rifles leaned against the gunwales.

'Them Yankee gunboats bit off mor'n they could chaw, eh, boys?" said one of the men.

"We gave 'em whatfor," said another.

The boat glided right into the stream and the oars stopped. Chip and Greg sank down into the wet bottom of the gig. The little craft had been liberally plastered with mud and was hardly distinguishable, but the men looking for them were sharp-eyed Mississippians, used to the swamps, who could spot a squirrel at a hundred yards no matter how tightly it clung to the bark of a tree. *They could shoot at it and hit it, too.*

"Yuh reckon them Yankee gunboats will come back, sarge?" asked one of the men.

"Naw! Some of ouah boys scouted upriver after 'em. They're gone all right." The sergeant laughed. "Thought they had a back way into Vicksburg. They didn't figger on Loring's Brigade and Ol' Fort Pemberton. Hawww!"

The men eyed the dank and misty swamp, and it seemed to the two boys that they were looking right into the gig.

"See anything?" asked the sergeant at last.

One of the men shivered. "Nothing but fever, sarge."

"Yeh."

Cold sweat rolled down Greg's face. He wanted to cough, sneeze, cry out, get up and run, do anything but lie there in the wet muddy bottom of that boat waiting for a rifle shot lo crack out and maybe to feel the impact of a minie ball in his back.

The oars grated and creaked in the rowlocks. Then the boat moved slowly out onto the broad Tallahatchie and was gone. Chip slowly let out his breath and looked at Greg. "I could 'a sworn they had us right in their sights, bub."

"Aye, bub!"

"Let's git!"

They pulled the gig farther upstream by means of the vines and overhanging tree branches. The sun was almost gone before Greg placed the oars in the rowlocks and began to pull steadily upstream conned by Chip, who sat in the stern sheets like an odd-looking gnome wearing a dirty white hat. Beyond them was the great swamp of the Yazoo Valley, thick and almost impenetrable. They had no map or chart, no way of knowing that they would come out onto the great Mississippi. But they were still free, and that was enough to spur them on.

―――――

THE RAIN SLANTED DOWN STEADILY. Greg pulled the gig around a sharp bend.

"Look!" said Chip.

A tumble-down structure lay on the muddy bank, thickly covered with vines. "Odd-lookin' house," said Greg.

Chip raised the carbine. "Ain't a house at all. Looks like an old boat, bub."

"Yup."

Greg eased the gig toward the shore and ran it into the soft mud. The rain was getting colder, and if the two of them stayed out in it much longer they'd come down with fever. They'd be too weak to travel. There were certainly no Federals left in that particular area. If they did come down with fever and the Confederates didn't find them, they'd die there. It wasn't a pleasant thought.

The two boys hauled the boat up a little higher and then walked slowly toward the odd-looking structure. It had been a boat all right, but someone had overturned it, raised it on props, then walled in the area between the boat and the ground. There were several oddly shaped and secretive-looking windows cut into the sagging walls and the door was set askew and was partly open.

Chip looked at Greg. Neither one of them wanted to probe into that crazy-looking structure but the rain was coming down harder and seemed to be colder.

"Here goes," said Greg. He had buckled the gun belt about his lean waist. He drew the heavy Colt from the holster and cocked it. He had never killed a man this way. He had no idea of how many men he had helped to kill by serving naval guns. But that was different. The gun did the dirty work. The gun crew were but its slaves.

Something clicked crisply behind Greg. He whirled and knew that Chip had cocked the carbine. The boy grinned weakly. "Go on, bub," he said softly, "you'll be a hero before your mother."

Greg stopped just outside the doorway and peered in. It was dark and dank. Then he gathered his courage and stepped inside with the Colt held at waist level and his finger tightening on the trigger. His eyes grew accustomed to the darkness. He walked forward and saw several crude bunks against the left wall, a battered and rusting stove at the rear, and a number of boxes and barrels scattered about. His foot struck something that clanked dully, and he looked down to see a tangled mess of rusted metal work and chain. He knew what those were. Traps. He had run a short trap line himself in Wisconsin.

Something scuttled behind a bunk and Greg's throat went dry. He could not cry out. Then a large rat scrambled through a hole in the wall and vanished. Greg wiped the cold sweat from his forehead. He peered at one of the boxes. It was sealed and the stenciled letters were easy to read. "Pilot Bread. U.S. Government Bakery, Evansville, Indiana," he read aloud.

Chip whistled softly.

Greg walked to the doorway. "No one here except us

swamp rats," he said. 'There's a full box of pilot bread here, so we won't starve anyway."

The towheaded boy peered about. "How'd it get here?" he asked suspiciously.

Greg grinned. "Why, the supply officer knew we were coming, bub, and he had it delivered here."

"You make my sides ache."

"If we don't get dry and get something to eat, it'll be more than your sides aching, bub."

They hauled the gig into thick willow withes along the shore and covered it with brush they gathered. Chip carefully filled in their footprints and dragged a branch over the ground to help conceal the marks.

They got inside the structure. Mosquitoes buzzed unpleasantly about them. Chip got to work with his sheath knife and pried open the box of bread. He tapped some of the food. "We could drive nails with these," he said thoughtfully. He looked about. "If we had some bacon grease, we could make hoosh."

"Hoss?"

"No! Hoooosh! Bread crumbled into hot fat. It ain't bad."

"Not if you have the fat, bub."

Chip prowled about. He pulled out a metal box from under one of the bunks and undid the hasp. He threw back the lid and then grinned up at Greg. "Found the larder," he said. He lifted up a side of bacon wrapped in greasy cloth.

"I wonder who uses this place?"

Chip shrugged. "Doesn't make much difference. If they don't come back, we have it all to ourselves. If they do come back, they'll either be trappers or soldiers. Either way, they'll be rebels."

They had to risk a fire. The smoke would be concealed by the rain and the mist, and maybe the odor of the burning wood would be diffused. There was fire-wood stacked beside the stove. Greg started a fire while

Chip whistled softly and got the food ready. The stove leaked smoke, which was hard on the eyes, but harder on the mosquitoes.

Chip prepared his "hoosh" and Greg had to admit it wasn't too bad. They ate the mess, along with thick strips of the salty bacon, and filled up with chunks of the pilot bread dipped into the grease. When they had finished, Chip began to slice up the rest of the bacon to fry it.

"I don't want any more right now," said Greg.

"You ain't getting any, bub. These will be our iron rations. Might be we won't have a chance to make a fire for a few days."

There was a faint suggestion of moonlight through the overcast when Greg went outside. It was a strange and eerie place. The wind moaned softly through the tangled woods. Now and then he heard a mysterious splashing noise. The mist seemed to boil up like steam from the water. The rain had stopped and the mosquitoes were out in full force whining about Greg's head. Somewhere, far off in the great swamp, a catamount screamed faintly and shrilly like a terrorized woman.

There was no sign of human life. Greg wondered how those Mississippians who trapped the swamp were ever able to find their way about in it.

He went back into the shelter. Chip had lighted a stub of candle and was busy exploring the place. He handed Greg a tattered shirt and a wide-brimmed hat, pierced with holes. Greg put them on and Chip grinned widely. "You look like Ol' Rip Van Winkle, bub."

They looked pretty bad, but it was better than running about in a fever swamp with nothing on from the waist up. The fire was still glowing in the old stove so they dried their clothing at it. Chip squatted beside the stove. "Best thing to do is stand guard tonight, eh, Greg?"

Greg nodded. "I don't want any of those Mississippians creeping up on us."

"Might be when we get farther west, we won't run into so many of them."

"I don't know," said Greg gloomily. "This whole Yazoo Valley is swarming with them, Zelah."

"Sure is, Gregory."

"You want to take first guard?"

"All right with me, bub."

Greg crawled into one of the rickety bunks. It was a little damp and it had a strong odor to it, but it was filled with dried fern and there were rough coverings made of sacking. He was tired enough to go to sleep almost at once.

———

GREG SLOWLY OPENED his eyes and raised his head. Then with a start he looked about. He was supposed to be on guard, but he knew now he had dozed off. It must be close to dawn. The swamp was quiet; it was almost *too* quiet.

He stood up and felt the stiffness in his muscles from the dampness. He looked down toward the misty shore fifty feet from where he stood with his back next to the old building. There was something just offshore. Something solid where nothing solid should have been. There was nothing out there but black swamp water. He knew that. But there *was* something out there!

He blinked his eyes, bent his head a little forward and stared hard. Then slowly, as though being formed from the swirling mist by the skillful hands of a master sorcerer, the shape of a man showed dimly. He was standing in a low-sided, flat-bottomed skiff, and it seemed as though he was staring right at Greg.

Greg opened his mouth and closed it. Then he raised the carbine slowly and leveled at his hip. Beyond the man in the skiff, he could see other indistinct and mysterious shapes in the dim gray light of dawn. More men, in flat-bottomed skiffs, perhaps a dozen of them, all told. There wasn't any doubt in his mind as to who they were either. Soldiers or trappers, it was all the same.

Greg eased back into the darkness of the structure. "Chip." he said softly.

"Yes?"

"There are men out there," said Greg in a low voice.

"Ours?"

"No. They're getting ready to land." Greg wet his dry lips. "They can't miss finding the gig."

They both knew what that would mean. They were on a sort of island and they could never get through the swamp without a boat.

Something bumped the shore. Chip was beside Greg in an instant. They peered through one of the crazy windows. Three skiffs were plainly seen. Four men stood on the muddy shore, with long rifles in their hands, looking directly toward the boathouse. Another man was standing near the willow withes. He whistled softly, then walked into the tangle. He had found the gig.

Out in the swirling mist was another boat, a bigger one, with five or six men in it.

"Trapped," said Chip faintly.

"No!"

"Talk big, bub, but you ain't going to get out of this mess!"

Greg gripped Chip by the arm. "Sneak out the back," he said softly. "Make a racket. Shoot! Yell! Anything! But draw them back there."

"Sure...sure! You got big ideas all right. What happens then? You get back to the fleet and tell 'em what a hero Ol' Chip was to save your life?" hissed Chip angrily.

Greg drew his lips back from his teeth. "Listen, Windy," he said harshly, Tm going to get one of those skiffs while you're making noises like a platoon of Yankee soldiers."

Chip swallowed hard. "Sorry, bub."

"Hide in the brush. When you have counted to about two hundred, you start your little show, bub." Greg handed him the Colt. "Use it to make noise, *or any other way you have to*."

"I get it."

They padded to the back of the structure and eased out of the big rear window. Chip gripped Greg hard by the arm and then vanished into the dripping brush. Greg bent low and padded to his left until he was in amongst the trees. He crawled through the clinging mud until he could see the boats. Four of the men stood close to the house. Another man was farther down the shore looking for tracks. The big skiff out in the mist had vanished as mysteriously as it had appeared, but Greg knew it was still out there, manned with men who could hear and see like Indians.

Greg lay down flat and bellied toward the end skiff. He reached the side of it and looked at the boathouse. The men were still standing there. If he tried to get into the skiff, they'd surely see him.

"Eee-yowww!" the wild scream came out of the thick tangle behind the house, and there wasn't any doubt as to who it was that gave voice. "Yipppeee! Yeow! Charge! Forward, men! First platoon follow me! Second platoon to the right! Third to the left! *Get them rebels*!" The last command was punctuated by the crack of a pistol shot.

Greg saw the men scatter into the brush at the sides of the shack, then he rolled over into the skiff and placed his carbine on a thwart. He gripped a pole and got up on his knees. He shoved off into the black waters. He was a good twenty feet from shore when the man who had been looking for tracks raised his rifle and fired. The slug whipped through the water inches from the stern of the skiff.

Chip was still at it. "Fix bayonets! Give 'em the cold steel, boys! *The Union forever*!" The Colt cracked again.

Greg poled into the mist, striving to reach the east

end of the low island. He rounded it slowly, ran aground and was forced to go over the side to get it into deeper water, and then he could hardly free his legs from the clinging mud. He reached the northern side of the island and saw a movement in a thicket. Then he saw a towhead bobbing up and down. Greg whistled shrilly and a moment later two rifles cracked from beside the boathouse. Chip disappeared and for one awful moment Greg stared at the island until he saw Chip plunge out of the brush and into the water, forcing himself toward the skiff. Greg shoved the skiff toward the boy, and Chip pulled himself over the side, gripped a pole, and shoved it into the water against the bottom.

"Git!" he yelled to Greg.

They swung about into the mist as rifle fire sparkled from the island and men yelled. Greg looked back. They were fairly safe. It was almost impossible to distinguish anything clearly in that mist and in the gray light.

"Look!" screamed Chip.

Greg turned. The big skiff was bearing down on them, with four men poling like mad toward the two boys, while another man stood up in the bow, aiming his rifle at them. Greg snatched up the carbine and cocked it. The cap was on the nipple. He raised the carbine, aimed at the sharpshooter and squeezed the trigger just as the man's rifle spat smoke and flame. The slug whispered past Greg's ear, and he saw the tall man sink slowly back into the skiff, dropping his rifle over the side. He fell against two of the other men and the skiff lost way.

"Larboard!" cried Chip.

They swung the skiff and darted between two huge rotting stumps that thrust themselves up from the water. They jabbed their poles down hard and drove the skiff on. It rocked crazily and water sloshed about their feet. Time and time again they had to duck to avoid over-hanging branches. Rifles spoke behind them and the unseen slugs whipped through brush and tree leaves searching for them.

Cold as it was, the hot sweat dripped from the faces of the two boys, and all the time Greg poled on he thought of the tall bearded man he had shot down back there near the island. There was a sickness within him that he could not dispel.

CHAPTER TEN

Cypress Bayou

"It's thunder, bub, as sure as I'm sitting here!" said Chip Powers pugnaciously. Greg shook his head.

"You think you know so much!" Greg leaned on his pole and held the skiff steady. They had been in the swamps for ten days now, forging ever slowly to the west. Somewhere in the tangle behind them they had crossed the Little Sunflower, or at least they had figured it was the Little Sunflower.

Once again, they heard the deep muttering sound from the southwest. "Thunder!" insisted Chip.

Greg listened to it. He had heard that sound too many times in recent months not to know what it was. It was the deep ringing of naval guns coming to them across the swampy land. There was a different sound to them as compared to army artillery. He really couldn't say how he knew they were naval guns, but he was willing to bet on it.

They waited there in the sunlit swamp. The mud had a sharp fetid odor to it as the sun warmed it. The sun had been coming out for the past few days, but this day there were heavy and ominous-looking clouds in the direction from which the sound was coming.

Both boys were tired-and edgy. Several times they had

been sure-they had been followed. Far behind them they thought they had seen skulking figures, and several times they had heard gunshots in the distance. Two nights they had been forced to sleep in the leaky skiff. Three nights had been spent in a ramshackle hut buried in vines on a tiny islet hardly bigger than the hut itself, while they patiently repaired the skiff with whatever materials they could find. Chip had managed to catch a few small fish. Their mainstay had been the hard pilot bread with which they had filled their pockets. Most of the time it was wet, but it was edible.

They had been lost innumerable times, forced to back trail, often winding up in a silent, brooding bayou with seemingly no inlet or outlet. Always there were the mosquitoes, gnats, red bugs and fleas. It seemed to be the vast breeding ground for every kind of flying, crawling and biting insect Greg had ever seen. Both boys were covered with lumps, swellings and scratches. They had tried everything to drive the pests away, using bacon grease, mud, ashes and various other concoctions with no results whatsoever.

The dull, muttering noise came again.

Chip looked at Greg. "If those *are* guns, bub, they could be ours, couldn't they?"

Greg nodded. Chip knew as well as he did that the rebels had gunboats in the rivers, too, and that some of them carried big guns. Rodmans, Parrotts, and Dahlgrens. Greg eyed the sun. They had been trending to the southwest the past few days. The courses of the rivers and creeks flowed in a general southerly direction toward the Yazoo, which in turn flowed diagonally in a southwesterly direction to the mighty Mississippi, meeting it west of Vicksburg.

Chip slapped at a mosquito. "I been thinking about that map. Greg. Now and then a chunk of it falls into place like a piece in a puzzle. We've been trending south-west, following the watercourses, which means we also been getting farther and farther south. More south than west in fact. There's a mess of waterways north of the Yazoo. Cypress Bayou, Deer Creek, Black Bayou, the Little Sunflower and Steele's Bayou, and they are all related to each other, like girls in Georgia."

"So?"

Chip rubbed at the mud on his dirty face. "I got a chilly feeling we've passed into one of them waterways, and that we're a heck of a lot farther south than we think we are."

"Nice."

"Yup."

The rolling thunder came to them again as the warm wind shifted. "There's a real hassle going on over there, Chip," said Greg quietly. "You *know* those are guns, don't you?"

"Yup."

"You want to take a chance and see if those are our gunboats?"

The towhead grinned. "I was waiting for you to ask me that."

"Let's go then."

"Keno!"

"Shove off forward! Shove off aft! *Mister* Powers!"

"Aye, aye, sir!"

"Take over the conn, sir, and mind you keep off the mud banks!"

"Aye, aye, sir!"

They moved slowly along the twisting waterway, getting ever closer to the sullen muttering of big guns dealing out death and destruction in the bitter fight to reach and capture Vicksburg, the Gibraltar of the Mississippi.

They saw the thick layers of smoke hanging over the treetops to the southwest. "Black smoke," said Chip. "Those must be our boats."

"We hope."

Now and then the swamp seemed to shake as a big gun let go, and white powder smoke swirled up to mingle with the black coal smoke.

There was a tired eagerness in the boys. They had bolstered each other's courage in the trying days that lay behind them and now they knew that they were close to success in finding the Federal forces. They glanced appreciatively at each other as they threaded their way through the mazes of water and trees. Greg thought back on the night they had made the pact between themselves, before they had left on the "Inland Cruise" of the *Dart*. *Let's promise to stick together, to help each other out, and if one of us weakens, the other is to straighten him out in a hurry, the hard way!*

It wasn't until Chip looked back at Greg with a tired smile that Greg realized he had unconsciously spoken aloud. "Aye, aye, mate," Chip said quietly.

Closer and closer they drew to the noise and the smoke, through the drowned land. Here, the channel was hardly distinguishable, for the water had flowed fifteen feet deep over the land. The heavy rains of the past weeks had virtually made a vast, tree-stippled lake of the Yazoo Valley, covering hundreds of square miles with water.

"If those *are* our boats," said Chip, "they must have come from the south, probably from the lower part of the Yazoo. Farther up the river is Haynes's Bluff and that's heavily fortified. Looks like our boys may be trying to find a way around it...it's a cinch we didn't do much good trying to outflank the rebs."

Greg looked about them. They certainly weren't in any channel now. "Looks like a road," he said.

Chip grinned. "It is, and a real wet one. Look up at the trees, bub."

The branches were strangely swollen and humped in places, and it wasn't until one of the humps moved that Greg realized the humps and swollen spots were actually raccoons, rats and mice. Even a bedraggled and wet wildcat crouched in a tree fork, glaring down at the two boys.

The trees came together high overhead and the boys moved in a shadowed world of water and brush. Something sailed slowly across an open patch, and Greg felt an uneasy feeling in the pit of his stomach. It had been a great, ragged-looking buzzard.

Here and there huge trees had fallen because the soaked ground had loosened about their roots. Ahead of the slowly moving skiff was a wide-open area. Chip looked back. "Probably a drowned cotton field," he said. "We'd better skin it."

They poled into the thick woods, forcing their way at times through thick willow growths. Chip held up a hand as they reached the far side of the cotton field. Greg rammed his pole down into the soft bottom to anchor the skiff. He looked past Chip and then whistled softly. There were levees ahead of them and the water lapped over them here and there. On a higher land area were a number of buildings, and in front of them was a long rickety wharf piled high with cotton bales beneath a roof supported on poles.

The smoke was thick over the trees a mile or so away from the two boys and the gunfire had died away, but the shifting wind brought other noises. Something mighty big was going on down there.

"Look at that cotton," said Greg. "A man could make a fortune if he could get that stuff out of here and to a northern mill, or to England. The blockade-runners on the run to the Bahamas or Halifax are making fortunes in one trip alone!"

Chip looked down at the leaky skiff. "Couldn't get much cargo in this thing, bub, and if we did, we couldn't outrun an angry mud turtle."

Greg rubbed his dirty face. "So, as long as *we* can't get it out of here, we could fix it so that no one else could."

Chip turned. "You mean?"

"You got it, bub. Have you any matches left?"

"Just enough, bub, just enough..."

They poled the skiff to the muddy shore and hid it in the willows. Chip eyed the water between the levees. "This *might* be Cypress Bayou, and if it is, we've sure made some miles from Fort Pemberton, bub."

They took the carbine and the revolver from the skiff and padded their way through the woods toward the buildings. There might be food in them. Greg could feel his stomach tighten. If they could reach those gunboats, they'd eat like kings, but they weren't aboard one of them yet.

They were close to a sagging shed when Chip stopped short and held out a warning hand to Greg. Three men walked quickly across a gap between the shed and another building and they carried rifles. "How close are them Yankees, Charlie?" one of them asked.

"Two—three miles, Ben."

"You think we can save the cotton?"

"How? No boats. No slaves to get it out of here. There's only one answer, Ben."

"The torch?"

"Yes."

The two boys edged close to the building and peered around the end. The three men were walking quickly toward the wharf. "Saves us a job," whispered Chip.

Greg looked at the buildings. "This place looks like it has been deserted for a long time."

"Yup. You often find 'em like that in this country. Sometimes the fever has run them out, or us Yankees. Ain't sure which is the worst, according to them."

"Look!" said Greg. He sank down to the ground and pulled Chip with him.

A small stern-wheel craft had rounded a bend and was chuffing slowly toward the wharf. It was towing a flatboat upon which was mounted a brass howitzer and a small coehorn mortar. Soldiers were on the stern wheeler and the flatboat. The steamer neared the wharf and they could see the faded letters on the side. "*Bayou Belle*," said Chip.

"Nice place for us," said Greg.

The steamer slowed down and then lost way. The paddle wheels thrashed in reverse to slow her down still further. A Confederate officer stood at the bow of the steamer. He cupped his hands about his mouth. "Burn that cotton!" he yelled.

One of the three men held up a torch. "We was just getting ready to, Captain! How close are they?"

"A few miles. It's that devil Porter and his boats! He has five ironclads, four tugs and some mortar boats. That madman Sherman has thousands of troops on transports along with Porter's boats."

"What about the rams at Yazoo City? Can't they come down and fight 'em, Captain?"

The officer waved a hand in disgust. "They're not a quarter finished and have no engines! Fire up, boys!"

The steamer went on up the bayou. In a short time, the smoke began to drift up from the cotton bales.

"They'll burn like those two or three days," said Chip.

"Thousands of dollars."

"Yup."

The three men walked to a skiff and boarded it, poling out into the bayou. On the far shore a thin line of butternut-clad figures plodded past in the mud. Confederate soldiers. It was getting on late in the afternoon.

Chip looked at Greg. "Ain't no use trying to get down to them ironclads with this country alive with rebels. Let's look for some grub and a place to hide out. Instead of us going to the gunboats, let them come to us, bub."

"Spoken like a real soldier," said Greg.

The place seemed deserted. The fire had begun to crackle amongst the stacked cotton bales. Down the bayou they heard the thudding of a big gun, and the mingled smoke of stack and gun rose high above the trees. The sun had disappeared and a cold wind arose, sweeping along the surface of the bayou and rustling amongst the trees.

Chip shivered. He turned his thin face to Greg. "Let's get under cover, Greg."

They worked their way slowly and carefully toward the main building. It had once been a fine structure, but now the paint was almost gone and the shutters sagged away from the windows. Boards had split away and shingles had dropped from the uneven roof. Birds fluttered away from under the eaves as the two boys neared the great house.

"Won't be any food in there," said Greg dubiously.

"No, but we'll be out of this wind, and maybe we can find some better clothes than these wet rags."

They rounded the house and stopped to listen. There was no sign of life. Chip peered in through a gaping window. He motioned Greg to give him a leg up and disappeared within. A moment later he looked out. "Empty," he said. "Looks funny though."

"What do you mean?"

"You'll see, bub."

Chip helped Greg in through the window. They were in a fine big room and the furniture was still in it. Some of it was shrouded with dusty covers, while here and there rats or mice had torn into the padding of stuffed furniture. Chip walked softly across the floor to a doorway. He cased open a door and looked into a hallway. He motioned Greg on. Greg felt his cold sweat greasy on the butt of the Navy Colt as he followed Chip.

The hallway was dark and musty. At the end of it a graceful staircase rose to the upper floors. Chip poked into a kitchen and looked about. Pots, pans and skillets still hung on hooks. He looked back at Greg. "Seems funny," he said. "If the people who left this place didn't take all this stuff, it's a wonder the place hasn't been looted long ago."

Greg nodded. He had a chilly feeling about him and wasn't sure whether it had come from the dank atmosphere of the house or from his wet clothing and the cold wind that had begun to moan through the open windows and partly open doors.

Chip was rattling around in a pantry. He whistled softly. "Hey, Greg," he said softly. "Come look!"

Greg walked into the pantry. The shelves were covered with bottles, canning jars, tins and containers of all kinds. The dust was thick on them and the tracks of mice, rats and other creatures threaded through the dust.

Chip look down a jar and pried open the lid with his knife. He sniffed at it. "Jiminy! Preserves! Blackberry preserves!" He scooped up some of it on his knife and tasted it "Delicious!"

Greg felt his mouth water, but he eyed the shelves. Why had this food been left here? The place looked as though it had been abandoned long ago.

Chip had no scruples. He muttered softly to himself as he poked about. "Canned lobster salad! Peach preserves! String beans! Squash! Apple butter! Sorghum molasses! Syrup!"

"Shut up!" said Greg irritably.

Chip turned and his sharp blue eyes were a little wild. "This is like Aladdin's Cave, bub! We're rich! Rich beyond our wildest dreams! Hallelujah!"

"You're making more noise than those gunboats!"

But Chip was bustling about. He took a box and began to select articles from the shelves with a perusing eye, as though he were shopping in a big general store back in Mound City.

Greg walked out of the kitchen into the hallway and toward the front of the house. He could see the fire on the distant wharf leaping and dancing against the dark waters, flaring up and smoking thickly, raising a pall of smoke high over the bayou. The wind swayed it back and forth like a great genie being risen from a bottle or lamp. Greg shivered a little. He glanced over his shoulder at the beautiful staircase that rose into the thick darkness at the head of the stairs, and a curious feeling, half of melancholy and half of fear, filled him.

Chip staggered into the hall, carrying the heavily laden box. "Grub up!" he said. "Where's the dining saloon, bub?"

Greg fingered the Colt. Maybe they could take the food out into the swamp and eat it. It would be safer. But the wind was cold, and even as he considered the idea, a cold spit of rain came through a broken window and chilled him. "We'd better go upstairs," he said. "We can keep a better lookout up there."

"Keno!"

Greg led the way up the carpeted stairs. He gripped the cold butt of the pistol, but it gave little comfort. The place seemed ghostly and long abandoned. He reached the top of the stairs and found a great room that looked out toward the distant bayou. The flaming bales, undefeated by the drizzling rain, would serve as light for the two boys to watch for the gunboats, or rebels.

"Some bed," said Chip as he bustled about prying open cans, bottles and jars. He jerked a thumb toward it

It *was* some bed. Wide, with a great dusty canopy over it, and with torn covers upon it.

"This must have been some place in the old days," said Greg quietly.

"Yup! You like blackberry preserves or peach?"

"Both."

"That's what I thought. Grub up, bub!"

They sat at the marble-topped table, looking out over the weedy ground between them and the wharf. The food was good, although it was a fantastic mixture such as only Zelah "Chip" Powers could have concocted. The boy ladled canned lobster salad, blackberry preserves, apple butter and hard crackers into his mouth as though he were stoking a boiler on the *Dart*. "Can't figure out how they left this bully grub here," said Chip around a mouthful of crackers and jam.

"Probably poisoned, bub."

The jaw hung down. Greg reached out and gently lifted it, closing Chip's mouth. "That ain't nice manners, bub," he chided gently.

"Yeh...heh...heh...yeh. You're a jolly one, bub."

When they had finished, Chip walked to the great bed and tested it. "Nice," he said. He dropped atop it and a cloud of dust arose. He crossed his legs, rested his hands on his chest and whistled softly. "In a way," he said softly, "this is better than loading ammunition, coal, food, guns, and anything else the old *Dart* needs. Swabbing decks, dumping ashes, rowing boats, patrolling, and so on and so on."

They could still hear the distant crackling of the fire and see the leaping flames.

"All the same," said Greg at last, "I'd rather be aboard her. I'd do *twice* as much work."

There was a strange wistful tone in Chip's usually cocky voice when he answered. "You can say that again, bub, and again..."

"I'll take first watch. Chip."

Chip's only answer was a gentle snore.

CHAPTER ELEVEN

The Haunted Mansion

It was just before the dawn when Greg opened his eyes. It was cold and a chilling wind whispered softly through the big room. He turned his head. Chip was not in sight at the sentry post near the great window that looked out upon the open area between the house and the river. Greg shivered. The house was cold and the bed was cold and the wind was colder still, but coldest of all was the feeling that had entered his mind. The silent house seemed haunted, but by what he did not know.

He sat up and reached for the carbine. He turned his head one way and then the other but he could not see Chip. Probably foraging. For all his slight size the boy could eat like a growing bird. Greg dropped his feet to the floor and walked to the window. The night's rain had tried hard to put out the fires but the cotton bales were still smoldering, and now and then a huge red eye of fire winked at him like a ruby upon velvet. The thick, cloying odor of the cotton smoke hung about the house, mingling with the fetid smell of the swamp behind the house. It was quiet except for the soft soughing of the wind. It was too quiet to suit Greg.

He left the room and padded down the dark stairway.

He had never felt so alone in his life, and now and then he turned his head as though he was being closely shadowed by some frightful fiend, and the impulse within him was to leap down those creaking stairs and burst out into the open where a man could run like the wind away from the unseen horror within the house and within his teeming mind.

He reached the bottom of the stairs and the cold sweat trickled down his body. He opened his mouth to call for Chip but nothing came except a hoarse, croaking sound. Surely his pal hadn't deserted him? Not Old Reliable Chip!

Greg turned and walked softly toward the back of the house. In a pitchy corner, where no light penetrated, he halted and a soft, dry rustling sound came to him as he stood there, hardly heard above the drumbeat thudding of Greg's heart, racing like a long-stroke steam engine.

He felt the cold greasy sweat beneath his hands as they gripped the carbine tightly enough to put an indentation in the stout walnut of the stock. He opened his mouth again. He couldn't speak.

The sound was still there. A steady rustling, mingled with a crunching and grating. Then his eyes saw the dim outline of a white figure, hardly more than a few feet from Greg, and he knew where the sound came from. The figure extended a hand at the end of an incredibly long and thin arm. Greg dropped his carbine, turned on a coin, and sprinted for the front door, slamming his feet down so hard that dust rose in thin spurts from between the floor boards. "Ahhh!" he gulped frantically. He reached the door and gripped the handle but the door would not open. He looked back over his shoulder and saw the white figure moving slowly toward him, extending that horribly thin arm, while the shoulders heaved convulsively up and down in some strange ritual of the undead.

Greg did not hesitate. There were long, narrow

windows at each side of the door and some of the panes were long gone. Greg hurled himself at one of the windows, smashed through and fell heavily onto the warped flooring of the front porch. The planking gave way and he was pinned there, half in and half out, unable to move. He did not dare look back as he struggled to get free. "Ahhh!" he cried hoarsely.

"You need help, bub?" a curious voice asked.

Greg turned in his temporary prison and saw Chip standing in front of the open door, draped in a ragged white blanket. "You!" snapped Greg.

"Yeh...*me*. How come you run so fast, bub?" There was a sly, knowing grin dancing on the freckled face of the boy.

"You...I saw...well...the arm...it was long and thin...like a bony arm...I..."

"Oh *that*," said Chip casually. He drew his right arm from behind his back and held it up. He clutched a long-handled fork in his hand, upon the tines of which were five thin pickles. "I got hungry," he said simply. "Found a barrel of gherkins and dug some of 'em out with this fork. I was only offering you some of them, old friend."

Greg scrambled out onto the porch. "Sure, sure," he said grimly as he rubbed his skinned shins. "You was only *offering* me some. Did you have to do it in a dark hallway, wrapped in a white blanket, acting like a ghost?"

Chip's jaw dropped. "You thought *I* was a ghost? Me, lil' ol' Chip? Hawww!"

Greg started for him and the boy sprinted for the end of the porch, plunged from it, darted into some bushes, plunged out of the other side and legged it for the rear of the house. Greg stopped at the corner of the house. Something was wrong. Then he realized it was just breaking daylight over the vast swamp to the east. It was no time to be playing hide-and-go-seek with Chip Powers. The rebels still held that country despite the presence of the Union gunboats upon Cypress Bayou.

Greg walked to the rear of the house and into the great kitchen. „Chip had vanished. Greg got his carbine and checked it. "Chip!" he called out. No answer.

Greg started up the stairs. "Chip!"

Utter silence.

He was almost at the top of the stairs when he heard the sound of Chip's voice coming from a gloomy chamber across the hall from the room wherein, they had spent the night.

"I was only joking, Greg!" said Chip earnestly. He laughed nervously. "Never seen you so mad before. Heck, bub, I was only offering you some pickles. Sure, it looked scary, but I figured you was one of these boys with cold steel for nerves, like Ol' Chip here. Let's shake and make up, pard!"

Greg's brow wrinkled. Whom was he talking to?

"Look, Greg," pleaded Chip. "I admit you got a right to be angry, but the joke is over now. Come on! Let's shake on it!"

Greg peered into the great gloomy room from which a dank miasma seemed to emanate. He shivered a little. He could just make out Chip near the fireplace standing facing something that looked rather vague and nebulous. A figure about the size of Greg, maybe a little taller and not quite so heavy. Greg stared at it and an eerie crawling feeling came over him. The dim figure moved toward Chip.

"That's it, pard!" said Chip holding out his hand. He bent his head a little and stared. "Sure are quiet, bub," he said a little uncertainly.

"You talking to me?" asked Greg.

Chip turned his head slowly. "Greg!" he said.

"The same."

Chip turned his head to look at the dim figure in front of him. "Then who...? I... Hey, this ain't right! How can you be in front of me and behind me at the same time?"

"I'm not," said Greg. "This is me back here, bub."

The dim figure moved. A faint, groaning sound came to the boys. There was a fast movement from Chip, a rush of displaced air, the thudding of feet on the floor and then on the stairs, a shattering tinkle of glass from down below, then a splintering of wood. "Ahhh!" yelled Chip hoarsely.

Greg backed slowly toward the door. The dim figure moved again and the groaning sound came, then it seemed as though an effluvium drifted from the figure toward Greg and it sickened him. He turned and went down the stairs three at a time and hurled himself at the front door. It swung outward. Chip had fallen through the decayed boards of the porch as Greg had done in his wild flight from Chip. Greg hit the ground and turned to look back at the house. Chip crawled from the hole and looked up, too. "*There*," he said shakily.

One of the dark windows seemed to fill with a dim whiteness and Greg could have sworn he saw a thin, sunken face, just yellowed flesh over bones, tautly, as though there was nothing behind the skin *but* hard bone. Then it was gone.

Something rattled near Greg. He turned and looked at Chip. The boy's teeth were rattling like castanets. "How come you run so fast, bub?" asked Greg casually. "Sure, it looked scary, but I figured you was one of these boys with cold steel for nerves like OF Greg here."

Chip passed a hand across his sweat-dewed brow. "For the love of heaven, Greg," he said hoarsely. "What was it?"

Greg looked up at the somber, brooding old house. "I don't know," he said quietly. All the time he had been in that damp, decaying pile he had had a feeling of intermingled melancholy and fear.

Both boys had slowly backed away from the house until they stood not far from the bayou bank, partially shrouded in mist and smoke. "We'd better get back to the boat," said Chip.

"Yeah, and quickly, too."

"I..."

Something roared thunderously out in the drifting mist and smoke. There was a rushing through the air and then a blasting explosion farther up the bayou. The stink of burnt powder drifted to the boys.

"Look!" said Chip as he whirled.

Through the dimness they could see a hulking shape in the middle of the dark waters. Even as they watched, a gun flashed and the shell whined through the air lo explode in the swamp to the north.

"Gunboat!" said Chip. "One of ours! We're going home, bub!"

"Let's get the boat! They won't come in after us for fear of an ambush, and we don't look like Union men in these rags."

The big gun thudded again and again. Neither of the boys could see what she was firing at, but they were more interested in getting to their boat than anything else. The skiff had filled somewhat with water and they struggled to turn her up on one side to empty it. Then they placed her in the water and shoved off, poling swiftly toward the bayou through the thick overhanging brush. The gunboat was still blasting away. Greg was so excited he drove his pole into the water too hard, thrust it into the soft bottom and could not pull it loose. He let go of it at the last instant. But Chip could pole fast enough for both of them.

They entered the bayou proper and peered through the swirling mist and smoke toward the squat, ugly iron-clad. "It's the *Mound City*, I think," said Chip excitedly. "Nope! It's the *Cincinnati*! See the blue-topped stack!"

They rounded the last bend between them and the thundering ironclad. A shell burst just short of them, sending up a vast spout of stinking muddy water. It rocked the frail skiff from side to side. Water slopped into it. Chip poled like a madman. They were within three hundred yards of the great monster when another shell struck the levee and hurled mud and shattered trees high into the air. Greg looked up. A pine trunk, at least twenty feet long, was sailing upward. It slowed, seemed to pause, then dropped swiftly downward gaining speed every second and to Greg it looked as though it was coming straight down toward the skiff. "Abandon ship!" he yelled hoarsely, shoving Chip over the side. He followed Chip, hitting the water in a clean, shallow dive. When he bobbed to the surface, he got sick. The pine trunk had pierced the skiff, pinning it to the bottom of the bayou. If they had stayed in the skiff...

Now the mist was thicker and the smoke heavier and they could not see the *Cincinnati*. She had stopped firing. The water was cold. Greg wiped the water from his eyes. "We'd better try swimming to her," he said. "Can you make it?"

"Half frog and half alligator," said Chip. He floated on his back and shot a stream of water upward from his mouth, lazily.

They swam slowly, using the breast stroke, peering through the swirling, drifting opaqueness of mist and smoke.

"Listen!" said Chip.

They could hear the thudding of an engine and the steady *frash, frash, frash* of paddles against the waters.

"We don't have to go to her," said Chip. "She's coming to us!"

"Nice," said Greg dryly. "Supposing she runs us down or we get sucked beneath the paddles? *There's* something to think about!"

"Jiminy! Ahoy! Ahoy! Ahoy!"

"Coming!" a man yelled through the dimness.

The sound of the paddles decreased a little. Then the

two boys saw the solid structure of a vessel moving slowly toward them. Chip grinned. Then his grin faded.

It wasn't the *Cincinnati* approaching them. It was a small stern-wheel craft with a flatboat lashed alongside. The faded lettering on the side of the steamer read *Bayou Belie*. A young officer stood at the bow, dressed in worn but neat rebel gray. "Take it easy,' he said in a pleasant, soft voice. "We'll pick you up, boys."

And that's just what they did. Greg and Chip looked up into the faces of a score of curious rebel infantrymen who leaned on their long muskets. "I'm Captain Douglas DeMaris," said the officer, "Seventh Mississippi Battalion, on special duty aboard the *Bayou Belle*. Who are you gentlemen?" He smiled.

Greg opened his mouth and then shut it. He glanced at Chip. Chip was the talker. If the witty Illinois boy could think quickly enough, he might save the both of them. If they were found out to be Union men, in civilian clothing, behind rebel lines, it might not turn out too pleasantly for them.

Chip wiped the water from his face. "Coupla Kentuck boys," he said, and Greg could have sworn Chip's voice and mannerisms had changed completely. "We belong to Forster's Independent Cavalry Scout Company. We had fever and were hospitalized. We heard the boys was near Vicksburg on scout duty so we come along to find 'em. My brother commands the second platoon. He'll be right worried about us, suh."

"Uh huh! I can imagine." DeMaris rubbed his lean jaw. "How did you happen to get into Cypress Bayou?"

Chip grinned. "We had a boat," he said. "That Yankee gunboat practically blew it out'n the water. We was trying to reach the *Bayou Belle* afore the Yanks captured we-uns. Lucky for us yuh come along at the right time, suh."

"No bother," said DeMaris.

"Now if yuh kin set us ashore we'd be right grateful, suh."

Greg felt his heart skip a beat or two. Somewhere to the south of them the *Cincinnati* opened fire, and they could hear a projectile crashing through the trees beyond the bayou.

DeMaris shook his head. "No need to set you ashore," he said. He signaled to the pilothouse. "Turn her around and head up the first branch! We can't do anything here with the popguns we have! The bayou is full of enemy gunboats!"

"Where we headin', suh?" asked Chip.

"Up Steele's Bayou to Black Bayou, thence to Deer Creek and down that to Haynes's Bluff. From there you can travel overland. It isn't very far."

"To *where*, sir?" asked Greg.

The officer looked surprised. "Why, to Vicksburg! Isn't that where you want to go?"

Chip swallowed hard. "Yup," he said hollowly.

"Yup," said Greg, "that's where we want to go all right, sir."

The *Bayou Belle* turned slowly and chuffed along the bayou through the clinging, swirling mist while behind them the Yankee guns rang and thudded. They passed the deserted house in which the two boys had spent the night.

A sergeant leaned on the rail and eyed the old house. He shivered a little. "Gives me the creeps to see that place, boys," he said quietly.

"How so, sergeant?" asked a young soldier.

"That's the old Commager mansion. It's called Avalon. Useta be a beautiful place in the old days."

"What happened to it?"

"Fever. It was just at the start of the wah. The fever killed most of 'em, or drove them away."

"All of them, sarge?"

The noncom nodded. "All the *living* ones." He felt for his pipe and filled it. "They say the living ones just left it like it was. Food in the pantry and the cellars. Sheets, pillows and blankets on the beds. Furniture and utensils. Everything."

A bearded soldier grinned. "Guess the locals or the slaves cleaned that all out 'in a hurry, eh?"

The sergeant lighted his pipe and puffed at it thoughtfully. "No," he said quietly. "They say all that stuff is still in theah. Won't no one go in that *place*, I tell yuh."

"Why?" asked Chip in a small, dry voice.

"It's haunted, it is! Big room on the second floor. That third window from your right is the one. They found more than one man lying dead in the hall just outside that room, staring with eyes that couldn't see, and a look of horror frozen on their faces like they had peeped into hell itself!"

"Yeh?" asked Chip in a wee, small voice.

"Sure, as I'm standing right heah! They say it's the ghost of old Elizabeth Commager. When the rest of 'em fled the place, she wouldn't come along. Stayed there she did, all alone, and they never knew whether she died or not. Ain't no one brave enough to go in there and find out for sure, because they just don't leave that room alive. Some say she's alive and some say she's dead. Me, I ain't interested in finding out."

"Look," said a lean soldier quietly. "Ain't that someone looking out'a that window now? Right at us?"

They all stared through the wreathing mist and smoke. There was *something*, or someone, standing in the window space, staring toward the river. Someone, or *something* in white; motionless as a statue. Then the mist and smoke swirled thickly up from the bayou. The *Bayou Belle* chuffed busily onward.

Captain DeMaris came to the forward deck. He smiled at Greg. "You two boys come and get some dry clothing and something to eat."

"Thanks, suh," said Greg. "Chip!"

Chip was lying on the deck.

"Fell asleep, I guess," said the sergeant.

The bearded soldier leaned toward Chip. "Funny thing," he said reflectively. "He was right alert there whilst you was tellin' us about that place, sarge. It was when you mentioned that ghost and he saw that something in the window he just dropped off like in a dead faint."

"That's funny," said Greg dryly. "Ol Chip there is one of those boys with cold steel for nerves. Wonder what made him faint?"

The little steamer moved steadily to the northwest, trending up Cypress Bayou toward its junction with Mud Bayou. Huge trees overhung the dark waters and the growing light of day hardly penetrated the gloominess. The thudding of the engine and the steady beating of the paddles echoed through the drowned woods, and scores of birds rose protestingly into the sky. Greg somberly watched a ragged buzzard floating high in the quiet air above the bayou, looking like a great floating scrap of charred paper borne aloft by an updraft. It seemed to be an ominous sign of the future to Greg, for instead of returning to the Federal fleet they were now on their circuitous way to Vicksburg, the heart of rebel resistance on the great river; the Gibraltar of the Mississippi.

CHAPTER TWELVE

Vicksburg, Gibraltar of the Mississippi

The pale April sunshine washed the plateau above the river* upon which stately old Vicksburg had spread out her flowing skirts in the quiet days before the war. Great bluffs sloped steeply down to the Mississippi, which wound its devious course past the town in a wide turbid yellow flood. Five thousand people had lived in the town at the start of the war, but now the population had increased many times as General Pemberton brought in more and more Confederate troops to defend the city, and the passage of the river, against the aggressive pushing Yankees of the Army of the Tennessee led by a quiet, cigar-smoking soldier of the bulldog breed, named Ulysses S. Grant.

The sounds of pick and shovel were hardly absent from Vicksburg day or night. White troops and Negro slaves worked like moles to spread ever-growing lines of trenches, stippled with batteries, redoubts and bombproofs across the sprawling terrain cut by deep gullies and precipitous hills. The garrison of the city was composed of Mississippians, Alabamians, Louisianians, Georgians, Tennesseans, Mary-landers, Arkansans, Virginians, Texans and Missourians, led by a Pennsylvanian, Lieutenant-General John C. Pemberton. They were determined to hold the river passage for most of them knew that the loss of Vicksburg would mean that the Yankees could control the Mississippi from its source to the Gulf of Mexico, and that, contrary to the belief of the Confederates who believed that the Confederate cause could be won or lost in Virginia, the loss of control of the great river would mean the loss of the war itself. They had that belief in common with more than a few Northerners, amongst them General Winfield Scott, who had suggested the famed Anaconda Scheme to strangle the Confederacy's commerce and means of supply by the Federal Blockade of Southern Ocean ports, and control of the Mississippi, thus splitting the Confederacy in twain. There were three other Northerners who believed firmly in this plan: Ulysses S. Grant, Abraham Lincoln and Zelah "Chip" Powers.

Greg Hollister, erstwhile "powder monkey," United States Light Draft Ship *Dart*, drove his spade deep into the soft, loamy soil of Mississippi and straightened his back to heave the dirt up upon the slowly rising embankment in front of the river battery that looked down upon the river. The sweat ran down his tired body and dripped from the end of his tired nose. In fact, he was tired all over, hungry, thirsty and was nursing the father and mother of all grudges against the labor boss who was standing on the embankment looking down upon the river.

"Yes, suh," said the boss as he shoved back his wide brimmed straw hat and wiped his face. "Them Yankees come down that ol' river theah and we'll blast 'em right out'a that watah!"

Greg shoved his spade down into the earth again and heaved a load of dirt perilously close to the man's feet. The boss glowered a little. "You heah me, boy?"

"Yup," said Greg. "You all from Kentucky, you say?"

"Yup."

The boss shook his head. "Beats me how you talk like

a Yank while that partner of yours talks like a real Southern boy."

"He would," said Greg sourly.

"What's that?"

"He's from farther south," said Greg quickly.

All up and down the long line of entrenchments and battery positions the dirt was flying. Now and then the sun flashed from the scoured metal of picks, spades and shovels as they rose and fell, digging deeper and wider, ever deeper and wider. Here and there along the line sweating engineers and artillerymen were practically manhandling heavy guns into the positions designated for them. There were a lot of them.

"Funny how you and that Chip boy ain't found your regiment yet," said the boss. "What was it again?"

Greg had to think quickly. "Forster's Independent Cavalry Scout Company."

"Yeah...yeah... Never heard of it, did you, Sergeant Hardy?"

The sergeant took his pipe from his mouth and his gray eyes studied Greg. "No," he said thoughtfully, "and I've been in just about every fight from Fort Donelson to Chickasaw Bluffs."

Greg did not dare look at him. More than once the quiet noncommissioned officer had dropped a few leading questions to Greg, and it had always been Chip who had readily supplied the answers.

"They might be with General Van Dorn," said Greg. "He has most of the cavalry."

"Yeah." The sergeant grinned. "Meanwhile we have you."

Greg wiped the sweat from his face. "Yup," he said.

Every able-bodied man in Vicksburg who could wield a shovel and pick was hard at work. Stragglers, unattached men, third-rate units had all been impressed into the labor battalions.

"That Chip boy," said the boss admiringly. "Sharp as a scythe. Smart, too, and brave as Achilles."

Greg scowled. "Who told you that?" he asked.

"Why, come to think of it, *he* did."

"That's what I thought."

Chip was smart all right. He was a lot smarter than Greg, and the first one to admit it was Greg himself, for Chip, with his assumed Kentucky accent and ingratiating ways, had wormed himself into the mess detail, and when he wasn't hauling the water cart up and down the line of entrenchments with drinking water for the soldiers and laborers, he was lolling about the mess tent, giving the amused cooks free advice on how to cook, meanwhile getting about three times as much to eat of the already scanty rations as anyone else.

"Time out!" called the boss.

Shovels, picks and spades clattered to the bottom of the long ditch and tired, sweating men scrambled up on top of the loose dirt to catch the faint breath of wind rising from the river far below them.

"Water boy!" yelled a big Irishman.

"Water boy!" cried a bearded Mississippian.

Chip appeared in the distance, driving a sad-looking caricature of a mule, hauling a big barrel set on wheels, while Chip rode one of the shafts.

"Wonder how long that mule will stay out'a the mess pots?" said a gap-toothed man.

"Not too long," said the Irishman. "Food is getting scarcer every day."

"How so?" asked a soldier. "They say there's aplenty back inland. How come we don't get it?"

"Yankees," said the Irishman gloomily. "They run them blasted-tinclads o' theirs up and down the rivers and the bayous burning and sinking, shooting up everything in sight. Then the Yankee cavalry takes a hand, too. Out in the Gulf they have cruisers stopping our supply

ships. It's getting worse and it ain't likely to get any
better."

"Just the same," said the soldier, "I'm sticking! I'll
help hold Vicksburg if I'm starving!"

Most of the men nodded their heads as they sat along
the humped lines of raw earth. Greg eyed them. Some of
them already showed the effect of short rations on their
pinched faces, but there was no lack of resolve on those
same pinched faces. They meant to hold that river city
and to block the passage of the Mississippi despite the
slowly growing strength and ponderous approach of the
veteran Army of the Tennessee.

Sergeant Hardy watched the engineers working on a
huge gun. "We've got plenty of artillery," he said quietly.
"I heard an engineer officer say we had two smoothbore
32-pounders, two smoothbore 24-pounders, one 30-
pounder Parrott gun, one English Whitworth gun and a
10-inch mortar."

A lean Mississippian yawned. "Ain't such a much," he
said.

"What do you mean?" demanded the labor boss. "You
all mean we ain't got enough guns to stop them Yankee
teakettles from coming down the rivah?"

The lean soldier tilted back his wide-brimmed hat.
"Sure! Sure! We got enough guns to keep the Yankees
from coming down the rivah in their *boats*, but supposing
they figure out a way to come 'round *behind* us, from
inland?"

"Hawww! Fat chance of that!"

The sergeant refilled his pipe. "Yeh," he said
thoughtfully.

The boss laughed again. "They can't do it! Besides,
even if they did, we'd have 'em between pincers! General
Pemberton could hit 'em from the west, and another
army could hit 'em from the direction of Jackson. Poof!
Just like a pecan in a nutcracker! No shell and all meat."

The lean soldier nodded. "Yeah," he said sourly, "but

ain't General Pemberton a Yankee, too?"

There was a moment's hushed silence and then the sergeant spoke. "Meaning what, Burroughs?"

"Well, he ain't no Southern man. Pennsylvania ain't exactly south of the Mason-Dixon Line, is it?"

"He's a good man and a fine soldier," said the sergeant.

"Maybe so. Seems to me, as important as Vicksburg is, they might' a sent us a real combat soldier like Joe Johnston, John Hood, James Longstreet or Pierre Gustave Toutant Beauregard!"

"Hear! Hear!" said the Irishman.

"How come he's with *us* anyways?" asked the gap-toothed man.

"Married a Southern woman," said the labor boss. He rubbed his jaw and half closed one eye. "Her pa's family is Virginia stock and her ma's side is Noth Cahlina. Fine people. Fine-looking woman."

"Just the same I'd like to see a born Southern general heah," said the lean man. "Besides, Pemberton ain't done any fighting yet in this wah. How do we know what he can do?"

Chip Powers had halted the water cart near Greg and as the laborers got water he winked at Greg, a silent message that he had something of importance to tell. Chip leaned back against the water barrel. "Ol' Pemberton seen fighting aplenty," he said in his assumed accent. "He fit at Palo Alto, Resaca de la Palma, the siege of Vera Cruz, Monterey, Cerro Gordo, Churubusco, Molino del Rey, the storming of Chapultepec and the storming of Mexico City. He was wounded twice and brevetted captain for gallantry."

"Sure, sure," said the lean skeptic in a dry voice, "but what's he done in *this* wah?"

Chip opened his mouth and shut it. There wasn't much of an argument he could make about that. Most of them knew that Pemberton had served at organizing and training recruits at Norfolk, Virginia; later as second in command to General Robert E. Lee at Charleston, South Carolina, where Pemberton had not been too popular. In time he had taken over command there after Lee had been called back to Virginia, and his unpopularity, much of it unfounded, had increased, despite the great trust placed in him by President Jefferson Davis. Later Pemberton had been transferred to Jackson, Mississippi, and in time had come to Vicksburg for the sole purpose of stopping the steady advance of General Grant. A skilled engineer and excellent artilleryman, a wounded combat veteran of the Mexican War, but as yet unblooded in the War Between the States, and a *Northerner* by birth. A highly capable man, but hardly the right man in a psychological sense, to lead soldiers of the Deep South in one of the most important posts of the entire Confederacy.

Chip got off of the cart and scrambled down into the ditch and up the other side to where he could see the great river far below. In a few minutes Greg joined him. Chip spoke out of the side of his mouth. "You want to make a break out'a here tonight?"

Greg was startled. "Why tonight?"

Chip glanced back over his shoulder. "I hear a rumor that some of our boats are going to try and run the batteries tonight."

Greg felt his heart thud erratically against his ribs. "You sure?"

"Pretty sure. I saw a man who I know to be one of our men. Civilian working as a spy for General Grant. He recognized me and tipped me off."

"So?"

"We'd better make a break for it, bub."

Greg nodded. "All right," he said, "but the less artillery these rebels have the better chances our boats will have."

"Meaning?"

Greg slid a hand into his pocket and drew out three spikes. "I'd like to ram these down the vents in some of the guns along here."

"Spike 'em?"

"Yup!"

"You're out'a your mind, bub."

Greg spat over the edge of the bluff. "Well," he said dryly, "I have a friend who is as brave as Achilles, or so these rebels *think*."

Chip flushed. "So?"

Greg grinned widely. "With such a partner, sharp as a scythe, smart, and brave as Achilles, how can we fail?"

"Yup." Chip wiped the sweat from his face. "You got any particular gun in mind, ginral?"

Greg nodded. "Whistling Dick," he said softly.

"Oh, Lord! I might'a know that! The best one they got!"

"Why not?"

Chip threw up his hands. "Why not?" he echoed. "We only got one life apiece to lose."

"Watahboy! Watahboy!"

"My master's call," said Chip dryly. He slapped Greg on the shoulder, sending up a cloud of dust. "I'm on, bub. See you at dusk."

Greg nodded. He watched Chip scramble down into the ditch and up the other side. *We only got one life apiece to lose*, he had said.

Greg walked along the ditch until he could see "Whistling Dick," the huge 18-pounder rifled gun made at the Tredegar Iron Works at Richmond, Virginia. It was the pet of the rebel gunners and had earned its colorful nickname because of the peculiar sound of its missiles speeding through the air. It was one of the most powerful guns in the possession of the Confederacy, and had been emplaced in a huge earthwork crowning a hill, named Fort Castle, one of the strongest defenses of Vicksburg itself.

If the Union gunboats tried to run the Vicksburg batteries that night, "Whistling Dick," with its trained crew, might make the difference between failure and success. Despite the heat of the sun Greg shivered a little at the thought of attempting to spike that powerful weapon which was sure to be well guarded by its doting gun crew. But somebody had to do it. As far as Greg knew, he and Chip were the only two Union men serving in Vicksburg under false colors. There was no one else to do the job.

As he walked slowly back to the work party, he thought of the construction of Fort Castle, for he had been part of a work crew there for a time. He knew the interior of the fort as well as any man there. Greg looked down the bluff toward the river. The wharves were still there, although precious little supplies came in these days. But there were plenty of small boats tied up to the sagging wharves, or run aground in the soft mud. the two boys managed to get down to the river, they *might* get a boat. But there were troops down there and small boat patrols. The Confederates had piled up huge masses of brush, barrels of turpentine and other inflammables to light when the Yankees tried to run the batteries. Many riverbank houses and other buildings had been emptied for that very same purpose and the guards would not hesitate to touch them off if need be.

He looked across the river to the small hamlet of DeSoto. It was a long way across and at night, if the gunboats tried to pass, the river surface would be illuminated like a torchlight parade. Guns would be thundering, both rebel and Union.

Despite the warmth of the spring day, he shivered in the wind. He had never felt so all alone in his life. There was a strong impulse within him to forget the whole thing; to wait for another chance to escape with a whole skin, but he knew he could not do that. Chip and he would make the attempt. *Somebody had to do it.*

CHAPTER THIRTEEN

Whistling Dick

The darkness covered Vicksburg thickly. Here and there, along' the lines of entrenchments, redoubts, forts and river batteries a faint, nickering pool of light would show from a bombproof or a tent, but for the most part the great sprawling fortifications were in darkness. It was quiet, but there was an uneasiness in the air, as though something was going to happen. Sentries and officers stood on fire steps and looked down upon the faintly glistening surface of the river. Guns in the river batteries had been shotted and the lanyards had been attached to the friction tubes in the fire holes of the great cold guns which gleamed with the night dew.

Greg Hollister raised his head. The rest of the occupants of his tent were sound asleep. A hard day's work on the entrenchments wasn't conducive to active nights, and with scant rations a man could sleep to forget his ever-gnawing hunger.

Greg eased out of his sagging cot, dropped to the floor, lifted the rear tent flap and rolled outside. It was a matter of minutes to reach the nearest deep trench and slide softly down into it. It was not occupied as it was not finished.

He padded quickly through the velvety darkness always expecting the sharp, ringing challenge of a sentry but it did not come. Chip was waiting for Greg on the rutted road that led up the scarred slope toward Fort Castle. The Illinois boy stood by the head of the caricature of a mule that drew the ramshackle water cart. "What'd you bring General Sherman along for?" fiercely demanded Greg, stabbing a thumb toward the dozing mule.

Chip spat casually. "Maybe you got a *better* way to get into that fort, bub?"

Greg was taken aback, and then he nodded. Maybe Greg had more foresight and a better head for the master plan, but when it came to shrewdness and quick thinking on the spot, it was Chip who took the honors. They made a good team. It was a hot, sultry night and the sentries would be thirsty.

"What's the plan?" asked Chip in a low, conspiratorial tone.

Greg looked up at the humped and sprawling silhouette of the fort. "I've got three spikes," he said quietly, "and a pair of mallets."

"Gee, how lucky can we get!"

"Shut up!" said Greg. He leaned against the side of the water cart. "We'll go in together. You got a big mouth and a load of rumors, and it's up to you to keep those sentries busy."

"Leave it to OP Chip."

Greg wiped the cold sweat from his face. "I'll try and work toward Whistling Dick."

Chip looked away. "One crack of that mallet against a spike in that gun's touchhole and the thing will ring like a church bell."

Greg nodded. 'That's the signal, Chip. After that happens you can grease out of there."

"Yup...but what about you?"

Greg shrugged. The words of Lieutenant Currie came

back to him as he stood there in the middle of the strongest rebel citadel in the western theater of the war, with three spikes in his pocket and a pair of mallets thrust through his belt, ready to attempt the foolhardy spiking of the best rifled gun in the works. *You will find yourselves in strange and weird places, fighting a mad sort of war on water that is half land, and the change may be hard on you, but...we fight on these waters as men of the United States Navy, and never forget that fact! Your discipline, training, and above all your courage, may help to decide whether or not we take Vicksburg.*

"Well?" asked Chip at last.

"I'll take my chances, Chip."

"Yup." Chip looked away again. "You only need one spike and one mallet. Be a good fella and loan me one of them mallets and the other two spikes. Never could drive the first nail true, bub. You see, there are other guns in that fort up there."

Greg passed a mallet and two of the spikes to Chip. Without another word they started up the rutted road.

"Halt!" cracked the challenge through the darkness. "Who goes there!"

"Water party!" said Chip.

The sentry hesitated. "*Water* party?"

"Yuh thirsty ain'tcha?"

Again, the hesitation. "Sure enough. Port Hudson!"

That was the sign, now Greg hoped Chip had the countersign. If he didn't, they might go down that hill with a minie ball feeling their shirttails.

Chip swallowed.

"Well?" growled Greg.

Chip opened his mouth and then shut it.

"*Port Hudson!*"

They heard a rifle hammer snick back in the quiet.

"General Beauregard!" squeaked Chip.

It was deadly quiet for a fleeting moment. "Pass," said the sentry at last.

Greg was holding shakily onto the side of the cart. "Blast you!" he snarled in Chip's ear. "Whyn't, you say it faster!"

Chip grinned weakly in the darkness. " 'Cause I wasn't sure, bub, *that's why!*"

They led General Sherman up the slope, and Greg's legs were as weak as water. Someday Zelah "Chip" Powers would be the death of his best friend and comrade.

The sentry slopped them, ladled water into his cedar-wood canteen, then allowed them to pass on into the interior of the fort. Here and there in the dimness men appeared, strolling casually over to the cart for water. Greg let Chip do the honors while he himself eyed the layout of the fortifications. There were plenty of heavy guns in it. Some of them mounted *en barbette* and others *en embrasure*. Whistling Dick was one mounted *en barbette*, set back from the ramparts, mounted on a heavy reinforced wooden carriage, with the muzzle of the rifle pointing over the top of the piled earth.

Greg looked about. Chip was keeping the soldiers occupied, kidding about with them, keeping them laughing. He was good at it, and Greg alone knew how scared the kid really was. Greg should know; he was frightened enough himself.

Greg strolled casually toward the great gun. A sentry leaned on his rifle, looking over the rampart down toward the dimly glistening river. "Thought I saw somethin' down there, Scully," he said to one of his mates.

"You always are seein' something, Bob." The second man heaved himself to his feet and looked at Greg. "Who are you?"

"Water detail."

"Water? Good! I could drink a cartload myself."

"Take my canteen, Scully," said Bob.

"Sure, mate."

It gave Greg just enough time to slip up on the heavy cypress wood carriage and feel for the touchhole. It was empty. He drew out the spike and gently inserted the tip of it in the hole. It was a close fit and he'd have to drive it hard to spike the gun.

He could hear voices from beyond the next gun. "Looks like something down there! I thought I saw a light!" cried out someone.

Greg gripped the mallet and set himself, lying close against the dew-wet metal of the great gun.

"By the Lord Harry!" yelled a man. "Those are Yankee boats down there! They're going to run the batteries!"

"Sound the alarm!" screamed a man running across the area just behind Greg's position.

Greg wet his lips. It was now or never. In a minute the gun crew would be upon him. He swung up the mallet and struck hard. It was just as Chip had said it would be. The gun seemed to ring like a church bell, but it was hardly heard above the thud of running feet, the calling of the officers and noncommissioned officers, the clattering of equipment and then the steady thudding and nerve-tingling sound of the drums beating the Long Roll.

He hammered harder and harder and the spike did not bend. It was flush with the top of the gun now. It would take time for them to drill it out. He slipped to the front of the gun and ducked under the thick barrel just as the gun crew double-quicked up behind the gun and fell in under the whiplash commands of the sergeant-gunner.

The drums sounded louder and more insistent, and the sound of them seemed to be echoed throughout Vicksburg as more and more commands were alerted and ran to their guns.

Then the noisy darkness was shattered by the thunderous blasting noise of a great gun as it belched flame and smoke and slammed back against its carriage. The projectile could plainly be heard as it hummed through the air. Gun after gun roared. Greg felt the cold sweat streak down his sides as he worked his way toward the rear of the gun he had spiked. The gunners were getting into their positions.

"You!" snapped the sergeant. "You on this crew?"

"No, suh!"

"Don't say sir to a noncommissioned officer!"

"No, suh!"

"Get out of the way then!"

Greg streaked for the darkness to one side just as an officer commanded a gun sergeant to open fire. The gun blasted, lighting up the interior of Fort Castle, and in the bright wash of light Chip Powers could be plainly seen standing on the carriage of a heavy gun that pointed downriver and was not manned as yet. His arm was up in the air, with the mallet in his hand, and he stopped there, transfixed, like a figure in a tableau.

"Who is that man!" yelled a rebel.

"Jump!" screamed Greg.

"Whistling Dick is spiked!" cried an officer.

"Oh, Lord," said Greg as he raced for the ramparts.

Chip was ahead of him. He leaped onto the right shaft of the water cart and gripped the reins of old General Sherman. He slapped him on the wrinkled hide. General Sherman came to life, aided by the roaring of the many guns. He jumped for the gateway. Greg swung up behind the cart. A sentry yelled at him from ten feet away. Greg stabbed a hand down the hill. "Fromisjesteritis detail for Colonel Bumbersnatch!" he cried out through cupped hands. "Urgent!"

Then they were in the clear, racking down the hill, bouncing in and out of the ruts. Chip drove like Jehu and General Sherman outdid himself.

"Stop those two men!"

A rifle cracked and the bullet thudded into something. Chip jerked. "Cany on, old friend!" he cried. "I'm hit hard!" Just then the cart hit a deep rut and tilted too far for comfort. Both boys left the cart like leaping frogs, hit what they thought was a ditch and found to their horror that there was nothing but empty space beneath their churning feet.

Greg yelled hoarsely. A second later his heels hit soft earth and he slid down the steep bluff unable to stop himself, while Chip Powers sailed gracefully past, turning slowly in mid-air. "Good-bye forever, partner!" he yelled as he disappeared into the darkness below.

Greg struck once again, surprisingly enough on a softer surface and he was startled by a hollow groan. He had landed on Chip. "Are you all, right?" he said.

"I'm bleeding bad."

A gun flashed from a nearby battery and Greg saw that Chip's shirt was darkly stained. His heart thudded erratically. He couldn't leave Chip lying there wounded, unable to escape, and sure to be shot as a spy if he was captured.

"Save yourself," said Chip faintly.

Greg stared at his partner. He seemed to be in pretty good shape for a man dying of a mortal wound. Greg passed a hand along the back of Chip's shin and fingered the wetness. It did not redden his fingers. He tasted it and it was not salty. He pulled back the thin shirt. There was no horrible wound on the boy's flesh. "Get up," he said flatly.

"Impossible, Greg. I'm mortal hit."

"Get up! The only thing that hit you was a spout of water from the cart when it got punctured by a minie ball!"

Greg glanced toward the river. It was ablaze with cannon fire from the river craft moving swiftly downstream through a pall of stack and gun smoke blossomed with red gun flashes and interspersed with great spouts of water as rebel missiles struck the river. The rebel batteries were in action along a four-mile line. Burning tar barrels blazed up to shed light and were soon joined by a large frame building, the railroad station, which illuminated a wide area. There was a continuous rippling of gunfire from the batteries.

Greg crouched beside Chip. "Look!" he said.

Dark shapes were moving along the far shore. Seven big ironclads were first in line, firing back steadily at the batteries; then came a towering ram, followed by two big side-wheel steamers and a stern-wheeler, and each of the three was towing barges. Far behind them came a lone barge.

"That's the *Benton* in the lead," said Chip.

Some of the steamers were well barricaded with cotton bales, and one of the "Cotton-clads" was already ablaze and drifting with the swift current. The gunboats now formed a line between the roaring batteries and the un-armored steamers, and the din assumed epic proportions. A gunboat had a steamer in tow and was valiantly pulling her to safety through a hurricane of exploding shells.

"That's the *Tuscumbia*!" said Chip. "She's towing *Forest Queen*!"

Greg glanced up the bluff. 'Time for us to pull foot," he said.

"Where to?"

Greg shrugged. "The river."

"You out'a your mind?"

"You got some other place to go, bub?"

"Nope."

"Then follow me."

Greg set off down the bluff, staying close to the sagging sheds and buildings of the decaying waterfront, hardly used since the advance of the Union forces. The air was alive with the humming rush of missiles traveling both ways. Union shells struck the raw earth of the forts and batteries and hurled earth, timbers and guns high into the air.

"There's a boat," said Chip. "Ain't no one near it."

Greg walked out onto a sagging wharf shielded from

the shore by a pile of decaying lumber. A skiff was moored to a piling and two pairs of oars were in it. There wasn't any hesitation on the part of the two boys. They dropped into the skiff, untied the painter and shoved off, each of them taking a pair of oars. They pulled swiftly with the current, skirting close to wharves, moored steamers and barges until they were almost at the southern limits of Vicksburg. Then a great blaze of light illuminated the western bank as many frame buildings in DeSoto, a hamlet across the river, burst into flame.

The boys pulled like a racing crew, with Greg at stroke, and the skiff surged up and down in the wash of the river. Luckily the rebel gunners had bigger and more important targets on the far side of the river.

They slanted across the river heading toward the battered Union vessels. It was darker there, and safer, but now and then a random shot hissed into the water or exploded in the smoky air. They were close to the steamers when a sharp challenge rang out from one of them. "What boat is that?"

"Two crew members of United States Light Draft Ship *Dart*!" called out Chip.

There was a moment's silence. "Come alongside! There are a dozen rifles aimed at you! No tricks now!"

The skiff bumped gently alongside the side of the ironclad. They stepped aboard and shoved off the skiff. They were home.

CHAPTER FOURTEEN

Disgrace and a New Assignment

The wagon stopped on the sagging wharf beside the familiar shape of the *Dart*. A wisp of steam floated up from her escape pipes. She looked much the same to the two boys, but there were more battle and campaign scars on the tinclad, A great patch had been neatly placed on the larboard stack. A shot hole on the starboard side, just above the first gun port, had been covered with raw lumber. But she looked fit and ready and best of all she was home for the two prodigals who dropped from the wagon and hurried toward the tinclad. It had been a long trip from the river below Vicksburg, roundabout, through swamps and across deserted plantations and farms, until the road meandered out to follow the river shore above Vicksburg, where the majority of the River Fleet was stationed.

It was almost dusk and the boys could smell food and coffee being cooked and brewed aboard the boat. A sentry stood at the foot of the gangplank, and as they approached, he snapped to attention, thrust forward his carbine and challenged. "Halt! Who goes there!"

Greg grinned. It was big Tom Bruce. "It's us, mate!" he cried. "Greg Hollister and Chip Powers!"

The gunner stared at them and then slowly lowered his carbine. "I'll be blowed! So, it is!"

Greg stuck out his hand. "Glad to be aboard!" he said.

Bruce did not take the hand. He stepped back and jerked his head toward the *Dart*. "Get aboard," he said coldly. "The Old Man will want to see you. Make it so!"

Chip glanced at Greg. Greg shrugged. They plodded aboard and stepped into the familiar interior of the tinclad. Men looked up at them but there were no smiles on their faces. "Hi, Taffy!" said Greg.

The wizened Irishman turned his back on them. Here and there men got up and walked away from the two puzzled boys.

Chip shivered. "Cold in here, ain't it?" he said to no one in particular.

Cavalry Corporal Sturgis spat leisurely through an open port. "*We* like it," he said dryly.

A big man came toward them. It was Boatswain Webb Downey. He stopped and placed ham-like hands on his hips. "Well," he said in a low voice. "You decided to show up at last."

Chip widened his eyes. "Wasn't much else we could do, Bos'n," he said cheerfully. "Now we..."

"Stow your blasted gab! Masthead for you two! Get up to the skipper's quarters! On the double!"

They walked to the ladder, glanced at the cold-eyed men, then went slowly up to the captain's quarters. Greg tapped on the door.

"Who is it?" called out the officer.

"Gregory Hollister and Zelah Powers, sir."

There was a moment of quiet. "*So?* Come in then."

They walked into the little cabin. Lieutenant Currie sat at his desk. He returned their salutes. He looked tired and pale and a good deal older than he really was. His eyes were cold as he looked at them. "What have you two to say for yourselves?"

Greg was puzzled. "Simply that we were lost overboard from the ship, sir, and when we saw that we couldn't rejoin her, we struck off through the swamps to try and reach other units of the river fleet."

"So? That was *weeks* ago, Hollister. You don't look as though you spent all of that time in the swamps."

Greg filled in the rest of the story, and as he related it his voice faltered and became slower and slower until he at last finished, for he knew all the time he was telling the tale that Lieutenant Currie did not believe it. Fact is, it *did* sound somewhat farfetched.

The officer slued his chair a little and gazed out of an open window toward the shore line where the ghostly evening mist was rising to shroud the swamps. Chip glanced quickly at Greg and raised his eyebrows questioningly.

Currie spoke quietly. "I will not doubt your word about your adventures since leaving *Dart*. They have the ring of truth about them. It is also true that you turned yourselves in to the commanding officer of the *Tuscumbia* and were ordered to report aboard the *Dart* for further orders. This you have done. Your conduct in reporting in as soon as you could is most commendable."

"Thanks, sir," said Greg with a feeling of relief.

"But..." Currie's voice changed, and it seemed to have been whetted and honed in the short interval since he had commended the boys, "*Both of you left the Dart without permission, deserting your posts in the face of the enemy*. Do you know the penalty for such an offense?"

Chip swallowed, opened his mouth, shut it. then squeaked out a shaky reply. "Execution by firing squad, sir."

"That is correct."

"But, sir," said Greg, "we did not desert! Zelah Powers went out in a gig to remove a torpedo from the course of the *Dart*."

"And Gregory Hollister came to my rescue, sir," said Chip. "He also pushed the torpedo out of the way. If he hadn't, there would be no *Dart* today, and maybe no one left alive of her crew."

"Who saw all this?" asked the officer quietly.

"*Someone* must have seen us," said Chip hotly.

"No."

The boys looked at each other. Despite the warmth of the spring night a curious feeling of coldness came over Greg.

"Where was your post of duty, Powers?" asked Lieutenant Currie.

"Captain's messenger, sir."

"And you, Hollister?"

"Powder monkey on the bow Dahlgren, sir."

"The *Dart* was afire and badly holed when you left the ship. You were a pumpman. You did not report for that necessary duty."

"No, sir." Greg swallowed hard. "But if we hadn't left the ship, she might have been lost by striking the torpedo."

"That is *your* story."

The officer stood up. "I closely questioned every member of the crew about your disappearance in the heat of action. Not *one* of them saw Powers leave the ship to go after a torpedo, nor did they see *you*, Hollister, go after Powers, as you say you did."

The ship's bell softly rang three bells. Steam hissed quietly in the escape pipes. A small steamer chuffed slowly past the *Dart*. Somewhere in the bowels of the tinclad a sailor was singing "Shenandoah," in a voice that betrayed his longing for the fresh salt sea, marble-hard white canvas, and the crying of gulls.

Currie walked to the window and looked out across the wide river. "There will be no charges pressed against either of you. You were absent without leave, I do not think you meant to desert or you would not have reported aboard the *Tuscumbia* as you did."

Chip breathed an audible sigh of relief.

"However, you *did* leave your posts in the face of the enemy, and no matter the reason, such conduct cannot be excused. I have permission from the commanding officer of the flotilla to dispose of the case as I see fit. Because of your ages and your previous good conduct in the service, there will be no punishment"

"Thank you, sir!" said Chip. "We'll make it up! The old *Dart* will be the better for it... Now I..." His voice trailed off and died away as he saw the look in Currie's eyes.

The officer sat down and reached for pen and paper. He wrote rapidly and signed the paper, then passed it across to Greg. "Those are your orders to report for duty aboard the Supply Ship *Elizabeth M. DePere*. She is moored a short distance away from here, up Raccoon Creek, undergoing repairs."

"A *supply* ship, sir?" asked Greg.

The hard, gray eyes seemed to stab at him. "I do not consider either one of you fit material for the crew of a *fighting* ship of the River Fleet. That is all! Dismissed!"

They saluted and walked outside. They went to their quarters and got their gear. Oddly enough, it seemed as though all their friends were busy elsewhere at the time. "You'd better say goodbye to your Uncle Tobias, Chip," said Greg out of the side of his mouth, as they saw Boatswain Webb Downey leaning against a bulkhead watching them with cold eyes.

"You out'a your mind! I'm hoping to get off this boat afore he knows I'm back. Jehosephat! If he sees me *first*!"

They quietly left the veteran tinclad. Greg did not have the heart to look back at her through the gathering swamp mist. Far from his first feeling when he had reported aboard her, he had grown to love the little scrapper and the men aboard her, and now he was no longer part of her complement.

Raccoon Creek was only a quarter of a mile from where

the *Dart* was moored. They passed supply boats and transports, tinclads and timberclads, ironclads and a huge hospital ship. The cheery sound of laughing men came to them and the tempting odor of cooking food. Somewhere on the deck of the hospital ship a banjo tinkled. Two soldiers wrestled in the glow of a lantern, cheered on by their mates. Greg began to feel lonelier and lonelier. A *supply* ship!

Chip cleared his throat. "Well," he said in an attempt at cheerfulness, "she *sounds* pretty good, bub. *Elizabeth M. DePere.* Might be a luxury steamer like some I seen. Crystal chandeliers, rosewood pianos, big staterooms, enough for one to each crew member. A real chef. You can't kick about that, Greg."

"No."

"We kin laugh at this someday when we look down on the ol' rusty *Dart,* bub."

"Shut up!"

They found the creek and walked along a muddy corduroy road toward the dim shape of a steamer moored to the bank. "That the *Elizabeth M. DePere?*" asked Greg of a soldier hurrying past.

"Yup."

They walked onto the rotting wharf. There wasn't any doubt that the boat that seemed to squat despondently in the muddy water was the *Elizabeth M. DePere.* The name was plain enough to see in peeling faded letters on her nameboard. She was a stern wheeler that had seen better days long, long ago. The twin stacks were bent and flaked with thick rust. The decks were splintered and torn and littered with filth and scraps. She had "hogged" sometime in her past, that is to say, she had bent in the middle, with a sort of humped effect, and great chains had been strung from bow to thick timbers amidships, then down to a fastening just forward of the paddle box, to pull up the sagging bow and stern. There was a sad, melancholy look about the boat. A light howitzer squatted on her bow, behind a flimsy shield of wood faced with boiler iron.

"Oh, Lord," said Chip.

"Yup. She sounds pretty good, bub. Elizabeth M. DePere. Might be a luxury steamer like some I seen. Crystal chandeliers, rosewood pianos, big staterooms, enough for one to each crew member. A real chef. We kin laugh at this someday when we look down on the ol' rusty Dart, bub."

"Oh, Lord," repeated Chip.

A potbellied man wearing a greasy cap came to the gangplank. The greening letters "Pilot" showed on his cap. "Howdy, boys," he said. "Kin I help you?"

"This *is* the *Elizabeth M. DePere*, isn't it?" asked Greg, hoping against hope that it wasn't by some fluke of fate.

"Yup," said the man. He grinned. "Ain't no one calls her the *Elizabeth M. DePere* though. She's just plain 'Lizzie' to the whole River Fleet. Ain't much to look at but she gets there and back when she ain't broke down, as she is most of the time."

The wind moaned softly through the swamp and hummed through the rusting wires of the boat.

"You boys assigned aboard?" asked the man.

"Yes."

"Come on aboard then. I'm Pilot Jonas Stringfellow. We been shorthanded for some time. Always seems as though every time we get a few good men they find some way of getting off the *Lizzie*."

"I wonder why?" breathed Chip hollowly.

They trudged aboard, and the smell of the ancient stem wheeler folded itself about them like an old familiar mantle. A mingled miasma of grease, stale food, caked filth and stagnant bilge water.

"Oh, Lord," said Greg as they followed the pilot aft.

CHAPTER FIFTEEN

Disaster on the Little Sunflower

I t was shady on the winding bayou beneath the thick overhanging branches of the trees hung with bearded Spanish moss, but the shadiness was a delusion, for the burning summer sun beat down upon the trees and the intense heat filtered down into the swamps and developed a humidity that was worse than the direct rays of the sun itself. The soaking heat brought out the rich but fetid smell of the thick mud and stagnant backwaters, and insects rose in myriad clouds, like a swiftly moving mist, to plague men and animals. Ants crept over anything and everything and now and then a sudden thrashing in the mud behind a thick screen of brush and trees revealed the unseen presence of a bull alligator.

The *Elizabeth M. DePere* slogged slowly and erratically along the chocolate waters of the bayou in a sort of aimless way, and it seemed as though the overhanging branches raking across her upper works would hold her fast at any moment. Steam leaked from pipes and breechings. The engine missed and hit, missed and hit in an irregular rhythm and the sound of it was maddening to Greg Hollister as he flaked down a muddy line on the forward deck.

"Wastin' your time, boy," said a stoker as he wiped the greasy sweat from his upper body. "This ain't no man-o'-war and it ain't likely to be. Rotten, leaking tub! Why, back in Cairo we would'a let this thing sink and then jump up and down on her hurricane deck to make sure she never came back up again!"

Greg nodded. The flies, gnats and mosquitoes swarmed about him as he walked out of the dappled shade of the foredeck. It was a waste of time trying to do anything worthwhile on the *Lizzie* for she was a laughingstock in the River Fleet. She should never have been taken for the service and should have been condemned even then, but some shrewd and unscrupulous contractor had supplied her to the service at an immense profit, and there she was and there she would stay until she sank, blew up, or the rebels, more out of pity than malice aforethought, would send a shot through her leaky boilers to put her out of her puffing misery.

"Have you seen Chip, Charlie?" asked Greg.

The stoker grinned. "Sure. He's up at the 'conn' now. Can't you tell by the way the boat is traveling?"

Greg raised his head angrily. "He's a good pilot and you know it!"

The stoker waved a placating hand. "Sure thing, kid. If it hadn't been for him, we'd never have got this far up this bayou, or whatever it is. Old Stringfellow is feeling poorly again. Malaria, dysentery, ague, bolts, consumption, gangrene and leprosy, for all I know! It was a lucky day for him when you and Chip come aboard. That boy knows the river better than a good many certificated pilots I know."

Greg nodded. He walked aft, ascended the ladder past the leaking, steaming pipes, and then walked forward to the ladder that led upward into the little pilothouse. The damp heat was even more intense in the pilothouse. Chip was handling the big wheel while Jonas Stringfellow dozed on a bench at the rear of the cubicle. Sweat was running down Chip's face. The boy was handling the cranky steamer all alone and his half-slitted eyes were studying the surface of the bayou as though it was a brown skein of ribbon running under the blunt bows of the *Lizzie*.

Chip turned the wheel sharply. "Deadhead," he said tersely.

"Who? Me?"

Chip shook his head. "Log lodged just below the surface so's you can't see it in bad light. This bayou is full of them."

"Just where are we, partner?"

Chip turned the wheel slowly. "Jonas *said* we were on Rolling Fork."

"So?"

Chip turned, shot a glance at Jonas, then looked at Greg. "We ain't," he said flatly.

"Where are we then?"

Chip jerked his head toward the chart that hung damply between two windows. "I calculate we're on the Little Sunflower."

Greg looked at the chart and then at Chip. "How far *south* on the Little Sunflower?"

Chip stared at the river, then quickly swung the wheel, then hastily "walked" the big wheel, planting his feet on the spokes and forcing them down to turn it more quickly. "Give me a hand!" he snapped.

Greg helped him with the stubborn wheel. "What's wrong?" he gasped.

"Sawyer! You see that 'boil' on the surface of the bayou?"

"Yes."

"Sawyer. Log with clay and earth clinging to roots. Root end sinks to bottom and points log right at us. Can ram through bottom, hit boilers and blow us up!"

Greg swallowed hard. He looked out onto the surface

of the bayou, or river, or whatever it was. They all looked alike to him. "How far south are we, bub?"

"Too far."

"Seems to me the Little Sunflower meets the Yazoo between the Big Sunflower and Deer Creek."

"Keno, bub."

Branches scraped murderously along the side of the pilothouse. Greg involuntarily ducked his head. 'That's northeast of Haynes's Bluff then."

"Keno."

Greg glanced back at the dozing pilot. "Doesn't he know that's solid rebel country?"

"He thinks we're on a branch of Rolling Fork."

Greg rubbed his sweating face. "I thought we were bringing supplies to a fork of Deer Creek and Black Bayou."

"That *was* the idea, bub."

"So now what?"

Chip shrugged and just as he did so there was a far-off booming noise somewhere within the tangled labyrinth of swamp and bayou. White cranes rose from the river-bank and disappeared. The echo of the noise slowly died away.

Chip looked at Greg. "What was that?"

"Big gun. You know that."

"Yeah...sure...only I didn't want to believe it."

Greg stared at the tangled walls of forest on each side of the meandering waterway. "*Ours*," he said in a soft voice.

"It better be!"

Greg nodded. It was late June and Vicksburg had been under close siege since the third week in May. General Grant's forces had crossed the Mississippi below Vicksburg and had come in from the rear, winning the battles of Port Gibson, Raymond. Jackson, Champion's Hill and Big Black River; then had settled down into a strangling siege of the town itself. There had been bloody assaults and bloody repulses. Porter's gunboats commanded the Mississippi and the Yazoo but the surrounding country was still alive with rebel guerillas. The rebels seemed to have plenty of ammunition, but they had a severe lack of musket caps, and without the caps, the ammunition was useless. Therefore, brave and enterprising rebels worked their way through the thick swamps bringing in the precious caps. Hollow logs were filled with them and floated down to the city. Many different stratagems were used to get them into the beleaguered city and most of them failed. But there were still men threading their way through the swamps with the caps, and the ubiquitous tinclads had been sent in after them and their source of supply. The first of the little fighting vessels to be sent in had been the *Dart*. Greg and Chip had stood silently on the deck of the *Lizzie* as the *Dart* had passed them a few days before on Rolling Fork headed for the heart of the guerilla country.

The gun thudded again and then again, and the uproar seemed louder and more continuous, and the *Lizzie* seemed to be getting closer to the sound of the firing. It was no place for a lady, even a lady as down at the heels as the *Elizabeth M. DePere*.

"We wouldn't have a chance if the rebels see us," said Chip.

Greg nodded. The only gun on the *Lizzie* was an ancient piece that was more fitted for a park ornament than the deck of a fighting craft. In the long weeks Greg had been aboard, he had never seen a gun drill, although he was assigned as powder monkey to the old gun. In fact, he had been laughed at when he had suggested such a practice. There was a stand or two of muskets on board, several rusty cutlasses and a brace or two of pistols, but little else, and the liny crew could hardly hope to hold off a party of bloodthirsty guerillas who were screaming to drink blood out of a boot.

Now the guns were snarling louder and louder.

Mingled smoke arose above the trees. Birds fled through the hazy air away from the scene of bitter conflict.

Jonas Stringfellow at last opened his eyes. The pilot had a bad case of malaria. His eyes were splotched, his skin had a yellowish tinge, and there were little blisters on his lips. "What's that racket, cub?" he asked Chip.

"Gunfire, Mister Stringfellow."

"Gunfire you say? Hawww!"

A big gun let go and the reverberation of the discharge even shook the flimsy structure of the *Lizzie*, as far away as she was.

The pilot was on his feet in an instant. "This is the Rolling Fork! Ain't no fighting around here!"

Chip shrugged. "Listen," he said dryly.

"It's the Rolling Fork, I tell you!"

"Look at the sun," said Greg quietly. "If we were on Rolling Fork, we'd see the sun almost dead ahead. It's been starboard of us for hours!"

"Then where are we?" faltered the pilot as he wiped his face with a bandana.

"The Little Sunflower," said Chip. "I'll swear to that."

"Oh, Lord," said Jonas. "I'm sick. Where's the captain?"

Greg glanced at him. "Flat on his back with malaria."

"And the mate?"

Chip turned the heavy wheel. "Went on French leave night before last. You're in command. Mister Stringfellow."

"*Me!*"

The thudding of the guns was now continuous and getting closer. Thick wreaths of smoke drifted along the bayou and the *Lizzie* plowed slowly through them. The pilot shoved Greg aside and snatched up the voice pipe. "Cut 'er back!" he screamed.

"Don't shut off steam, Mister Stringfellow!" pleaded Chip.

It was too late. The power was gone and the big

stern-wheel slowed down, beating the water impotently into chocolate froth. The current took control and drifted the craft toward the bank. Greg saw a suspicious-looking boiling of the water surface. "Sawyer!" he yelled.

Chip glanced at the pilot but the little man had been unnerved. "Steam up!" yelled Chip into the voice pipe. "Reverse steam! Full speed astern!"

The *Lizzie*'s engineers had never been noted for speed, and this day they were more lethargic than usual. Greg watched in helpless horror as the steamer moved inexorably toward the sawyer. Then slowly the big wheel went into reverse but the current and the forward impetus were too much. The boil vanished beneath the muddy prow of the *Lizzie*. There was a horrible scraping and wrenching noise from beneath the steamer and then a ripping, splintering crash.

Chip looked at Greg. "If that hits the boilers!"

His voice had hardly died away when something blew upward and outward in a rending, thunderous noise. The pilothouse seemed to lift lazily upward, tilt to one side and then it fell with terrible swiftness down toward the lower deck. It struck hard, split apart, hurling the three occupants into the bayou, then collapsed on the riven deck of the sinking stern wheeler.

Greg went down deep, then shot toward the surface. He came up not far away from Jonas Stringfellow. "Help!" screamed the pilot. "I can't swim!"

There was no sign of Chip. The current was sweeping Greg away from the shattered mass of timber and metal that had been the *Elizabeth M. DePere*, now a total wreck caused by the explosion of her own boilers.

Greg struck out for Jonas but the little man had gone down. He came to the surface with his mouth squared like a Greek tragic mask, but no sound came from it. Greg was five feet from him when he went down. The last thing Greg saw was a hand clawing up toward the light of day and then that, too, was gone.

The *Lizzie* was now submerged to her hurricane deck, and the water was slowly sweeping away debris from the shattered craft. There was no sign of life aboard her nor were there any heads bobbing about on the water. Greg felt sick. He swam slowly toward the muddy shore and crawled out. A curious-looking figure sat on a log, covered from head to foot with thick, clinging mud. A pair of sharp blue eyes peered through the mud. It was Chip.

"You see any of the others, Chip?" asked Greg.

The boy shook his head. "Just you n' me, partner."

The guns were still thundering to the south of them. Where there was cannonading there would be fighting and where there was fighting there would be Union men and Confederates. If the two boys didn't reach the Union forces and were captured by the rebels, they might be taken to Vicksburg and recognized as the two boys who had spiked rebel guns and escaped from the city. They would be considered traitors or spies. Either way it would be a quick walk-up Ladder Lane and down Gallows Street.

It was getting along toward dusk. An aura of tragedy had settled along the Little Sunflower. The setting sun picked out the broken upper works of the *Lizzie* for a moment, then slowly the stern wheeler turned on her side, and with a swift rushing and gurgling of the turbid waters she was gone from sight.

It turned cool as the boys stood there, side by side, looking at" the brown skein of the bayou. Just the two of them, unarmed, without food, in enemy country. Castaways who had lost their ship. Not much of a ship it was true, for the *Lizzie* wasn't like the *Dart*, that somehow engendered a sense of faith and loyalty in her crew as some ships do. But no sailor or steam boatman likes to lose a ship, and the *Lizzie*, in her way, had done the best she could and had died in the war as surely in service as many a gunboat had done in the heat of battle.

The gunfire had died away a little. "Let's go, Greg," said Chip. They turned away and waded through knee-deep mud toward firmer and drier land. Already the mosquitoes had sent out an alert to their mates in the far reaches of the swamp. They were gathering posthaste now, winging swiftly in from all quarters, for there was fresh game along the Little Sunflower: Zelah Powers and Gregory Hollister.

———

THE SOUND of steady slapping of flesh and the tattoo of heavy rain aroused Greg from a sluggish, miserable sense of being half asleep and half awake. He opened his eyes. Chip squatted at the entrance to the thickly vined place between two huge logs that they had crawled into the night before for shelter. He was industriously slapping at the elusive mosquitoes, ants, gnats and other little friends of bayou and woodland who like fresh food.

The leaden-looking rain was slanting down steadily just beyond the entrance, pocking the flat surface of the bayou, dripping from the trees and brush, flowing in ever-increasing rivulets across the half-drowned land.

"Mornin'," said Chip. "You want eggs or a kipper for breakfast?"

"Hardtack and bacon would do me."

"Yup."

Greg sat up and felt a slow, cold worm of rain work down his back. "How long has this been going on?"

"'Bout an hour. This ol' bayou will rise like the River Jordan, bub, and we're right on the edge of it."

"You hear or see any of our boys?"

"No," said Chip gloomily.

Greg shivered a little in the searching dampness. He vividly remembered the last time they had been cast away in the Yazoo Valley swamps. This time they might not be so lucky.

"What do we do now?" asked Chip.

Greg stood up and began to work his stiffening muscles. "They have a saying in the Army in situations like this."

"So?"

"March to the sound of the guns."

"Sure! Sure! Fine and dandy! But what guns?"

As though in answer there was a distant crashing noise and the hard ringing sound of a big gun. It reverberated throughout the swamp. "*That* gun," said Greg. "Let's go! Rise and shine! Show a leg!"

Greg led the way through the slanting rain. He was outright miserable but he didn't want Chip to see it. Chip never did bear up well in such situations

Now and then, Greg sank up to his knees. He navigated by guess and by gum, but the strain of picking a path through the tangled mess, half land and half water, and getting to be more water by the minute, began to tell heavily upon him. Fear came sailing over the dripping swamp on silent, velvety wings, to keep the boys unwelcome company.

Don't be afraid, thought Greg, as he slogged onward. *Don't be afraid, for if you are afraid, you're half licked before you get started. Don't be afraid!*

It was a weird, eerie landscape through which they plowed their slow way, pulling each foot out of the stinking mud with a squelching, sucking noise, tiring out their leg muscles. Vines seemed to lash across their faces. Wait-a-bit creepers caught at their wet, torn clothing. The insects had sent in fresh levies to crawl beneath clothing, into ears and nostrils, and to bite afresh into lumps that still itched horribly from the bites of the night before.

But the guns still thudded sullenly and erratically, and the two tired boys marched to the sound of them.

Greg came out upon the quaking edge of a labyrinth of winding runnels of blackish water with hardly a foothold between them. He stopped to study the terrain. The fighting was going on beyond the tangled mess of waterways. They needed a boat, or a raft to get afloat.

"Look," said Chip.

Something was drifting toward them. A thick panel of wood. It bobbed up and down a little and the faded letters ELIZ showed on the flaked surface. It was part of the paddle-box sheathing of the *Elizabeth M. DePere*. Chip waded into the water and gripped the panel. He looked at Greg. "Bad as she was, bub," he said quietly, "she didn't forget us."

Greg tore loose two decaying saplings and climbed aboard. "Ready to clear, sir!" he said.

"Ahead a quarter, Mister Hollister!"

"Order out the leadsman, Mister Powers!"

"Aye, aye, sir!"

They grinned wetly at each other as they poled their way slowly out into a broader reach of water. The sound of the guns was still ahead of them. They neared a bend in the waterway.

"Hold to the outside of the bend. Mister Hollister," said Chip. "Traveling downstream we can profit best from depth and current! Cramp over, sir! Cramp over!"

They rounded the bend and Greg jabbed his pole down into the soft bottom to hold the raft steady. "We found our fight. Mister Powers," he said quietly.

The swamp here had been cut back some years past, and there were open areas on both sides of a straight, broad reach of the bayou, stippled with second-growth timber and tangled creepers. A point thrust itself out into the rain-pocked waters, and on it squatted a number of rain-blackened timber buildings. Beyond the buildings, close to a stand of timber, was a small redoubt formed of timbers and sandbags, cotton bales and mud, and several field guns were in angry voice from within it, shooting steadily at something across the wide bayou.

"Rebels," said Greg. He looked across the river and

saw a pair of tall smokestacks thrusting above treetops beyond another point. Smoke and steam drifted up from them. Now and then there was a heavy detonation from the hidden vessel and a projectile, hardly to be seen in its swift flight, arced through the streaming air and struck in the mud on the far shore.

"Lousy shooting," opined Chip.

"They can't get a good sight on that redoubt," said Greg. "Too much defilade."

"Oh, sure, sure..."

"Wonder what boat it is?"

Chip shrugged. "What difference does it make? We can't get to her across land, if you can *call* it land, and we can't float down on her without getting a shell or solid shot down our collars."

Greg shoved at his pole and eased the raft into the shelter of some trees that stood deeply in water. He leaned against a tree and studied the savage and seemingly impotent battle. While the rebels fired, they seemed to do little damage to the boat, and the return fire of the boat hardly bothered the rebels. But what was all the fuss about? A fight for a group of worthless ramshackle buildings guarded by a two-bit redoubt?

"What do you think is in them buildings?" said Chip.

"Something the rebels want to guard and something the boat wants to get"

"Such as?"

Greg looked at Chip. "Such as musket caps, bub."

"You really think so?"

"Yup."

Mist and smoke seemed to boil along the surface of the bayou, shielding the boys from the rebel position. Greg suddenly shoved the raft from the tree, and without a word began to pole swiftly toward the buildings. Chip poled steadily, too. They had no need to say anything to each other.

They floated into an inlet not far from the buildings.

The crackling sound of musketry came to them. There was a line of butternut-clad infantry standing amongst the trees shooting toward the boat across the bayou.

Chip was off the raft and through the wet brush before Greg could open his mouth. Greg shored the raft and began to follow Chip. He saw Chip slip in through a sagging window of the closest building. Greg swallowed hard.

Minutes ticked past and then Chip reappeared. He scuttled toward Greg and dropped beside him on the soaked earth. "Look," he said quietly. He opened his left hand. There was a small box in it. "British made musket caps," said Chip quietly. "Eley's! 'Bout the best you can get. That there building is stacked full of cases of 'em, bub. *Thousands* of 'em."

"Now we know what the fuss is all about."

"Yup."

Greg looked toward the concealed Union vessel. There was something familiar about those rusty stacks. Chip walked toward the bayou. "Greg" he called back.

Greg walked toward Chip. The boy pointed silently out toward the middle of the bayou. A body floated out there. A man wearing a naval uniform. He bobbed up and down in the current and floated closer to the boys. Chip swallowed and looked away. Greg felt sick. Both of them had recognized the pale face of Perry Shepherd, their shipmate on the *Dart*.

"That's the *Dart* around there all right," said Chip.

"In trouble, too."

They walked back to the raft. "Drop!" said Chip suddenly.

They hit the ground. Two rebel soldiers passed beyond the screen of brush. "We've got her like cold meat, Jerry," said one of them. He laughed. "She's hard aground, been on fire twice, full of holes and with most of her guns out of action."

"What do you think them Yanks will do, Cass?"

"What else can they do but wait until it's dark and leave her? They can't get the musket caps. There's a detail coming through the swamps for these caps tomorrow."

"They'll be here, eh, Cass?"

The other man laughed. "Why not? Them Yanks will be lucky to get out of here alive, much less with our caps, Jerry."

When the men had passed on, Greg looked at Chip. Greg felt sick and he knew Chip wasn't feeling any better. It was the end of the *Dart* for certain.

"Now what?" asked Chip.

"I think we'd better try to reach the *Dart*. Maybe we can join the crew when they pull out of her."

Chip nodded gloomily. The rain slashed down piti-lessly. The rebel guns had redoubled their firing, while the return fire of the tinclad was. slackening. The smoke and mist hung in a thick, rifted blanket across the river. Chip and Greg poled out onto the water, then worked their way across to the far bank. There was no use trying to reach the tinclad across land. They'd have to wait until they could move down to her under cover of darkness. *If she was still there when darkness came.*

CHAPTER SIXTEEN

Rescue of the U.S.S. Dart

The bayou was shrouded in a white woolly blanket of thick mist. Here and there in the mist could be seen the dim outline of trees. It was quiet except for the soft rushing of the bayou water and the dripping from the trees. Somewhere, high overhead, the moon was trying valiantly to pierce the shroud of mist. As it was, a sort of vague, ghostly light filtered down into the drowned land. Chip was at the front end of the raft, flat on his belly, trying to see along the surface of the water, while he conned Greg with quick motions of his dirty hands. Greg had no idea how his partner knew where he was going but the Illinois boy was like a muskrat born to those waters. Greg softly shoved against a cypress, giving the raft enough impetus to move it along a few feet.

"Listen." said Chip softly.

Greg strained to listen. Then he heard it. An unmistakable sound to a sailor. The creaking of oars in rowlocks somewhere out on the quiet bayou and the gurgling of water about the prow of a boat.

They drifted along. Chip stared through the clinging mist. Greg was standing up, and as the mist rifted he suddenly saw three heavily laden boats moving with

muffled oars toward the far shore. The lead boat was
steered by a man he knew well; a pale-faced man with his
left arm in a sling and a dirty bandage about his head
beneath his officer's cap. "Mister Currier said Greg.

"Shhh!" hissed Chip.

The mist boiled up then rifted again and Greg saw
that the boats were manned by the men of the *Dart* and
those who were not pulling an oar were clutching pistols,
cutlasses and carbines. He saw Tom Bruce, Webb
Downey, Ab Cory, Mister Luscombe and many others.
He opened his mouth to call out and then shut it. He
knew what they were up to. They were going to raid the
buildings on the far shore in a last desperate effort to
destroy those valuable musket caps. But they were
outnumbered by far. It was Lieutenant Currie's way
though, and the way of the *Dart*'s crew. Then the boats
vanished again.

Chip looked back. "You see 'em?" he asked.

"Yes."

"What do we do?"

"Follow them!"

Chip stared into the mist. The current was fast; too
fast for the raft. The water had risen and was rising
higher and higher because of the heavy rains. The current
took control of the raft and moved it down-river. There
was nothing the boys could do about it. They swirled
about a muddy point and something loomed up in the
mist. The rusty slab side of a lightly armored tinclad.
There was no mistaking her. *It was the Dart!*

The raft bumped alongside and both boys without a
word stepped easily from their frail craft onto the guard
rail of the tinclad.

Chip grinned. "Wait until the boys aboard see us!"

"We're lucky we don't get a bullet through the head."

Chip poked his head into the port that was close
beside him. Softly he whistled "The Battle Hymn of the
Republic." They waited. Chip poked his head in again.

"Ahoy, the *Dart*," he said. His voice echoed softly. "Ahoy, the *Dart*. Ahoy, the *Dart*... Ahoy, the...Ahoy..."

Chip shivered. He eased a foot inside and Greg followed him. It was dark inside the armor shield of the tinclad. Dark and damp and smelling of wet burned wood and smoke.

They padded aft, then across to the larboard side, then up the ladders and along the other decks, ending up in the empty pilothouse. The *Dart* had been abandoned. Her decks were atilt. She was fast aground. She had seen a lot of action. Holes gaped in her sides. Two of her howitzers lay smashed on the splintered gun deck. Two were missing altogether and the last two had been spiked. There were suspicious-looking dark stains on the decks.

Chip shivered again as he looked from one of the peepholes of the tinclad's pilothouse. "I can see where the boys had a rough time, Greg." His voice echoed hollowly.

"You think they might come back?"

"Not a chance. She's hard aground and badly hurt. Well, she did her job when she was able to. No boat in the River Fleet did more. Maybe the reason they sent her in here was because they knew she'd do her job or sink trying. Well, she's done for." There was a catch in the boy's voice.

The thick mist swirled along the river in the rising wind. Suddenly there was a popping noise like the sound of hot grease in a gigantic skillet. Men yelled and the clang of metal came echoing across the waters.

"Hot fight!" said Chip.

There was nothing they could do to join their mates. The *Dart* was hard aground and not a boat had been left aboard her. The fight raged back and forth pinpoints of gunfire prickling through the wavering mist and then suddenly the gunfire died away and a ragged rebel yell arose and echoed through the swamp.

Greg looked at Chip. They knew what that meant.

The outnumbered crew of the *Dart* were dead, wounded or prisoners, and the musket caps were still safe in rebel hands.

Chip kicked at the big wheel of the boat. He turned and slid down the ladder. Greg could have sworn he had heard a dry, sobbing noise.

Greg peered from a loophole. The moon slanted down through the dimness and he could see over the top of the low-lying mist. Figures in butternut uniforms were herding figures in navy and army blue along the shore toward the redoubt. It was the end of the *Dart*'s crew and the end of the *Dart* itself. But Greg wasn't through yet. If they captured the two boys, their age wouldn't save them from a hanging.

Greg went below. Chip was standing beside the thick breech of the big bow Dahlgren. "Old Abe isn't much use any more," he said quietly.

The port had been triced up and the big 32-pounder had been run out, peering myopically through the mist with her one red-rimmed eye. Greg nodded. He looked at the breech. "They didn't spike Old Abe," he said.

"I wonder why?"

"Maybe they figured they might win over there and be able to come back and get the *Dart* afloat."

"Yup. Well, we might as well do the job ourselves and then get off of her in a hurry."

Greg rubbed a hand across the cold damp breech of the big Dahlgren, remembering the many fights he had been in. It would be hard to spike the old boy.

"What's that?" said Chip suddenly.

Greg looked up. He peered through the. port. The sound of creaking oars came to him. Then he saw one of the *Dart*'s boats and for a moment he thought the crew was returning, but his dream exploded when he saw the butternut uniforms. "Rebels!" he said.

"Oh, Lord!"

They were heading for the *Dart*. No doubt about it.

Chip gripped Greg by the arm. "We can hide in the paddle box!" he said. They raced aft and opened the door that led into the dark interior of the great housing of the stern wheel, and closed it behind them just as they heard a boat bump alongside. Then the scuffling of feet and the muffled sound of voices came to them.

Feet grated on the deck not far from the door. "Loot her, Sergeant Hardy," said a soft, cultured voice.

"Any chance of getting her off. Captain DeMaris?"

"No. She's fast aground. But the river is rising. She might float free, but we won't have time to wait. The battalion will move out of here tomorrow when the flat-boats come for the caps."

The sergeant laughed. "*And* the Yankee prisoners."

"Yes."

"I hate to leave her sitting here like this, suh. You reckon some Yankees might come in here and free her?"

"Probably not, but we can take care of that anyway. Get up steam on her. Weight down the safety valves. She can blow herself to Kingdom Come, sergeant."

"Yes, suh!"

Feet grated on the decks and a little while later the boys heard the ringing of shovels on the deck plating as coal was fed to the fires in preparation for the self-destruction of the *Dart*.

"Wouldn't you know it?" whispered Chip. "It *would* have to be Captain Douglas DeMaris and Sergeant Hardy of the Seventh Mississippi Battalion! Oh, Lord, if they catch us again, bub!"

Greg shivered.

They stood there in the darkness on a narrow walkway above the dark bayou waters, listening to the steady clanging of the coal scoops as they fed coal to the growing fires, and the pungent smell of hot oil drifted to the boys as the rebels used it to get greater heat under the boilers.

Then they heard the fire doors clang shut and the

shuffling of feet on the decks above the hissing of escaping steam. "Should we spike the big bow gun, suh?" a man called out.

"The explosion will take care of it," answered the captain.

"But she's double-shotted, suh! Ready to fiah!"

"The louder the explosion then, Carter."

"Yes, suh! Hawww!"

Chip pressed his ear against the door and listened. "Can't hear any voices," he said.

"Don't take a chance."

The boy turned and his face was ghostly white in the dimness. 'Take a chance? You joshing, bub? They've weighted down them safety valves. We stall around here much longer and we won't have to worry about *flying* up to heaven." Chip eased open the door. They slipped out and headed forward. Chip stopped suddenly. Greg bumped into him. A tall figure in butternut was standing near one of the safety valves, wiring a heavy weight on to it. It was Sergeant Hardy.

The sergeant was grinning and whistling "Dixie" between his teeth. He turned suddenly and saw Chip. He stared at him. "Why aren't you in the boat, soldier?" he demanded.

"Goin' right now, sergeant!"

The two boys faded into the darkness and lay down flat behind an upturned howitzer. Feet scuffled on the deck and the noncom passed them, left the boat by a port, and a moment later they heard the splashing of oars.

The boilers were humming. Steam hissed here and there. The fire doors glowed red hot through the dimness.

"What do we do?" demanded Chip. "Take off the weights? Open the fire doors and flue caps? Douse the fires?"

Greg wasn't listening. He was peering through the

port behind the gun. It was almost dawn. The wind was pushing the mist away. He could see clearly across the bayou. The buildings stood out starkly, and he could see the muzzles of the rebel guns as they were hauled out of the redoubt to be hitched to the teams for withdrawal.

"Look!" snapped Chip. "We've got to abandon ship or else take off them weights! One or the other! Make up your mind or the boilers will make it up for you."

The river was rising all the time. The swift current moved the hull of the grounded *Dart*.

"Greg!" snapped Chip.

Greg turned slowly as though in a dream. "We won't do either one," he said quietly.

"You out'a your mind?"

"The rebels need those caps to help hold Vicksburg. Our mates from the *Dart* will soon be on their way to a rebel prison. The *Dart* herself is doomed unless we do something about it."

"Agreed! But *what?* And you'd better answer in a hurry!"

Greg hurried forward and looked at Old Abe. He picked up a rammer and gingerly tested the depth of it in the gun. It didn't go far enough in for one load of powder bag and projectile, and by the feel of it the gun must be double-shotted as the Confederate soldier had said it was.

"Hurry!" said Chip.

Greg peered from the port. The gun was not lined up on the building where the caps were stored and he knew that he and Chip could never train it to aim at the building because of the great weight of the Dahlgren. But the *boat* could be moved. Greg turned to Chip and swiftly told him his plan. The boy paled. "All right," he said. "I'll conn her, but you'll have to handle the engine room *and* the gun."

"Let's get those weights off."

They rushed into the hellish heat of the engine room

and staggered a little as the heat seemed to strike at them with invisible strength. There was certainly enough pressure in the boilers to move the grounded *Dart*, and the water was rising. They worked swiftly, yanking the weights from the safety valves, expecting the boilers to go any minute. Steam began to hiss from the overloaded valves. The boys darted from the engine room. Chip gripped Greg by the arm. "You know what to do now?" he demanded.

Greg nodded. He had watched the engineers on the *Dart* and on the *Lizzie*. He had no stokers to keep up pressure but they might have enough pressure for what they intended to do.

"Take over then, Mister Hollister!" said Chip. He raced for the ladder that led upward to the pilothouse.

"Aye, aye, Mister Powers!"

Greg walked back into the familiar and greasy engine room. He felt uneasy as he looked at polished brass and shining steel. Then a sharp whistle sounded down the voice pipe. Greg picked it up. The squeaky voice of Chip came down to him. "From now on I'll signal by bell, bub. You know the signals?"

"Yes."

"Then let's get cracking. I just saw some barges coming up the bayou towed by a paddle tug. Looks like the rebels comin' for their caps and their artillery."

Greg's throat went dry. He turned away from the mouthpiece.

The bell tapped three times to alert him. Then it clanged once. Slow ahead. He engaged the engines and felt the big paddle wheel thrash slowly at the water, but the boat did not move. She could not break the bottom suction. The bell clanged twice. Stop. Then the signal came for slow astern and he engaged the reversing gear. Then Chip went to work in earnest, all alone in the pilot-house high overhead. Forward slow; stop; reverse; stop; forward slow; and so on and so on until the sweat poured down Greg's body and his hands slipped on the mechanism. Then above the crackling of the steam exhausts he heard another sound; a familiar sound; the smacking of lead against iron. The rebels had been alerted and had opened fire with their muskets, probably because they had already hauled their artillery guns out of the redoubt and did not yet have them in position to open fire.

The *Dart* creaked and groaned and then with a soft rushing sound she broke free from the clinging bottom and careened from side to side. Three quick taps came on the bell, then two harsh clangs, followed by four bells. Full ahead! The *Dart* surged forward. Greg staggered to the voice pipe as heard the whistling sound. "I'm aiming the jack staff at the storage building, bub!" squeaked Chip.

"Get on Old Abe!"

Greg jumped from the engine room and ran forward to the great gun. He worked like a demon, capping the gun-lock and attaching the lanyard. Out of the corner of his eye he could see the surface of the water lighted by the rising sun. Musket balls patted against the metal sheathing of the hull. One of them rang from the red-painted muzzle of Old Abe.

Greg took his courage in his hands and peered from the port. The *Dart* was aimed straight and true at the storage building. Gun flashes sparkled all along the shore and Greg could see a rebel gun crew cramming powder and shot into one of their guns aimed right at the onrushing tinclad. Even as he watched he saw the gun crew clear the gun and the gunner step aside with the long lanyard in his hand.

The storage building seemed to grow in size. Greg squatted and peered over the sights. Straight and true! He patted the plump breech of the gun and stepped aside just as a musket ball struck the breech where his face had been and sang eerily off into space to strike with a dull thud against a beam. Even as he stepped aside, he heard the dull coughing roar of the rebel field piece and the shot struck into the racing *Dart* with a crushing of limbers. She seemed to stagger and slow down, but it wasn't really from the shot. The steam pressure was lowering because the fires were not being fed. It was now or never!

He could see the gunners reloading with swift precision, then stepping aside to let the gunner insert friction tube and attach his lanyard.

Greg prayed quickly, then jerked the lanyard cleanly with a steady pull. Old Abe roared mightily and reared back against the hurters with a hard slamming sound. wreathing his muzzle with thick smoke. Then, almost like an echo, there was a thunderous roar from the shore of the bayou and as the gun smoke cleared, Greg saw the roof of the building sailing skyward, bent in almost a concave shape, with streamers of smoke and bits of shattered wood hurtling outward. The crashing echo reverberated through the swamp.

There was no time to gloat. Greg raced toward the engine room in answer to the frantic ringing of the signal bells. He slipped on the wet deck, gripped the edge of the engine room door, glanced over his shoulder at the rapidly growing shore, then darted into the room and gripped the reversing gear and shot it home. The engines shuddered and the whole boat seemed ready to collapse. Things broke and things fell as the great wheel groaned into reverse with a clashing of metal and a frantic screaming sound that seemed to come from the pilothouse. Tree branches smashed along the upper works of the tinclad and there was a heavy crashing noise as one of the tall stacks broke in half and fell into the bayou.

Then the *Dart* was roaring back across the bayou as she had been racing forward. The bell clanged into life. Greg stopped jumping about as two bells rang crisply. He stopped the engines but way was still on. Then the bell was tapped three times. Alert. One bell. Slow ahead. Four bells. Full ahead! The *Dart* moved forward. She was losing pressure. Greg jumped from the engine room. Chip must have gone out of his mind. Greg raced for the ladder to the pilothouse and then he saw why Chip had rung for full ahead. The rebel tug had turned in midstream to haul her barges clear of the wild movements of the tinclad.

The *Dart* was overhauling the tug with the last of her strength. Pale faces peered at her from the deck of the tug and then one after the other the crew dived overboard like great ungainly frogs. They had abandoned ship just in time, for the blunt prow of the *Dart* struck the little tug amidships and smashed through the thin hull. The barges broke free, wallowed heavily in the wash and then began to fill with water. The battered *Dart* plowed on, losing speed as the steam pressure went down.

Greg ran to the engine room and opened a fire door. He snatched up a scoop and began to hurl coal into the maw of the hungry furnace. Vaguely he could hear hoarse cheering from the nearby shore, and he knew it wasn't the rebels cheering this time.

The pressure gauge was creeping up but it was going to be a losing battle as Greg was just about through. He turned and slid the scoop under the coal pile. Something made him turn. Half a dozen men in muddy blue uniforms were standing there watching him. Lieutenant Currie, Boatswain Webb Downey, Gunner Ab Cory, big Tom Bruce, little Taffy Hayes and Pilot Tobias Powers. Someone pushed his way through them to come and stand beside Greg. It was Chip. "You can drop the scoop now, bub," he said out of the side of his mouth. "I think we're heroes."

Lieutenant Currie eyed the two tired boys. "Welcome," he said quietly. "Glad to have you aboard."

"Glad to be aboard, sir," chorused the two boys.

Mister Luscombe appeared and saluted Lieutenant Currie. "Captain DeMaris, Seventh Mississippi Battalion, has sent out a flag of truce, sir."

"So?"

The young officer smiled. "Captain DeMaris states, that inasmuch as his transportation has been destroyed, that he is cut off from his base and own forces, with no supplies, he is ready to consider terms of surrender, sir."

Lieutenant Currie looked at his men. "Unconditional surrender," he said. Then he smiled.

Suddenly the whistle cord of the tinclad was yanked down, and all the precious pounds of pressure Greg had built up in the boilers blew out of the whistle in a shower of spray and droplets, while the melodious sound echoed and re-echoed throughout the swamps and bayous.

CHAPTER SEVENTEEN

A Double Victory!

The United States Light Draft Ship *Dart* left Mud Bayou and steamed out onto the broad Mississippi River in the full hot glory of the July sun. She was battered and worn, and she seemed to limp a little in her movements as she met the strong current of the Father of Waters. Great holes had been shorn through her thin plating and wooden sides. One stack was bent and the other was missing. Rust and mud streaked her bedraggled sides. But her flags flew crisply in the hot wind. Her brass howitzers were polished, and the big Dahlgren in the bow had a dull polished sheen to it and a fresh coat of red paint, man-o'-war style, on her muzzle.

A good part of the River Fleet was there, but most of the bigger vessels were missing. As the *Dart* moved quickly down the stream, the crew could hear hoarse cheering from the crews of the other vessels.

Chip Powers casually inspected his fingernails. "Guess they know a *real* fighting ship when they see one, bub," he said to Greg Hollister.

"Yup," said Greg. He shoved back his flat hat and eyed the vessels. They had run up all their flags. Men were jumping up and down on their decks and armored casemates. "Funny they should be giv'n us the big welcome. No one around here knows what we did."

Chip rubbed his jaws. "Yup," he said in a puzzled tone.

Ab Cory came out on the little forward deck where the two boys stood. He cupped his hands about his mouth and hailed the nearest vessel. "Ahoy there, mates! What's the excitement about?"

"You don't *know*?" yelled a sailor in an incredulous tone.

"Would I be asking ye if I *did* know?" roared Ab.

The sailor grinned. "The rebels were defeated at Gettysburg, Pennsylvania, by General Meade and the Army of the Potomac after a hard three-day fight! General Lee and the Army of Northern Virginia is in full retreat!"

The crew of the *Dart* began to cheer, too. "Now all we have to do is take Vicksburg!" yelled Webb Downey in a voice like a steam calliope.

"Where have you been?" yelled back a marine aboard an ironclad. "General Pemberton surrendered Vicksburg three days ago! On the Fourth of July no less! The same day on which Lee retreated from the field of Gettysburg! If you hadn't been fooling around in the swamps in that rusty teakettle, you might have learned the news!"

"Go boil your shirt!" yelled Chip. He spat contemptuously over the side. "Fooling around in the swamps in that rusty teakettle! I'd like to straighten out his hook of a nose for him."

The *Dart* plowed on down the great river, now flowing unvexed to the Gulf of Mexico. The engines thudded steadily and the *frash-frash-frash* of the paddles had a monotonous beat to them. The sun sparkled on the water and a hot wind snapped out the flags.

Greg Hollister stood beside Chip Powers and thought of the days of fighting aboard the *Dart*. Of Jimmy Haslett who had died with a sharpshooter's bullet in his head before he had even been able to report aboard for duty. Of Assistant Pilot Dan Gregg blinded for life by a bullet on the Tallahatchie. Of Lieutenant-Commander Watson Smith, who had collapsed physically and mentally from the strain of the Inland Cruise. Of the men who had died on the decrepit old *Elizabeth M. DePere* on the Little Sunflower. Of Perry Shepherd floating in the bayou with his pale face staring at Greg and Chip. Of all the others who had been buried in the stinking mud, or who had floated away on the dark waters, who had died of sharp-shooters' bullets, or crashing shells, or insidious malaria, while fighting with The Mosquito Fleet.

But they had done their job. Vicksburg had fallen at last. The war wasn't over yet, but a bright glimmer of victory was beginning to show through the dark clouds of the adversities which had beset the Union the first two years of the war.

Lieutenant Currie had been right that day long ago, or so it seemed, when he had welcomed the new draft aboard the *Dart* on a nameless bayou in a forgotten swamp. "You will find yourselves in strange and weird places, fighting a mad sort of war on water that is half land, and the change may be hard on you, *but*...we fight on these waters as men of the United States Navy, and never forget that fact! Your discipline, training, and above all your courage, may help to decide whether or not we take Vicksburg."

The *Dart* whistled for a bend in the great river. The melodious tone echoed back and forth across the waters. Greg felt at peace with the world, or so for a time at least. The war was still on. He looked at his tough little partner, Zelah "Chip" Powers, who had formed a pact with Greg so long-ago. The Illinois boy would surely have something important lo say on this occasion. "What are you thinking about, Chip?" he asked seriously.

Chip yawned. "I was thinking of them pickles and them blackberry preserves we found in that old

Commager mansion on Cypress Bayou. Maybe we could borrow a wherry some day and go back there for some of 'em, but then you was so afraid of that ghost back there I guess I couldn't ever get you back into it again."

"Oh, Lord," breathed Greg. He closed his eyes and shook his head.

The whistle sounded again, half in joy and half in a melancholy tone. Joy for a double victory; sorrow for the brave dead of the *Dart*.

TAKE A LOOK AT ROANOKE RAIDERS AND POWDER BOY OF THE MONITOR:

Two Full Length Historical Civil War Novels

Spur Award and Owen Wister Award-Winning Author Gordon D. Shirreffs spins tales of the Old West that are exhilarating and bigger than life. In this double volume, Shirreffs turns his authority toward thrilling Civil War-era naval stories, both of which will take you on an incredible journey through a time before modern naval warfare.

In *Roanoke Raiders*, the subject is Admiral William Cushing, renowned for his skill as a naval officer. Fourteen-year-old David Scott tells the tales as a young Cushing rises through the ranks, making his mark and building a legacy many still reference today.

Powder Boy of the Monitor follows Dick Morgan, responsible for ensuring the *USS Monitor*'s armaments are supplied with dry powder and cartridges to sustain—and win—every battle they undertake. His adventures aboard the country's first 'ironclad' warship are the stuff of legend. But when the *Monitor* encounters the second 'ironclad,' the *Merrimack*, naval warfare is changed forever as the age of wooden vessels is forgotten in favor of more durable iron vessels.

"Excitement is high; action is authentically drawn as are the characters..." —Kirkus Reviews

AVAILABLE NOW

ABOUT THE AUTHOR

Gordon D. Shirreffs published more than 80 western novels, 20 of them juvenile books, and John Wayne bought his book title, *Rio Bravo*, during the 1950s for a motion picture, which Shirreffs said constituted *"the most money I ever earned for two words."* Four of his novels were adapted to motion pictures, and he wrote a Playhouse 90 and the *Boots and Saddles* series pilot in 1957.

A former pulp magazine writer, he survived the transition to western novels without undue trauma, earning the admiration of his peers along the way. The novelist saw life a bit cynically from the edge of his funny bone and described himself as looking like a slightly parboiled owl. Despite his multifarious quips, he was dead serious about the writing profession.

Gordon D. Shirreffs was the 1995 recipient of the Owen Wister Award, given by the Western Writers of America for "a living individual who has made an outstanding contribution to the American West."

He passed in 1996.

Printed in France by Amazon
Brétigny-sur-Orge, FR

23476599R00205